Competition Law in Austria

Competition Law in Austria

Second Edition

Viktoria H.S.E. Robertson

This book was originally published as a monograph in the International Encyclopaedia of Laws/Competition Law.

Founding Editor: Roger Blanpain
General Editor: Frank Hendrickx
Volume Editors: Francesco Denozza & Alberto Toffoletto

Wolters Kluwer

Published by:
Kluwer Law International B.V.
PO Box 316
2400 AH Alphen aan den Rijn
The Netherlands
E-mail: lrs-sales@wolterskluwer.com
Website: www.wolterskluwer.com/en/solutions/kluwerlawinternational

Sold and distributed by:
Wolters Kluwer Legal & Regulatory U.S.
920 Links Avenue
Landisville, PA 17538
United States of America
E-mail: customer.service@wolterskluwer.com

ISBN 978-94-035-3239-4

e-Book: ISBN 978-94-035-3249-3
web-PDF: ISBN 978-94-035-3259-2

The Author

Viktoria H.S.E. Robertson is a Professor of Commercial Law, Competition Law and Digitalisation at the Vienna University of Economics and Business, where she heads the Research Group on Competition Law and Digitalization. She is also the Director of The Competition Law Hub. She holds a diploma in law and a doctorate from Graz University and an MJur from Oxford University and has clerked with the Austrian Supreme Court on competition and intellectual property matters. Among others, she has been a visiting academic with Oxford University's Centre for Competition Law and Policy (CCLP), the Max Planck Institute for Comparative and International Private Law, Stanford University and the FGV-Rio Law School. She has taught competition law at Oxford University, the European University Institute, the College of Europe, Graz University and the Vienna University of Economics and Business. She is a member of the European Law Institute and the Academic Society for Competition Law. Her current research focuses on the application of competition law in digital market environments as well as on computational antitrust. She is the author of *Competition Law's Innovation Factor: The Relevant Market in Dynamic Contexts in the EU and the US* (Oxford, Hart Publishing 2020) and of an Expert Report on *Digital Merger Control* for the European Commission (2022).

The Author

Table of Contents

List of Abbreviations

AAC	Average Avoidable Cost
ABGB	Allgemeines Bürgerliches Gesetzbuch (General Civil Code)
AG	Advocate General
AktG	Aktiengesetz (Stock Corporation Act)
AußStrG	Außerstreitgesetz (Non-contentious Proceedings Act)
AVG	Allgemeines Verwaltungsverfahrensgesetz (General Administrative Procedure Act)
BER	Block Exemption Regulation
BG	Bezirksgericht (District Court)
BGBl	Bundesgesetzblatt (Federal Law Gazette)
B-VG	Bundes-Verfassungsgesetz (Federal Constitutional Act)
BWB	Bundeswettbewerbsbehörde (Federal Competition Authority)
CbC	Call by Call
CJEU	Court of Justice of the European Union
CPS	Carrier Preselection
dBGBl	deutsches Bundesgesetzblatt (German Federal Law Gazette)
dRGBl	deutsches Reichsgesetzblatt (German Imperial Law Gazette)
ECLI	European Case Law Identifier
ECN	European Competition Network
E-Control	Energy Regulator
EEA	European Economic Area
EFTA	European Free Trade Association
ELI	European Law Institute
EO	Exekutionsordnung (Execution Act)
EU	European Union
EUMR	European Union Merger Regulation
FMA	Finanzmarktaufsicht (Financial Market Authority)
FWBG	Faire-Wettbewerbsbedingungen-Gesetz (Fair Conditions of Competition Act)
GC	General Court

List of Abbreviations

GDP	Gross Domestic Product
GmbHG	GmbH-Gesetz (Limited Liability Company Act)
GP	Gesetzgebungsperiode (Legislative Period)
ICN	International Competition Network
IEL	International Encyclopaedia of Laws
IT	Information Technology
JGS	Justizgesetzsammlung (Collection of Judicial Acts)
JN	Jurisdiktionsnorm (Jurisdictional Norm)
KartG	Kartellgesetz 2005 (Cartel Act 2005)
KaWeRÄG	Kartell- und Wettbewerbsrechts-Änderungsgesetz (Competition Law Amendment Act)
KG	Kartellgericht (Cartel Court)
km	kilometer
KOG	Kartellobergericht (Supreme Cartel Court)
KommAustria	Kommunikationsbehörde Austria (Austrian Communications Authority)
LG	Landesgericht (Regional Court)
LIDC	Ligue internationale du droit de la concurrence (International League of Competition Law)
LRAIC	Long-Run Average Incremental Cost
m	million
NCA	National Competition Authority
no	number
nos	numbers
NVG	Nahversorgungsgesetz (Local Supply Act)
ÖBB	Österreichische Bundesbahnen (Austrian Federal Railways)
OECD	Organisation for Economic Co-operation and Development
OGH	Oberster Gerichtshof (Supreme Court)
OJ	Official Journal of the European Union
OLG	Oberlandesgericht (Higher Regional Court)
ORF	Österreichischer Rundfunk (Austrian national broadcaster)
P2B	Platform to Business
pa	per annum
PCK	Post-Control Kommission (Post-Control Commission)
pt	point
RGBl	Reichsgesetzblatt (Imperial Law Gazette)
RIS	Rechtsinformationssystem (Legal Information System)
RS	Rechtssatz (Legal Proposition)

RTR-GmbH	Rundfunk und Telekom Regulierungs-GmbH (Regulatory Authority for Broadcasting and Telecommunications Limited Liability Company)
SIEC	Significant Impediment of Effective Competition
SSNIP	Small but Significant Non-transitory Increase in Price
StGB	Strafgesetzbuch (Criminal Code)
StPO	Strafprozessordnung (Code of Criminal Procedure)
TCK	Telekom-Control Kommission (Telecoms-Control Commission)
TEU	Treaty on European Union
TFEU	Treaty on the Functioning of the European Union
TTBER	Technology Transfer Block Exemption Regulation
UGB	Unternehmensgesetzbuch (Commercial Law Act)
UNCTAD	United Nation Conference on Trade and Development
US	United States
USACA	US Allied Commission for Austria
UWG	Unlauteres Wettbewerbsgesetz (Unfair Competition Act)
VABER	Vertical Agreements Block Exemption Regulation
VwGH	Verwaltungsgerichtshof (Higher Administrative Court)
WettbG	Wettbewerbsgesetz (Competition Act)
WKStA	Wirtschafts- und Korruptionsstaatsanwaltschaft (Central Public Prosecutor's Office for the Prosecution of White-Collar Crime and Corruption)
ZPO	Zivilprozessordnung (Code of Civil Procedure)

List of Abbreviations

General Introduction

§1. General Background of the Federal Republic of Austria

1. The Federal Republic of Austria (hereinafter: Austria) covers an area of 83,883 km^2 and consists of nine Federal States ('Bundesländer'): Burgenland, Carinthia, Lower Austria, Salzburg, Styria, the Tyrol, Upper Austria, Vienna and Vorarlberg. It is a parliamentary democracy with a population of almost 9 million, of which about 2 million inhabitants live in its capital city of Vienna. Austria joined the European Union (EU) on 1 January 1995, making it one of the Union's twenty-seven current Member States.[1]

§2. Economic System of Austria

2. Austria relies on a social market economy ('soziale Marktwirschaft'), i.e., a free market economy with a focus on social welfare. In 2023, its gross domestic product (GDP) amounted to EUR 478.2 billion and its GDP per capita amounted to EUR 49,400.[2] Austria's economy is largely based on small- and medium-sized enterprises,[3] a fact which is reflected in the Austrian competition law framework as it also protects smaller companies vis-à-vis powerful business partners.

§3. Austrian Legal System

3. As a Member State of the European Union, EU law enjoys supremacy over any Austrian national law.[4] In the hierarchy of norms, EU law therefore stands above national constitutional law, followed by primary legislation – i.e., acts passed by the Austrian Parliament and signed into law by the Federal President – and secondary legislation, which is typically adopted by members of the Federal Government in the form of regulations ('Verordnungen').

1. Statistik Austria, 'Österreich: Zahlen, Daten, Fakten' 8, 9, 12, 24 (2023). For the current EU treaties, *see* Treaty on European Union (TEU) [2016] OJ C202/13; Treaty on the Functioning of the European Union (TFEU) [2016] OJ C202/47.
2. Statistik Austria, 'Bruttoinlandsprodukt und Hauptaggregate' (1.8.2024), https://www.statistik.at/web_de/statistiken/wirtschaft/volkswirtschaftliche_gesamtrechnungen/index.html last accessed 8.8. 2024.
3. Statistik Austria, 'Österreich: Zahlen, Daten, Fakten' 52 (2023).
4. CJEU Case 6/64 *Flaminio Costa v. ENEL*, ECLI:EU:C:1964:66.

4. Austria's Parliament is bicameral, consisting of the National Assembly ('Nationalrat') and the Federal Assembly ('Bundesrat'). The head of state is the Federal President ('Bundespräsident:in'), while the Federal Chancellor ('Bundeskanzler:in') heads the Federal Government.

5. Austria relies on a civil law system. Its Constitutional Act dates from 1920 and, after World War II, fully re-entered into force on 19 December 1945.[5] The constitutionally guaranteed rights can be found in the Basic Constitutional Act ('Staatsgrundgesetz') of 1867 and in the European Convention of Human Rights of 1953, which is of constitutional rank.[6] In addition, the European Union's Charter of Fundamental Rights applies.[7]

6. Austria has three supreme courts: the Constitutional Court ('Verfassungsgerichtshof'), the Higher Administrative Court ('Verwaltungsgerichtshof') and the Supreme Court ('Oberster Gerichtshof' or OGH). Unless there is a particular constitutional right at stake, cases that involve questions of competition law are decided by the Austrian Supreme Court in the last instance, in its composition as the Supreme Cartel Court ('Kartellobergericht' or KOG). If the basis of a competition law claim is general civil law, for instance, in the case of a damages claim, then the regular civil courts deal with the matter. In that case, the Supreme Court decides in the last instance.

7. Where a question arises on the interpretation of EU law – including EU competition law –, Austrian courts can make a request for a preliminary ruling to the Court of Justice of the European Union (CJEU) in Luxembourg.[8] Requests for preliminary rulings are regularly made by Austrian courts in relation to European competition law provisions. Should proceedings before the Supreme (Cartel) Court require a new interpretation of EU law, then the Supreme (Cartel) Court is even obliged to make such a request for a preliminary ruling. A substantial number of competition law-related preliminary rulings by the CJEU originated in Austria, thereby contributing to the harmonious development of EU competition law (on these, *see* §§ 110, 224 f., 357 ff., 388, 533, 536 and 545 of this monograph).[9]

---

5. Bundes-Verfassungsgesetz (B-VG; Federal Constitutional Act), BGBl 1930/1 as amended.
6. Staatsgrundgesetz vom 21. December 1867 über die allgemeinen Rechte der Staatsbürger für die im Reichsrathe vertretenen Königreiche und Länder, RGBl 1867/142 as amended; Konvention zum Schutze der Menschenrechte und Grundfreiheiten (European Convention on Human Rights), BGBl 1958/210 as amended, and BGBl 1964/59 (constitutional rank).
7. Charter of Fundamental Rights of the European Union [2016] OJ C202/389.
8. Article 267 TFEU. Since April 2024, the General Court has jurisdiction to give preliminary rulings related to specific areas of EU law; competition law is not among those; *see* Art. 50b of the Statute of the Court of Justice of the European Union. contained in Protocol (No 3) annexed to the Treaty on European Union, the Treaty on the Functioning of the European Union and the Treaty establishing the European Atomic Energy Community [2016] OJ C202/210, as amended.
9. *See* CJEU Case C-7/97 *Oscar Bronner v. Mediaprint*, ECLI:EU:C:1998:569; CJEU Case C-273/06 *Petschenig v. Toyota Frey Austria*, ECLI:EU:C:2007:66; CJEU Case C-138/11 *Compass-Datenbank GmbH v. Republik Österreich*, ECLI:EU:C:2012:449; CJEU Case C-536/11 *Bundeswettbewerbsbehörde v. Donau Chemie*, ECLI:EU:C:2013:366; CJEU Case C-681/11 *Bundeswettbewerbsbehörde v. Schenker*, ECLI:EU:C:2013:404; CJEU Case C-557/12 *Kone and others v. ÖBB-Infrastruktur*,

8. Austria has a long tradition of a so-called economic and social partnership ('Wirtschafts- und Sozialpartnerschaft'), whereby the four major national interest groups – the Austrian Chamber of Commerce ('Wirschaftskammer Österreich'), the Austrian Chambers of Agriculture ('Landwirtschaftskammern Österreichs'), the Austrian Federal Chamber of Labour ('Bundesarbeiterkammer') and the Austrian Trade Union Federation ('Österreichischer Gewerkschaftsbund') – work together with the Federal Government in order to further Austria's economic and socio-political interests. While the three chambers are self-governing bodies under public law with a statutory membership, the Trade Union Federation is organised as an association. In terms of the legislative process, these four interest groups have the right to submit expert opinions on proposed legislation and to propose legislation coming under the interest groups' main area of expertise.[10] The social partnership forms an advisory board for economic and social affairs ('Beirat für Wirtschafts- und Sozialfragen'), which also carries out work on competition policy.[11] In addition, in the area of competition law, the Austrian Cartel Act foresees that the three Chambers (i.e., statutory interest groups) propose expert lay judges for the Cartel Court who are then nominated by the Federal Minister of Justice (§ 68 KartG; on this *see* further § 474 of this monograph).[12]

§4. HISTORICAL BACKGROUND OF AUSTRIAN COMPETITION LAW

9. Towards the end of the nineteenth century, the idea for competition law-type rules first took a proper hold in Austria, which was then part of the Austro-Hungarian Empire. At that time, Austrian laws already contained a provision in the Criminal Code of 1803 that prohibited anti-competitive agreements,[13] a decree which prohibited tendering cartels dating from 1838,[14] and legislation dating from

---

ECLI:EU:C:2014:1317; CJEU Case C-248/16 *Austria Asphalt v. Bundeskartellanwalt*, ECLI:EU:C:2017:643; CJEU Case C-435/18 *Otis v. Land Oberösterreich*, ECLI:EU:C:2019:1069; CJEU Case C-151/20 *Bundeswettbewerbsbehörde v. Nordzucker*, ECLI:EU:C:2022:203; CJEU Case C-2/23 *FL und KM Baugesellschaft and S* (pending) [2023] OJ C127/17.

10. *See* Österreichische Sozialpartnerschaft, https://www.sozialpartner.at/ last accessed 8.8.2024.
11. For instance, *see* Beirat für Wirtschafts- und Sozialfragen, 'Zukunft der Wettbewerbspolitik in Österreich' (Beiratsstudie Nr 84/2010); Beirat für Wirtschafts- und Sozialfragen, 'Effizienz – Rechtsstaatlichkeit – Transparenz im österreichischen Wettbewerbsrecht: Wettbewerbspolitische Herausforderungen für die 25. Gesetzgebungsperiode (2013–2018)' (Beiratsstudie Nr 87/2014). More recently, also *see* the joint position paper by these four national interest groups and the Federation of Austrian Industry: Bundesarbeiterkammer, Landwirtschaftskammer Österreich, Österreichischer Gewerkschaftsbund, Industriellenvereinigung & Wirtschaftskammer Österreich, 'Aktuelle Herausforderungen für ein modernes Wettbewerbsrecht – Handlungsempfehlungen für den europäischen und nationalen Gesetzgeber' (September 2020).
12. Kartellgesetz 2005 (KartG; Cartel Act 2005), BGBl I 2005/61 as amended.
13. Strafgesetzbuch 1803 (Criminal Code), JGS 1803/626 as amended, § 227. After the reform of 1852, this provision was Strafgesetzbuch 1852 (Criminal Code), RGBl 1852/122 as amended, § 479.
14. Hofkanzleidekret vom 6. Juni 1838 über die Ungültigkeit von Verabredungen bei öffentlichen Versteigerungen (Court Chancellery Decree on the voidness of agreements at public auctions), JGS 1838/277. There has even been research pointing towards the word 'cartel' being of Austrian origin,

1870 that declared cartel agreements null and void.[15] However, these laws lacked an effective enforcement mechanism. After economic liberalism had largely failed in the mid-1800s, multiple cartels started to form in Austria.[16] When these cartels were seen as increasingly problematic towards the end of the nineteenth century, this led to the emergence of competition law ideas as a possible solution. These ideas were first developed and voiced by the legal scholar Adolf Menzel as early as 1894, who underlined the economic and societal harm that cartels could lead to.[17] In what followed, the Austrian government prepared a legislative proposal based on Menzel's ideas in 1897, but that proposal was never adopted. Nevertheless, it provided an important impetus for the future development of competition law in Austria and also in Germany, where the Austrian proposals were used in parliamentary and scholarly debates at the turn of the century.[18]

10. After World War I, Austria introduced an Act on Unfair Competition in 1923.[19] While this Act did not aim to ensure a competitive economy as such, it wanted to give companies a tool to take action against competitors that acted unfairly in the competitive process.[20] Cartelisation of the Austrian industry continued when Austria became part of the National-Socialist German Reich in March 1938 ('Anschluss'). After the end of World War II in May 1945, the Allied Forces undertook to sever German interests in Austrian enterprises and to decartelise the Austrian industry, with the aim of ensuring that pro-Nazi interests would not resurge through financial interests in Austrian companies.[21] At that point, Austria was found

---

having first been used with its current meaning in 1873, and then spreading throughout the world; *see* Helmut Schulte, *Das Österreichische Kartellrecht vor 1938* 1 (Münster 1980) (containing further references).

15. Koalitionsgesetz (Coalition Act), RGBl 1870/3 as amended, § 4: 'The provisions contained in §§ 2 and 3 shall also apply to agreements between tradespeople that have the purpose of increasing the price of goods to the detriment of the public' (own translation). However, this law lifted the criminal sanction on price cartels.
16. On this development, *see also* Otto Auracher, 'Werden des österreichischen Kartellrechts und Kritik an seiner Anwendung' (1962) *Recht der Arbeit* 317; Helmut Schulte, *Das Österreichische Kartellrecht vor 1938* (Münster 1980). *See also* the concise treatise tracing the development of competition law in Austria in Hans-Georg Koppensteiner, *Österreichisches und europäisches Wettbewerbsrecht* § 3 paras 1–25 (3d ed., Orac 1997) .
17. Adolf Menzel, 'Referat über die wirtschaftlichen Kartelle und die Rechtsordnung' (1895) 61 *Schriften des Vereins für Socialpolitik* 23.
18. On this, *see* David J. Gerber, 'The Origins of European Competition Law in Fin-de-Siecle Austria' (1992) 36 *American Journal of Legal History* 405; Bernhard Grossfeld, 'Zur Kartellrechtsdiskussion vor dem Ersten Weltkrieg' 255, 260–268, in: Helmut Coing & Walter Wilhelm (eds), *Wissenschaft und Kodifikation des Privatrechts im 19. Jahrhundert*, vol. 4 (Klostermann 1979). On the rise of cartels in Austria, *see* Friedrich Kleinwächter, *Die Kartelle: Ein Beitrag zur Frage der Organisation der Volkswirthschaft* (Wagner 1883). On the historical development of competition law in Germany, *see* Florian Wagner-von Papp's competition law monograph in the International Encyclopaedia of Laws.
19. Bundesgesetz gegen den unlauteren Wettbewerb (UWG; Unfair Competition Act), BGBl 1923/531 as amended.
20. Helmut Schulte, *Das Österreichische Kartellrecht vor 1938* (Münster 1980) 81.
21. This was known as the SAFEHAVEN project; *see* US Allied Commission for Austria (USACA) Section – German External Assets Branch, Records M1928: 'Examination of the Severance of German Interests in Austrian Enterprises and Decartelization of Austrian Industry (1945–1950)', file number 1-43, https://www.fold3.com/image/271457636 last accessed 8.8.2024.

to be among the most cartel-friendly countries worldwide.[22] This can also be seen in Austria's so-called Cartel Act of 1951, which highlighted that cartels were not always harmful and could also have a stabilising force on the economy. For that reason, said Act only foresaw a register for cartels rather than their prohibition.[23] Anecdotal evidence supports the conclusion that in some sectors of the Austrian economy, the sentiment that cartels are not harmful persists to this day.

11. In 1972, Austria adopted its first proper Cartel Act (Kartellgesetz 1972) prohibiting cartels, which was called 'Act through which provisions on cartels and regulations to maintain free competition are enacted'.[24] In 1988, the Austrian legislator adopted another Cartel Act (Kartellgesetz 1988),[25] which entered into force on 1 January 1989 and was called the 'Act on cartels and other restrictions of competition'. Through an amendment in 1993, Austria for the first time introduced provisions on merger control.[26] The Cartel Act of 1988 contained a number of provisions that criminally sanctioned certain competition law infringements.[27]

12. Austria's accession to the European Union in 1995 was an important milestone for Austrian competition law,[28] for it was against the background of EU competition law that Austria introduced its modern antitrust provisions with the Cartel Act of 2005 (Kartellgesetz or KartG), this time again entitled 'Act against cartels and other restrictions of competition'.[29] The main Austrian competition law provisions were reworded in a way that is clearly modelled upon today's Articles 101 and 102 TFEU. The main difference between the two principal EU competition law provisions and the ones contained in the Austrian KartG is that the latter are much more detailed than the two European provisions. In some cases, the Austrian KartG contains provisions that the European Commission introduced through soft law, such as the European *de minimis* provisions. In other cases, the Austrian KartG contains specific market share thresholds that are only found in case law on the European level, such as market share thresholds for market power.

13. EU accession in 1995 also meant that EU competition law became directly applicable in Austria. This direct applicability of EU competition law was strengthened by Regulation 1/2003. The regulation abolished the previous notification system for possibly anti-competitive agreements, in which the European Commission

22. Hans B. Thorelli, 'Antitrust in Europe: National Laws after 1945' (1959) 26 *University of Chicago Law Review* 222, 227.
23. Kartellgesetz 1951 (Cartel Act 1951), BGBl 1951/173 as amended.
24. Kartellgesetz 1972 (Cartel Act 1972), BGBl 1972/460 as amended. On the developments leading up to this Act, *see* Thomas Schröcksnadel, *Die Entstehung des österreichischen Kartellgesetzes von 1972: die Entwicklung seit 1937* (Münster 1992).
25. Kartellgesetz 1988 (Cartel Act 1988), BGBl 1988/600 as amended.
26. BGBl 1993/693.
27. *See* Kartellgesetz 1988 (Cartel Act 1988), BGBl 1988/600 as amended, §§ 129, 130, 131, 132, 133.
28. As a Member of the European Free Trade Association (EFTA), Austria was also a founding Member of the European Economic Area (EEA) which was established on 1.1.1994. The EEA Agreement contains competition law provisions that are identical to those in the TFEU; *see* Agreement on the European Economic Area [1994] OJ L1/3, Arts 53, 54.
29. Kartellgesetz 2005 (KartG; Cartel Act 2005), BGBl I 2005/61 as amended.

played the central enforcement role. Instead, Regulation 1/2003 established that the legal exemption foreseen in Article 101(3) TFEU became directly applicable.[30] This also heightened the importance of companies' individual self-assessment of their agreements.

14. Austria's two main public enforcers of competition law, the Federal Competition Authority ('Bundeswettbewerbsbehörde') and the Federal Cartel Prosecutor ('Bundeskartellanwalt'), were both installed on 1 July 2002, with the entering into force of the relevant provisions in the Competition Act (Wettbewerbsgesetz or WettbG).[31] Together, they are known as the two official parties ('Amtsparteien'), as they are parties in all cases that come before the Cartel Court and the Supreme Cartel Court, no matter whether these cases were initiated by one of the official parties or by private applicants (§ 40 KartG). The Federal Competition Authority replaced the social partners' former status as official parties, while the Federal Prosecutor's Office lost its previous position as an official party in favour of the Federal Cartel Prosecutor.[32]

15. Since its introduction in 2005, the KartG has seen three major amendments, one in 2012, one in 2017 and another in 2021. The 2012 amendment introduced a single provision on damages for competition law infringements (on this, *see* § 212 of this monograph) and new rules on the publication of the Cartel Court's decisions and the calculation of fines.[33] The 2017 amendment introduced an additional threshold into Austrian merger control, based on the value of the transaction (on this, *see* § 87 of this monograph).[34] It also introduced a range of provisions on private enforcement of competition law, which implemented the Damages Directive (on this, *see* §§ 209–243 of this monograph).[35]

16. The 2021 amendment[36] implemented the ECN+ Directive,[37] introduced a new sustainability exemption (§ 2(1) KartG; *see* § 71 of this monograph) and a new provision on digital companies (§ 28a KartG; *see* § 93 of this monograph). In addition to a range of further changes, it also added a second national merger threshold (§ 9(1) no 2 KartG; *see* § 86 of this monograph) and established the SIEC test as the substantive test of Austrian merger control (§ 12 KartG; *see* §§ 371 and 609 of this monograph).

30. Council Regulation (EC) No 1/2003 of 16 December 2002 on the implementation of the rules on competition laid down in Articles 81 and 82 of the Treaty [2003] OJ L1/1.
31. Gesetz über die Einrichtung einer Bundeswettbewerbsbehörde (Wettbewerbsgesetz, WettbG), BGBl I 2002/62 as amended.
32. 1005 der Beilagen XXI. GP (Erläuterungen zur Regierungsvorlage), pp. 17, 18, 41.
33. Kartell- und Wettbewerbsrechts-Änderungsgesetz 2012 (KaWeRÄG 2012), BGBl I 2013/13.
34. Kartell- und Wettbewerbsrechts-Änderungsgesetz 2017 (KaWeRÄG 2017), BGBl I 2017/56.
35. Directive 2014/104/EU of the European Parliament and of the Council of 26 November 2014 on certain rules governing actions for damages under national law for infringements of the competition law provisions of the Member States and of the European Union [2014] OJ L349/1.
36. Kartell- und Wettbewerbsrechts-Änderungsgesetz 2021 (KaWeRÄG 2021), BGBl I 2021/176.
37. Directive (EU) 2019/1 of the European Parliament and of the Council of 11 December 2018 to empower the competition authorities of the Member States to be more effective enforcers and to ensure the proper functioning of the internal market (ECN+ Directive) [2019] OJ L11/3.

Part I. Structure of Austrian Competition Law and Its Enforcement

Chapter 1. Sources of Austrian Competition Law

17. The sources of Austrian competition law can be categorised as national and supranational. As a Member State of the European Union, European competition law – as supranational law – is directly applicable in Austria and has had a profound influence on many national provisions. As European competition law will be the subject of a separate monograph in the IEL Competition Law series, the following refers to national sources of Austrian competition law and the European influence on these.

§1. National Sources

18. Substantive law: The main national source of Austrian competition law is the Cartel Act of 2005 (Kartellgesetz, hereinafter: KartG), the latest amendment having been made in 2021.[38] The Fair Conditions of Competition Act (Faire-Wettbewerbsbedingungen-Gesetz, hereinafter: 'FWBG')[39] of 1977 equally contains provisions concerning the conditions of competition in the local supply of goods. While only the German language version of the Acts is authentic, the Federal Competition Authority provides an English translation of several laws.[40]

19. The Criminal Code (Strafgesetzbuch, hereinafter: 'StGB')[41] contains two provisions related to anti-competitive conduct, namely § 168b StGB on bid rigging and § 292c StGB on collusion during certain auctions.

20. While competition or antitrust law is comparatively new in Austria, the country has a well-established law of unfair competition, which is predominantly privately enforced by consumers, competitors and consumer or trade organisations. The provisions of the Unfair Competition Act (Unlauteres Wettbewerbsgesetz)[42] are

38. Kartellgesetz 2005 (KartG; Cartel Act 2005), BGBl I 2005/61 as amended.
39. Faire-Wettbewerbsbedingungen-Gesetz (FWBG), BGBl 1977/392 as amended. Until 2021, this act was called Nahversorgungsgesetz (NVG) or Local Supply Act.
40. *See* Bundeswettbewerbsbehörde, 'Legal Basis' https://www.bwb.gv.at/en/factual_information/legal_basis last accessed 8.8.2024. *See also* Viktoria H.S.E. Robertson (ed.), *Kodex Competition Law* (3d ed., Collection of legal materials, LexisNexis 2024).
41. Strafgesetzbuch (StGB), BGBl 1974/60 as amended.
42. Bundesgesetz gegen den unlauteren Wettbewerb (UWG), BGBl 1984/448 (recast) as amended.

not the subject of the present treatise.[43] Note, however, that the Federal Competition Authority has the power to enforce the Unfair Competition Act.[44]

21. Procedural law: The Non-contentious Proceedings Act (Außerstreitgesetz, hereinafter: AußStrG)[45] is the law that governs procedural matters before the Cartel Court and the Supreme Cartel Court. Where compensation for damages due to competition law infringements is sought, or if a preliminary injunction is sought based on unfair competition law in combination with the competition law provisions, this is governed by the Jurisdictional Norm (Jurisdiktionsnorm, hereinafter: 'JN').[46] The Code of Criminal Procedure (Strafprozessordnung, hereinafter: 'StPO') contains a single procedural provision relating to competition law, namely on the prosecution stepping back from a criminal investigation under certain circumstances.[47]

22. §§ 38 to 49 KartG contain specific provisions on the course of proceedings before the Cartel Court and the Supreme Cartel Court. §§ 58 to 74 KartG provide details on the composition of those two courts (for further details, *see* §§ 468 ff. and 625 of this monograph).

23. The Competition Act (Wettbewerbsgesetz, hereinafter: 'WettbG') sets up the Austrian Federal Competition Authority.[48] It also contains rules on the authority's powers, including investigatory powers and the leniency programme. The WettbG was last amended in 2023.[49]

24. Directive 2019/1, also known as the ECN+Directive, foresees a harmonisation of the laws on national competition authorities (NCAs) within the European Union. Among others, this Directive concerns the powers of NCAs, their independence and the need for sufficient resources to support the NCAs' work. Austria implemented this Directive through an amendment of 2021.[50] In the course of this amendment, however, the legislator introduced a new reporting obligation from the Federal Competition Authority to the Minister of the Economy which has led to some public debate.[51]

---

43. But *see*, for instance, Axel Anderl, Andreas Wiebe & Georg E. Kodek (eds), *Kommentar zum UWG: Gesetz gegen den unlauteren Wettbewerb* (2d ed., Manz 2020).
44. § 14 UWG.
45. Außerstreitgesetz (AußStrG), BGBl I 2003/111 as amended.
46. Jurisdiktionsnorm (JN), RGBl 1895/111 as amended.
47. Strafprozessordnung (StPO), BGBl 1975/631 as amended, § 209b.
48. Gesetz über die Einrichtung einer Bundeswettbewerbsbehörde (Wettbewerbsgesetz, WettbG), BGBl I 2002/62 as amended.
49. *See* Bundesgesetz, mit dem das Bundesgesetz über die Einrichtung einer Bundeswettbewerbsbehörde (Wettbewerbsgesetz – WettbG) geändert wird, BGBl I 2023/172.
50. *See* on this Natalie Harsdorf, Erika Ummenberger-Zierler & Axel Reidlinger, 'Europäische Vorgaben für Befugnisse und Unabhängigkeit von nationalen Wettbewerbsbehörden: Eine erste Analyse der am 3.2.2019 in Kraft getretenen ECN+-RL' (2019) 68 *Österreichische Blätter für Gewerblichen Rechtsschutz und Urheberrecht* 63. For the legislative amendment, *see* Kartell- und Wettbewerbsrechts-Änderungsgesetz 2021 (KaWeRÄG 2021), BGBl I 2021/176.
51. *See* Luise Ungerboeck & Renate Graber, 'Aufregung um Berichtspflicht für Kartellwächter' (26.4.2021) *Der Standard* https://www.derstandard.at/story/2000126170222/aufregung-um-berichtspflicht-fuer-kartellwaechter last accessed 8.8.2024.

25. The Law on Cooperation among Consumer Protection Authorities contains provisions on additional competences of the Federal Cartel Prosecutor and the Federal Competition Authority.[52]

26. The law governing the Austrian national broadcaster (Österreichischer Rundfunk, ORF) also contains provisions related to competition law,[53] as do several laws on regulated sectors.[54]

27. To implement Directive 2020/1828[55] on representative actions, Austria adopted an Act on qualified entities that also gives a role to the Federal Cartel Prosecutor.[56] Competition law provisions are among those that a qualified entity may address in the interest of consumers.

§2. Supranational Sources

28. With Austria's accession to the European Union in 1995,[57] EU competition law became directly applicable in Austria. In addition, since the entry into force of Regulation 1/2003 on 1 May 2004,[58] Articles 101 and 102 TFEU are now directly enforced by the Federal Competition Authority, the Federal Cartel Prosecutor and the Austrian courts by virtue of Articles 5 and 6 of Regulation 1/2003. This is also referred to in § 83 KartG and § 3 WettbG. Where an antitrust case may affect trade between Member States, there is a system of parallel application of the national and European competition law provisions. Based on the principle of the supremacy of EU law, the parallel application of national and Union competition law may not prejudice the uniform application and full effect of EU competition law.[59]

29. Article 3 of Regulation 1/2003 ensures some substantive harmonisation among the national and European competition law provisions, as its paragraph 2 requires national competition law on anti-competitive agreements not to be stricter than Article 101 TFEU wherever there is an effect on trade between Member States. Similarly, national competition law on unilateral conduct may not be more lenient than Article 102 TFEU wherever there is an effect on trade between Member States. It may, however, be stricter. In Austria, the provisions contained in the Fair Conditions

52. Verbraucherbehörden-Kooperations-Gesetz, BGBl I 2006/148 as amended, §§ 3(1) no 1, as well as Annex, no 1.
53. ORF-Gesetz, BGBl 1984/379 as amended, §§ 6a, 6b, 31b, 31c.
54. On these, *see* below in § 61 of this monograph.
55. Directive (EU) 2020/1828 of the European Parliament and of the Council of 25 November 2020 on representative actions for the protection of the collective interests of consumers [2020] OJ L409/1.
56. Verbandsklagen-Richtlinie-Umsetzungs-Novelle, BGBl I 2024/85.
57. Treaty of Accession of Austria, Finland and Sweden [1994] OJ C241/1.
58. Council Regulation (EC) No 1/2003 of 16 December 2002 on the implementation of the rules on competition laid down in Arts 81 and 82 of the Treaty [2003] OJ L1/1.
59. CJEU Case 14/68 *Walt Wilhelm v. Bundeskartellamt*, ECLI:EU:C:1969:4, para. 4.

of Competition Act are understood to constitute such stricter rules on unilateral conduct.[60] A further such provision is contained in § 4a KartG on relative market power.[61] While Article 3(2) of Regulation 1/2003 exclusively applies to cases that have an effect on trade between Member States, in practice, it has led to national competition laws increasingly resembling the European provisions both in the legal texts and in their interpretation and application.

30. As soon as a case has a (potential) effect on trade between Member States, the European Commission's legally binding block exemption regulations (BERs) are directly applicable in Austria based on Article 288 TFEU.[62] These BERs foresee under which conditions certain types of agreements come within the safe harbour of Article 101(3) TFEU. They include the following:

a. Vertical Agreements BER 2022/720[63]
b. Technology Transfer BER 316/2014[64]
c. Research & Development BER 2023/1066[65]
d. Specialisation BER 2023/1067.[66]

In addition, there are a number of sector-specific block exemptions, for instance, relating to agriculture[67] and motor vehicle distribution.[68]

---

60. KOG 25.3.2009, 16 Ok 2, 3/09 – *Sägerundholz II*.
61. Note that the Supreme Cartel Court has argued that former § 4(3) KartG (now: § 4a KartG) is already encompassed by Art. 102 TFEU; KOG 12.7.2018, 16 Ok 1/18k – *Fachverband Reisebüros/Lufthansa*. This finding, however, is controversial. In the first instance, the Cartel Court had held that Lufthansa enjoyed relative market power under (then) § 4(3) KartG, but not under § 4(1) KartG or Art. 102 TFEU; *see* KG 6.12.2017, 27 Kt 13/16p – *Fachverband Reisebüros/Lufthansa*.
62. *See also* Council Regulation 2821/71/EEC of the Council of 20 December 1971 on application of Article 85 (3) of the Treaty to categories of agreements, decisions and concerted practices [1971] OJ L285/46 as amended.
63. Commission Regulation (EU) 2022/720 of 10 May 2022 on the application of Article 101(3) of the Treaty on the Functioning of the European Union to categories of vertical agreements and concerted practices (VABER) [2022] OJ L134/4.
64. Commission Regulation (EU) No 316/2014 of 21 March 2014 on the application of Article 101(3) of the Treaty on the Functioning of the European Union to categories of technology transfer agreements (TTBER) [2014] OJ L93/17.
65. Commission Regulation (EU) 2023/1066 of 1 June 2023 on the application of Article 101(3) of the Treaty on the Functioning of the European Union to certain categories of research and development agreements [2023] OJ L143/9.
66. Commission Regulation (EU) 2023/1067 of 1 June 2023 on the application of Article 101(3) of the Treaty on the Functioning of the European Union to certain categories of specialisation agreements [2023] OJ L143/20.
67. Commission Regulation (EU) No 702/2014 of 25 June 2014 declaring certain categories of aid in the agricultural and forestry sectors and in rural areas compatible with the internal market in application of Articles 107 and 108 of the Treaty on the Functioning of the European Union [2014] OJ L193/1.
68. Commission Regulation (EU) No 461/2010 of 27 May 2010 on the application of Article 101(3) of the Treaty on the Functioning of the European Union to categories of vertical agreements and concerted practices in the motor vehicle sector [2010] OJ L129/52. The application of this BER was prolonged until 31 May 2028.

31. The practical relevance of block exemption regulations in Austria can also be seen in a preliminary reference that the Commercial Court Vienna sent to Luxembourg, in which the interpretation of a block exemption regulation was a decisive issue in a case on damages.[69]

32. Where a set of facts has no (potential) effect on trade between Member States, the Federal Minister of Justice may adopt Austrian regulations that can refer to the European BERs (§ 3(1) KartG). However, this has not yet occurred. In practice, the European Commission's BERs are regularly relied upon, thus ensuring a harmonious interpretation of EU and Austrian competition law.

33. In merger cases, Regulation 139/2004 (European Union Merger Regulation or EUMR) ensures that mergers of a certain size are exclusively reviewed by the European Commission as the only competent authority ('one-stop-shop principle' contained in Article 21 EUMR), while the national merger control regimes continue to deal with cases below the European turnover thresholds ('Union dimension', Article 1 EUMR).[70] Where EU merger control applies due to a concentration's Union dimension, Austrian merger control rules therefore become inapplicable.

34. The Geoblocking Regulation,[71] the P2B Regulation[72] and the Digital Markets Act[73] contain provisions that are relevant to competition in digital markets. As European regulations, they are directly applicable and enforceable in Austria. Austria has not yet adopted provisions that give the Federal Competition Authority investigatory powers under the Digital Markets Act.[74]

§3. Secondary Sources

I. Regulations

35. While the Federal Minister of Justice could issue regulations on exemptions for anti-competitive agreements based on § 3 KartG, this power has not yet been used. As mentioned above, the EU block exemption regulations are applicable in Austria as long as a case has a (potential) effect on trade between Member States. In practice, they are also applied where no such potential effect is established.

69. CJEU Case C-273/06 *Petschenig v. Toyota Frey Austria*, ECLI:EU:C:2007:66.
70. Council Regulation (EC) No 139/2004 of 20 January 2004 on the control of concentrations between undertakings (EUMR) [2004] OJ L24/1.
71. Regulation (EU) 2018/302 of the European Parliament and of the Council of 28 February 2018 on addressing unjustified geo-blocking and other forms of discrimination based on customers' nationality, place of residence or place of establishment within the internal market (Geoblocking Regulation) [2018] OJ L60 I/1.
72. Regulation (EU) 2019/1150 of the European Parliament and of the Council of 20 June 2019 on promoting fairness and transparency for business users of online intermediation services (P2B Regulation) [2019] OJ L186/57.
73. Regulation (EU) 2022/1925 of the European Parliament and of the Council of 14 September 2022 on contestable and fair markets in the digital sector (Digital Markets Act) [2022] OJ L265/1.
74. Article 38 para. 7 Digital Markets Act.

36. The Federal Minister for Economic Affairs is empowered to set out detailed provisions on the Austrian leniency programme by regulation (§ 11b(4) WettbG). Such a regulation was adopted in November 2021, after hearing the Federal Competition Authority, the Federal Cartel Prosecutor and the Competition Commission.[75]

37. If mergers on specific markets adversely affect competition despite low turnover, the Federal Minister of Justice can issue a regulation stating that sales revenues achieved on a specific market have to be multiplied by a certain factor when applying the turnover thresholds of Austrian merger control (§ 18(1) KartG). To date, no such regulation has been adopted.

38. The Federal Minister of Justice, in agreement with the Federal Minister for Economic Affairs, could issue regulations detailing the format and content of merger notifications (§ 10(2) KartG), but no such regulation has been adopted to date. On the Federal Competition Authority's soft law in this respect, *see* the following section.

39. The Federal Minister for Economic Affairs, after hearing the Federal Competition Authority, can issue a regulation detailing the implementation of a new section on notification of documents and enforcement in the European Competition Network (§ 14a WettbG). Such a regulation was adopted in November 2021.[76]

II. Guidelines

40. The Federal Competition Authority issues soft law instruments in order to inform companies of the way it intends to apply Austrian competition law. These are usually published under the name of either 'position' (Standpunkt) or 'guideline' (Leitfaden). A regularly updated list of soft law instruments issued by the Federal Competition Authority can be found on its website.[77] These currently include:

1. Competition Law and Compliance (Kartellrecht und Compliance)
2. Defective/incomplete merger notifications – actions by the official parties (Mangelhafte/unvollständige Anmeldung eines Zusammenschlusses – Vorgehen der Amtsparteien)
3. Fairness catalogue for companies – position paper for good business conduct (Fairnesskatalog für Unternehmen – Standpunkt für unternehmerisches Wohlverhalten)

---

75. Verordnung der Bundesministerin für Digitalisierung und Wirtschaftsstandort über die Anwendung der Kronzeugenregelung des Wettbewerbsgesetzes, BGBl II 2021/487.
76. Verordnung der Bundesministerin für Digitalisierung und Wirtschaftsstandort über die Zustellung und Vollstreckung im Europäischen Wettbewerbsnetz, BGBl II 2021/486.
77. *See* Bundeswettbewerbsbehörde, 'Standpunkte der BWB' https://www.bwb.gv.at/recht-publikationen/standpunkte last accessed 8.8.2024. Many of the position papers are also available in English: Bundeswettbewerbsbehörde, 'Standpoints' https://www.bwb.gv.at/en/factual_information/standpoints last accessed 8.8.2024.

4. Federal Competition Authority treatment of anonymous submissions (Behandlung anonymer Eingaben durch die BWB)
5. Focus paper on sector inquiry into the food industry - Price comparison platforms (Fokuspapier Preisvergleichsplattformen)
6. Guidance on pre-notification procedures in merger control (Leitfaden Pränotifikationsverfahren in der Zusammenschlusskontrolle)
7. Guidance on transaction value thresholds for mandatory pre-merger notification in Austria and Germany (Leitfaden zur neuen Transaktionswert-Schwelle in der Zusammenschlusskontrolle in Österreich und Deutschland)[78]
8. Guidelines – merger control and insolvency proceedings (Leitfaden – Zusammenschlusskontrolle und Insolvenzverfahren)
9. Guidelines on dawn raids (Leitfaden zu Hausdurchsuchungen)
10. Guidelines on the Application of Sec. 2 para. 1 Cartel Act to Sustainability Cooperations – Sustainability Guidelines (Leitlinien zur Anwendung von § 2 Abs 1 KartG auf Nachhaltigkeitskooperationen – Nachhaltigkeits-LL)
11. Issuance of waivers of investigation (Abgabe von Prüfungsverzichten)
12. Leniency programme guidelines (Leitfaden zur Kronzeugenregelung)
13. Notification requirement for concentrations – turnover calculation at the time of the acquisition (Anmeldebedürftigkeit von Zusammenschlüssen – Umsatzberechnung zum Zeitpunkt des Erwerbs)
14. Paper on fine reductions in the leniency programme (Papier Geldbußenreduktionen im Kronzeugenprogramm)
15. Position on funeral services (Standpunkt zum Bestattungswesen)
16. Position on media cooperation in the radio broadcasting market (Standpunkt zu Medienkooperationen im Hörfunkmarkt)
17. Position on motor vehicle distribution (Standpunkt zum KFZ-Vertrieb)
18. Position on questions on the applicability of the group exemption under competition law (Standpunkt zu Fragen der Anwendbarkeit des kartellrechtlichen Konzernprivilegs)
19. Position on settlements (Standpunkt zu Settlements)
20. Position on vertical price-fixing (Standpunkt zu vertikalen Preisbindungen)
21. Position paper – macroeconomic effects of mergers in the context of the COVID-19 crisis (Standpunkt – Gesamtwirtschaftliche Auswirkungen von Zusammenschlüssen im Kontext der COVID-19 Krise)
22. Position Paper on National and European Champions in Merger Control (Positionspapier zu nationalen und europäischen Champions in der Fusionskontrolle)
23. Proposition Paper Digitalisation and Competition Law (Thesenpapier Digitalisierung und Wettbewerbsrecht)
24. Withdrawal of a request for investigation following the withdrawal of a notification (Zurückziehung eines Prüfungsantrages infolge der Zurückziehung einer Anmeldung)
25. Working Paper Competition Monitoring (Arbeitspapier Wettbewerbsmonitoring).

78. This Guidance was issued together with the German NCA, the Bundeskartellamt. It is currently available in its second edition.

41. The soft law of the European Commission – frequently named Notices or Guidelines – is avidly read and applied not only by competition practitioners in Austria but also by the national competition authorities and the courts. This soft law is in no way legally binding but has a persuasive power.

§4. Sources' Relation and Hierarchy

42. Austrian national competition law needs to be in line with the Austrian Constitution, of which the European Convention on Human Rights[79] forms an integral part.[80] This is particularly important for procedural rights.

43. As a Member State of the European Union, Austrian national competition law generally needs to be in line with EU competition law where company behaviour may also affect trade between Member States. The general principle of the direct effect of EU law was already acknowledged in *van Gend en Loos*,[81] while the principle of the supremacy of EU law was established in *Costa v. ENEL*.[82]

44. Regulation 1/2003 requires that – at least where company behaviour may have an effect on cross-border trade within the European Union – national rules on anti-competitive agreements are in line with Article 101 TFEU, while national rules on unilateral conduct may be stricter but not more lenient than Article 102 TFEU. The only exceptions are national provisions that pursue a goal that is different from the EU provisions.

45. As for mergers, the EU Merger Regulation 139/2004 foresees a one-stop-shop for mergers that surpass the European turnover thresholds ('Union dimension'), effectively meaning that only mergers below that threshold may be assessed under national merger provisions. Where the European Commission considers that a national competition authority is better placed to assess a concentration that has been notified to it, it can refer such a concentration to that national competition authority (Article 9 EUMR). For mergers below the Union dimension threshold, however, there is the possibility to refer these to the European Commission, either upon application by a notifying party (Article 4(5) EUMR) or upon the request of a national competition authority (Article 22 EUMR). While the European Commission issued guidance explaining that national competition authorities can refer mergers to it even where they themselves are not competent to review them under national merger control laws,[83] the Federal Competition Authority has only referred

79. Konvention zum Schutze der Menschenrechte und Grundfreiheiten (European Convention on Human Rights), BGBl 1958/210 as amended.
80. On the constitutional rank of the Convention, *see* BGBl 1964/59.
81. CJEU Case 26/62 *van Gend en Loos*, ECLI:EU:C:1963:1.
82. CJEU Case 6/64 *Flaminio Costa v. ENEL*, ECLI:EU:C:1964:66.
83. European Commission, Guidance on the application of the referral mechanism set out in Article 22 of the Merger Regulation to certain categories of cases [2021] OJ C113/1.

mergers where it was competent to review said merger. This is in line with the CJEU's recent ruling in *Illumina Grail*.[84] On Austrian referrals to date, *see* § 622 of this monograph.

46. Although the soft law instruments issued by the European Commission and the Federal Competition Authority provide much-needed guidance in practice, the Austrian courts are not bound by either.

§5. Role and Authority of Precedents

47. The Austrian legal system is a civil law system, meaning that it does not adhere to the legal doctrine of stare decisis. Nevertheless, in practice, lower courts regularly apply the law as interpreted in the judgments of the Supreme Cartel Court very much as if they constituted binding precedent. The Supreme Cartel Court will remain true to its own prior judgments, and its main statements of interpretation are collected in so-called legal propositions ('Rechtssätze') that can easily be accessed online.[85] These legal propositions are numbered and the judgments relying on them are listed in the database, with a direct link to their full text. For practical purposes, this is of great value. At the time of writing, the database contained 919 legal propositions on the KartG alone[86] and a further 43 on the WettbG.[87] In this monograph, the legal propositions summarising the Supreme Cartel Court's case law are referred to in the footnotes as 'RIS-Justiz RS' followed by a running number.[88]

48. Cases decided by the Supreme Cartel Court ('Kartellobergericht' or KOG) and the Cartel Court ('Kartellgericht' or KG) are not given an official case name. Therefore, one and the same case will often be referred to by different names in the

84. CJEU Case C-611/22 P *Illumina Grail v. European Commission*, ECLI:EU:C:2024:677.
85. *See* Rechtsinformationssystem des Bundes, https://www.ris.bka.gv.at/Jus/ last accessed 8.8.2024.
86. *See* Rechtsinformationssystem des Bundes, Rechtssätze zum KartG (26.2.2025) https://www.ris.bka.gv.at/Ergebnis.wxe?Abfrage=Justiz&Fachgebiet=&Gericht=&Rechtssatznummer=&Rechtssatz=&Fundstelle=&Spruch=&Rechtsgebiet=Undefined&AenderungenSeit=Undefined&JustizEntscheidungsart=&SucheNachRechtssatz=True&SucheNachText=False&GZ=&VonDatum=&BisDatum=26.02.2025&Norm=KartG&ImRisSeitVonDatum=&ImRisSeitBisDatum=&ImRisSeit=Undefined&ResultPageSize=100&Suchworte=&Position=1&SkipToDocumentPage=true last accessed 26.2.2025.
87. *See* Rechtsinformationssystem des Bundes, Rechtssätze zum WettbG (26.2.2025) https://www.ris.bka.gv.at/Ergebnis.wxe?Abfrage=Justiz&Fachgebiet=&Gericht=&Rechtssatznummer=&Rechtssatz=&Fundstelle=&Spruch=&Rechtsgebiet=Undefined&AenderungenSeit=Undefined&JustizEntscheidungsart=&SucheNachRechtssatz=True&SucheNachText=False&GZ=&VonDatum=&BisDatum=26.02.2025&Norm=WettbG&ImRisSeitVonDatum=&ImRisSeitBisDatum=&ImRisSeit=Undefined&ResultPageSize=100&Suchworte=&Position=1&SkipToDocumentPage=true last accessed 26.2.2025.
88. RIS-Justiz stands for Rechtsinformationssystem-Justiz; this is the Austrian federal legal information database. RS stands for Rechtssatz (legal proposition).

literature. To ensure some consistency, the case names referred to throughout this monograph are those assigned to the cases in Johannes Gruber's collection of Austrian competition law cases.[89]

49. As a Member State of the European Union, and when applying EU competition law, Austrian courts – including the Supreme Cartel Court – are bound by the legal interpretations of EU competition law given in the judgments of the Court of Justice of the European Union, which includes the Court of Justice (CJEU) and the General Court (GC).[90] In addition, the almost identical wording of the Austrian and EU competition law provisions has led the Austrian Supreme (Cartel) Court to rely on European interpretations even when applying Austrian competition law (e.g., *see* §§ 76, 80 of this monograph). This is in the interest of a harmonious interpretation of the two overlapping competition law regimes.

89. Johannes P. Gruber, *Österreichisches Kartellrecht* (3d ed., Manz 2020). This publication contains a comprehensive list of Austrian decisions, including the decision's date, file number and assigned name. The online edition of this work also contains direct links to the cases (*see* rdb.manz.at). Cases decided after the publication of that collection are assigned a name by the author.
90. For example, *see* Article 267 TFEU.

Chapter 2. Scope of Application

§1. Territorial Reach

50. Austria's national competition law covers the territory of the Federal Republic of Austria, consisting of its nine Federal States.

51. According to § 24(2) KartG, the Cartel Act applies where a set of facts has effects on the Austrian market, no matter whether the anti-competitive behaviour at issue originates in Austria or whether the anti-competitive agreement is agreed upon in Austria (effects doctrine). This rule also applies to the Fair Conditions of Competition Act.[91] It is of no consequence where the undertaking engaging in the anti-competitive conduct has its seat.[92] The effects doctrine is also relied upon in EU competition law.[93]

52. Pursuant to § 24(3) no 1 KartG, the Cartel Act does not apply to credit institutions, building societies and private insurance companies in so far as they are supervised by the Financial Market Authority.[94] Furthermore, it does not apply to transport undertakings in so far as they are supervised by the Federal Ministry for Transport.

53. The merger rules contained in the Cartel Act apply whenever the turnover or transaction value thresholds foreseen in § 9 KartG are surpassed by a concentration (on this, *see* §§ 82 ff., 153 ff. of this monograph).

§2. Special Sectors

54. Due to its concentrated media landscape, Austria has a special merger regime for media concentrations (*see* §§ 89, 157, 374, 553, 559 of this monograph).

55. To allow companies to advance the goal of a greener economy, the Austrian legislator introduced a sustainability exemption in 2021 (*see* § 71 of this monograph).

56. In the publishing sector, resale price maintenance is permitted as long as it is necessary to guarantee a nationwide and non-discriminatory distribution of these print products ('Buchpreisbindung'). On this exemption for the book and magazine trade, *see* § 2(2) no 2 KartG and § 303 of this monograph.

---

91. Faire-Wettbewerbsbedingungen-Gesetz (FWBG), BGBl 1977/392 as amended; KOG 16 Jul. 2008, 16 Ok 3/08 – *Sägerundholz I.*
92. KOG 6.9.2017, 16 Ok 10/16f – *BWB/Semperit.*
93. For example, *see* CJEU Case C-413/14 *Intel v. Commission*, ECLI:EU:C:2017:632.
94. Finanzmarktaufsicht or FMA.

57. Certain restrictions of competition are allowed among members of cooperatives, and between the cooperative itself and its members so as to allow cooperatives to fulfil their purpose. On this so-called cooperative privilege ('Genossenschaftsprivileg') of § 2(2) no 3 KartG, *see* § 291 of this monograph.

58. Agricultural producers and associations of agricultural producers may conclude agreements and decisions or engage in practices that relate to the production or sale of agricultural products as well as to the use of joint facilities for storage, treatment and processing of agricultural products (§ 2(2) no 5 KartG).[95] However, these agreements may not include an obligation to charge identical prices.

59. Where other legal provisions fix prices or allow for the fixing of prices, price limits or pricing guidelines, these shall not be prohibited by the Cartel Act (§ 25 KartG).

§3. State-Owned Enterprises and Public Utilities

60. The Cartel Act does not apply to state-granted monopolies, as long as the latter are acting within their statutory monopoly power (§ 24(3) no 2 KartG). Apart from this restriction on the application of competition law to state-granted monopolies, the provisions of the KartG also apply to the actions of state-owned enterprises, particularly where they participate in the private sector. For instance, while the Supreme Cartel Court has acknowledged that the Austrian Post had a state-granted monopoly on producing and issuing stamps, this monopoly could not be extended to the distribution of stamps; consequently, the latter came under the provisions of the KartG.[96]

61. State-granted monopolies cannot generally rely on their immunity under this Austrian provision when it comes to the application of Articles 101 and 102 TFEU.[97] In order to establish whether they also escape antitrust liability under the European provisions, one needs to have regard to the (European) notion of undertaking.[98]

62. Where public utilities are concerned, such as electricity, gas, railways, sewage, telecommunications, waste collection or water, these are frequently subject to sector-specific regulation, particularly in previously state-owned monopolies that were liberalised. Here, sector-specific regulation and general competition law work

95. On this specific exemption and its relationship with EU competition law, *see* Johannes P. Gruber, 'Wettbewerb in der Landwirtschaft – Teil II' (2009) *Österreichische Zeitschrift für Kartellrecht* 188, 193–194.
96. KOG 17.11.2003, 16 Ok 14/03 – *Verschleißerprovision*.
97. Franz Urlesberger, '§ 24 KartG' para. 13, in: Alexander Petsche, Franz Urlesberger & Claudine Vartian (eds), *Kartellgesetz 2005* (2d ed., Manz 2016).
98. For example, *see* CJEU Case C-41/90 *Höfner & Elser v. Macrotron*, ECLI:EU:C:1991:161; CJEU Case C-364/92 *SAT Fluggesellschaft mbH v. Eurocontrol*, ECLI:EU:C:1994:7; CJEU Case C-138/11 *Compass-Datenbank GmbH v. Republik Österreich*, ECLI:EU:C:2012:449.

hand in hand. Examples of such regulation can be found in the Telecommunications Act,[99] the Electricity Industry and Organisation Act,[100] the Gas Industry Act,[101] and the Ground-Handling Services Act.[102] In the case of infringements of certain aspects of these sector-specific rules, the regulatory authority can ask the Cartel Court to issue a fine.[103] In the area of telecommunications, § 2(4) of the Telecommunications Act states that this Act does not affect the competences of the Cartel Court, the Federal Cartel Prosecutor or the Federal Competition Authority. Therefore, the Supreme Cartel Court has ruled that abuses of a dominant position can be penalised under the KartG irrespective of the possibility to also penalise them under the Telecommunications Act.[104] This can lead to a certain overlap between the two regimes.

§4. Sensible Effect and De Minimis

63. An anti-competitive agreement needs to have an appreciable effect on competition in order to attract scrutiny under the KartG. For this reason, § 2(2) no 1 KartG contains a *de minimis* rule for minor anti-competitive agreements. This provision was introduced in order to mirror the European Commission's (non-binding) *De Minimis* Notice and the case law of the CJEU.[105] While the CJEU has ruled that the Commission's *De Minimis* Notice was not legally binding on either national courts or national competition authorities,[106] the Austrian legislator decided to make these thresholds contained in the Notice legally binding through the KartG. The *de minimis* rule in § 2(2) no 1 KartG applies to minor cartels ('Bagatellkartelle') that are concluded among competitors with a combined market share of up to 10%, or among non-competitors with a market share of up to 15% each. These thresholds refer to the market shares that the parties to the agreement have on a relevant market, which is not necessarily confined to the relevant market that is affected by the cartel. The companies in question may not have surpassed these market share thresholds during the entire duration of the agreement that wants to benefit from the *de minimis* rule.[107] It is for the party wishing to rely on the *de minimis* rule to show that it fulfils the conditions for this exception.[108]

64. The Austrian *de minimis* rule, as the European *De Minimis* Notice, only exempts minor cartels from the prohibition of § 1(1) KartG provided that these

99. Telekommunikationsgesetz 2003 (TKG), BGBl I 2003/70 as amended.
100. Elektrizitätswirtschafts- und -organisationsgesetz 2010 (ElWOG), BGBl I 2013/6 as amended.
101. Gaswirtschaftsgesetz 2011 (GWG), BGBl I 2011/107 as amended.
102. Flughafen-Bodenabfertigungsgesetz, BGBl I 1998/97 as amended.
103. For example, *see* § 104 ElWOG, § 164 GWG.
104. *See* KOG 1.3.1999, 16 Ok 1/99 – *One*.
105. 926 der Beilagen XXII. GP (Erläuterungen zur Regierungsvorlage), p. 5.
106. CJEU Case C-226/11 *Expedia*, ECLI:EU:C:2012:795, para. 29; European Commission, Notice on agreements of minor importance which do not appreciably restrict competition under Article 101(1) of the Treaty on the Functioning of the European Union (*De Minimis* Notice) [2014] OJ C291/1.
107. KOG 26.6.2006, 16 Ok 51/05 – *Asphaltmischanlage II*.
108. Astrid Ablasser-Neuhuber, Florian Neumayr, Gerhard Fussenegger & Sebastian Reiter, 'Austria' § 2.02[3][a], in: Frank L. Fine (ed.), *European Competition Laws*, vol 1 (loose-leaf, Matthew Bender Elite Products, release 21-11/2022).

agreements do not fix selling prices, restrict production or distribution, or share markets. This latter restriction for hardcore cartels was only introduced in 2012, in order to align the Austrian provision with EU competition law.[109] For instance, the Cartel Court has held that vertical price-fixing, as a hardcore restriction, cannot benefit from the *de minimis* rule.[110]

109. 1804 der Beilagen XXIV. GP (Erläuterungen zur Regierungsvorlage), p. 6. Arguing that the alignment is not complete in light of more recent revisions of the European *De Minimis* Notice, *see* Astrid Ablasser-Neuhuber, Florian Neumayr, Gerhard Fussenegger & Sebastian Reiter, 'Austria' § 2.02[3][a], in: Frank L. Fine (ed.), *European Competition Laws*, vol 1 (loose-leaf, Matthew Bender Elite Products, release 21-11/2022).

110. KG 3.3.2016, 26 Kt 2/16 – *BWB/Rauch Fruchtsäfte*.

Chapter 3. Overview of Substantive Provisions

65. The substantive provisions of Austrian competition law are contained in §§ 1 to 25 KartG and cover restrictive agreements (§§ 1 to 3 KartG), abuse of a dominant position (§§ 4 to 6 KartG) and mergers (§§ 7 to 19 KartG). §§ 20 to 25 KartG contain provisions that apply to all three areas of competition law, for instance, on an economic approach to cases, on the calculation of turnover and of market shares, and on the scope of application of the Cartel Act and its relationship with other legal provisions. The remainder of the Cartel Act (§§ 26 to 96 KartG) contains provisions on the enforcement of competition law, the (Supreme) Cartel Court and competition law proceedings before these courts, the Federal Cartel Prosecutor, application of EU competition law, and final provisions.

§1. Restrictive Agreements

66. §§ 1 to 3 KartG contain the rules on anti-competitive agreements. § 1(1) KartG prohibits '[a]ny agreements between entrepreneurs, decisions of associations of entrepreneurs and concerted practices which have as their object or effect the prevention, restriction or distortion of competition (cartels)'. § 1(2) KartG goes on to list types of agreements which, according to the legislator, fall under § 1(1) KartG, including the fixing of prices or other trading conditions, the limiting or controlling of production, as well as the sharing of markets or sources of supply. This list is non-exhaustive.

67. § 1(3) KartG foresees that '[a]ny agreements and decisions prohibited pursuant to para. 1 shall be automatically void'.

68. Recommendation cartels whereby certain prices, price limits, calculation guidelines, trade margins and discounts are recommended, and that aim at or result in a restriction of competition, are also considered to constitute a cartel within the meaning of § 1(1) KartG (§ 1(4) KartG). This does not apply to non-binding recommendations of this kind, as long as these are not enforced through economic or social pressure.

69. § 2(1) KartG contains an exemption provision with two positive and two negative conditions that need to be fulfilled in order to qualify for individual exemption:

1. the cartel contributes to improving the production or distribution of goods or to promoting technical or economic progress;
2. consumers are allowed a fair share of the resulting benefits;
3. the restrictions imposed on undertakings are indispensable to achieve these objectives; and

4. undertakings are not put in a position in which they could eliminate competition in respect of a substantial part of the products in question.[111]

It is for the company wanting to rely on this exemption provision to show the pro-competitive effects of its behaviour.[112]

70. The Supreme Cartel Court has emphasised that the individual exemption can only be relied upon where benefits are actually passed on to customers.[113] While reliance on § 2(1) KartG does not regularly succeed, the Supreme Cartel Court has found that benefits were passed on to consumers in a case involving a system of cross-guarantees between savings banks, as this was beneficial for customers.[114]

71. In 2021, the Austrian legislator introduced an additional exemption into § 2(1) KartG: a sustainability exemption. It comes in the form of an additional sentence at the end of that provision which states: 'Consumers shall also be considered to be allowed a fair share of the resulting benefit if the improvement of the production or distribution of goods or the promotion of technical or economic progress substantially contributes to an ecologically sustainable or climate-neutral economy.'[115] This means that one of the conditions that is hardest to fulfil under § 2(1) KartG – the passing-on of the benefit to consumers – is automatically presumed under the new sustainability exemption once it is ascertained that the benefit resulting from an anti-competitive agreement substantially contributes to the green economy. In 2022, the Federal Competition Authority issued guidelines on how to apply this new exemption.[116]

72. In addition to the general exemption provision of § 2(1) KartG and its new sustainability exemption, § 2(2) KartG contains four further exemptions from the prohibition on anti-competitive agreements, including a provision on minor cartels (*de minimis* rule; *see* above at §§ 63–64 of this monograph), an exemption for resale price maintenance for books and similar goods (so-called Buchpreisbindung; *see* § 303 of this monograph), a provision on restrictions of competition among members of a cooperative (so-called Genossenschaftsprivileg; *see* § 291 of this monograph), and certain exemptions for agricultural producers.

73. Based on § 3(1) KartG, the Federal Minister of Justice can issue regulations exempting certain categories of agreements from the prohibition of § 1(1) KartG

111. On the cumulative nature of these four conditions, *see* KOG 26.6.2006, 16 Ok 51/05 – *Asphaltmischanlage II.*
112. KOG 8.10.2015, 16 Ok 2/15b & 16 Ok 8/15k – *Spar.*
113. KOG 20.12.2005, 16 Ok 45/05 – *Honorarordnung der Baumeister.*
114. KOG 21.3.2007, 16 Ok 12/06 – *Haftungsverbund II.*
115. On this provision and its relationship with EU competition law, *see* Viktoria H.S.E. Robertson, 'Sustainability: A World-First Green Exemption in Austrian Competition Law' (2022) 13 *Journal of European Competition Law & Practice* 426.
116. Bundeswettbewerbsbehörde, Guidelines on the Application of Sec. 2 para. 1 Cartel Act to Sustainability Cooperations – Sustainability Guidelines (September 2022).

(block exemptions). These regulations may also refer to the European Commission's block exemption regulations under Article 101(3) TFEU. So far, no such Austrian regulation has been issued. This is problematic, as it means that while competition law practice heavily relies on the European block exemption regulations when applying both European and Austrian competition law,[117] there is no Austrian legal basis that explicitly provides for this application where a case does not have an effect on trade between Member States.[118]

74. Together, the first and second paragraphs of § 1 KartG mirror Article 101(1) TFEU, while § 1(3) KartG contains the nullity of anti-competitive agreements that is also foreseen in Article 101(2) TFEU. § 2(1) KartG contains an exemption provision that is modelled upon the one found in Article 101(3) TFEU. This is a sensible approach, as Regulation 1/2003 makes Article 101 TFEU directly applicable in all Member States, including Austria. Where a company's behaviour may affect trade between Member States – a condition which is easily fulfilled under the case law of the CJEU – the application of national competition law may not prohibit agreements that would not be prohibited under Article 101(1) TFEU, that fulfil the conditions of Article 101(3) TFEU or that would come under one of the Commission's block exemption regulations (Article 3(2) of Regulation 1/2003). In other words: as soon as the (potential) effect on cross-border trade is fulfilled, national provisions on anti-competitive agreements may not be stricter than the European provisions to the same effect. The only exception that Article 3(3) of Regulation 1/2003 foresees is for national rules that predominantly pursue objectives different from those of the EU's competition law provisions.

75. Austria's sustainability exemption can only apply where the agreement in question does not have such a (potential) effect on trade between Member States, making its sphere of application quite limited.

76. Because the Austrian provisions are modelled upon the European ones, the Supreme Cartel Court has emphasised that the decisional practice of the European Commission and the case law of the CJEU need to be referred to when deciding cases under §§ 1, 2 KartG.[119]

§2. Dominant Undertakings

77. § 4 KartG defines market dominance. This is a decisive provision because companies that are found to be dominant on the relevant market are subsequently subject to stricter antitrust rules. § 4(1) KartG defines what is considered to be single dominance, while § 4(1a) KartG sets out that two or more companies may also be

117. Heinz Keinert, 'Innerösterreichische Anwendung von EG-GVO auch ohne ausdrückliche Rezeption?' (2008) *Österreichisches Recht der Wirtschaft* 565.
118. *See* Walter Brugger, 'Braucht Österreich eine Verordnung nach § 3 KartG?' (2009) *Österreichische Zeitschrift für Kartellrecht* 3.
119. KOG 26.6.2006, 16 Ok 51/05 – *Asphaltmischanlage II*.

collectively dominant. § 4(2) and (2a) KartG set out different presumptions of dominance that are based either on market shares or on market shares together with the number of competitors active on the market. If a company (paragraph 2) or several companies together (paragraph 2a) are subject to these presumptions, then it or they bear the burden of proof that the conditions for single or collective dominance are not fulfilled. The market shares contained in these presumptions are considerably lower than the respective rules established by the CJEU for EU competition law.[120]

78. Should a company or several companies collectively not fulfil the conditions for market dominance as set out in paragraphs 1, 1a, 2 and 2a of § 4 KartG, then § 4a KartG foresees a further alternative, namely a predominant market position in relation to a company's purchasers or suppliers (relative market power). Such a predominant market position is thought to exist where a company's 'purchasers or suppliers depend on maintaining business relations in order to avoid serious economic disadvantages'. This provision on market dominance is specific to Austrian competition law and does not have a counterpart in EU competition law.[121] Such a stricter national rule is possible thanks to Article 3(2) of Regulation 1/2003.

79. Where a company is dominant pursuant to §§ 4 or 4a KartG, it needs to abide by the rules of § 5 KartG. That provision prohibits the abuse of a dominant position and contains a non-exhaustive list of abusive behaviours, including excessive pricing, discriminating among contract partners, tying, or selling below cost price without objective justification. For the latter type of abusive behaviour, § 5(2) KartG foresees a reversal of the burden of proof for companies engaging in such behaviour. While the list of possible abusive behaviour is modelled on Article 102 TFEU, its final instance of selling below cost price cannot be found in the European provision. In addition, the Austrian list is somewhat more detailed than the one in Article 102 TFEU.

80. Overall, the Austrian Supreme Cartel Court considers that due to the close similarity of Article 102 TFEU and § 5 KartG, the European case law on Article 102 TFEU can be relied upon in order to interpret the Austrian provision on abuse of dominance.[122]

81. For more details on dominance, *see* §§ 121 ff. of this monograph; for types of abuse of dominance, *see* §§ 145 ff. of this monograph.

---

120. For single dominance and the *Akzo* presumption of a 50% market share for dominance, *see* CJEU Case C-62/86 *AKZO Chemie v. Commission*, ECLI:EU:C:1991:286, para. 60.

121. The Supreme Cartel Court has stated, however, that it believes Art. 102 TFEU to also cover relative market power; *see* KOG 12.7.2018, 16 Ok 1/18k – *Fachverband Reisebüros/Lufthansa*. For the opposite view, *see* the Cartel Court in the same case; KG 6.12.2017, 27 Kt 13/16p – *Fachverband Reisebüros/Lufthansa*.

122. RIS-Justiz RS0110382; e.g., KOG 18.6.1998, 16 Ok 5/98 – *Power-Pack III*; KOG 8.10.2015, 16 Ok 9/15g – *Verpackungen II*.

§3. Concentrations

82. § 7(1) KartG defines what is considered to be a concentration for the purposes of merger control under the KartG 2005:

1. the acquisition of an undertaking, as a whole or of a substantial part of it, by an undertaking, especially by way of merger or conversion;
2. the acquisition by an undertaking of rights in the business of another undertaking by means of operational lease or management agreements;
3. the direct or indirect acquisition of shares in an undertaking by another undertaking if as a result the participation held after the acquisition is or exceeds 25%, or is or exceeds 50%;
4. as a result, at least half of the management or members of the supervisory boards of two or more undertakings are identical;
5. any other connection of undertakings which allows one undertaking to have a direct or indirect dominant influence over another undertaking.

83. § 7(1) KartG therefore covers any scenario in which the joining of undertakings allows one undertaking to have direct or indirect control over another.

84. The establishment of a joint venture that fulfils all functions of an independent economic entity on a lasting basis is also considered to constitute a concentration for the purposes of merger control (§ 7(2) KartG).

85. For more details on the nature of concentrations under Austrian merger control, *see* §§ 153 ff. of this monograph.

86. § 9 KartG sets out which concentrations need to be notified to the Federal Competition Authority. That provision contains both a turnover threshold (paragraph 1) and an alternative transaction value threshold (paragraph 4). The turnover threshold consists of:

a. an aggregate worldwide turnover exceeding EUR 300 million;
b. an aggregate Austrian turnover exceeding EUR 30 million, with at least two undertakings concerned each exceeding a turnover of EUR 1 million in Austria;[123] and
c. an individual worldwide turnover exceeding EUR 5 million for at least two of the merging undertakings.

87. In addition to the turnover thresholds, a transaction value threshold was introduced into § 9(4) KartG in the summer of 2017. It was intended to target the acquisition of promising start-ups in digital markets that leave markets devoid of meaningful (potential) competitors.[124] It is actually the combination of two turnover

---

123. This second Austrian turnover threshold was introduced by the 2021 amendment.
124. 1522 der Beilagen XXV. GP (Erläuterungen zur Regierungsvorlage), p. 3. On this new provision, *see* Maximilian Mertel, 'Ausweitung der Zusammenschlusskontrolle durch das KaWeRÄG 2017'

thresholds in addition to the transaction value threshold and the need for domestic activity. Under the transaction value threshold, there is a duty to notify a merger when:

a. the merging companies' aggregate worldwide turnover exceeds EUR 300 million;
b. their aggregate domestic turnover exceeds EUR 15 million;
c. the value of the transaction exceeds EUR 200 million; and
d. the undertaking to be acquired carries out significant domestic activity.

88. The notification requirements in § 10(1) KartG ensure that the Federal Competition Authority, to whom the notification needs to be addressed, receives all relevant information to appraise whether the concentration may create or strengthen a dominant position.

89. §§ 8, 9(3) and 13 KartG specifically deal with media concentrations, reflecting the need to keep an eye on the already concentrated media markets in Austria to maintain media pluralism. § 8 KartG lays down which companies are considered to be media companies or media support companies, and when a concentration is deemed to constitute a media merger. This concern for media mergers is also reflected in the notification requirements, as § 9(3) KartG foresees that the turnover of media companies and media services needs to be multiplied by a factor of 200 when applying the turnover thresholds relied upon for merger notification. Furthermore, the notification of a media merger must include 'exact and exhaustive information on circumstances that might affect media pluralism' (§ 10(1) no 2 KartG). § 13(2) KartG sets out the concept of media pluralism that needs to be taken into account in merger control.

90. While the Austrian rules on anti-competitive agreements (§ 1 KartG) and on abuse of a dominant position (§ 5 KartG) are directly modelled upon the respective European provisions, the Austrian provisions on mergers differ a little from their European counterparts. This is also due to the different relationship that national merger regimes have with EU merger control. Article 21 EUMR contains a one-stop-shop rule according to which any concentrations that reach one of the two turnover thresholds of that regulation have a Union dimension. The European Commission is exclusively competent to assess mergers with such a Union dimension. Contrary to the rules on anti-competitive agreements and unilateral conduct, there is therefore no parallel application of national and European rules. Only mergers that do not have a Union dimension may be assessed under national merger regimes, such as the Austrian one.[125]

(2017) *Österreichische Zeitschrift für Kartellrecht* 91; Judith Feldner, '§ 9 Abs 4 KartG – Die praktische Bedeutung des neuen Schwellenwerts' (2017) *Österreichische Zeitschrift für Kartellrecht* 149; Teresa Eckhard, Anton Hartl & Stefan Ruech, 'Digitisation, Transaction Value Thresholds in Merger Control and Associated Challenges' (2019) *Österreichische Zeitschrift für Kartellrecht* 3.

125. Article 21(4) EUMR contains a small exception to that rule, as national merger control can apply to protect legitimate interests that are not taken into consideration under the EUMR, such as public security or media pluralism.

91. As already set out above (§ 45 of this monograph), there are several possibilities under the EUMR to refer cases from national competition authorities to the European Commission and vice versa (e.g., *see* Articles 4, 9, 22 EUMR). The substantive test for mergers under the EUMR is the SIEC test (significant impediment of effective competition), which includes not only the creation and strengthening of a dominant position but also goes beyond that. Since September 2021, this has also been the substantive test under Austrian merger control (§ 12 KartG).

§4. Other Prohibitions

92. § 6 KartG contains an additional prohibition that is closely related to the abuse of a dominant position: where a company is directly affected by a dominant undertaking's abuse of dominance and initiates proceedings against said dominant undertaking (§ 26 KartG) or complains to one of the official parties about such abuse (§ 40 KartG), the dominant undertaking may not engage in retaliatory measures against that company – such as cutting it from further supplies or selling to it on unreasonable terms.

93. While Austria did not introduce a prohibition as the German one (§ 19a GWB)[126] for digital gatekeepers, the 2021 amendment introduced § 28a KartG, which allows the two official parties to request the Cartel Court to find whether an undertaking enjoys a dominant position on a multisided digital market. This new provision cannot be relied upon by private parties (*see* § 36(2a) KartG). Also, it stops at the finding of a dominant position and does not concern the abuse of said dominant position, which is why the provision has been criticised for being of little practical use.[127]

94. The Fair Conditions of Competition Act (FWBG) contains provisions concerning the conditions of competition in the local supply of goods. These rules apply to unilateral conduct but are not premised upon the existence of a dominant position. § 1 FWBG prohibits commercial behaviour that endangers competition on the merits, while § 2 FWBG targets discriminatory conditions in supplier-reseller relationships. § 3 FWBG prohibits retaliatory measures. § 4 FWBG foresees a possibility for compulsory contracting where a company usually sells to final sellers and the local supply of goods is in jeopardy. § 5 FWBG contains a coverage obligation for commercial final sellers. §§ 5a ff. FWBG implemented Directive 2019/633 on unfair trading practices in business-to-business relationships in the agriculture and food supply chain.[128]

---

126. Gesetz gegen Wettbewerbsbeschränkungen (GWB; Act against Restrictions of Competition), dBGBl I 2013/1750 as amended.
127. On this criticism, *see* Dieter Thalhammer & Maximilian Mertel, '§ 28a KartG' para. 43, in: Alexander Egger & Natalie Harsdorf-Borsch (eds), *Kartellrecht – Kommentar* (Linde 2022).
128. Directive (EU) 2019/633 of the European Parliament and of the Council of 17 April 2019 on unfair trading practices in business-to-business relationships in the agricultural and food supply chain [2019] OJ L111/59.

95. The Criminal Code (StGB) prohibits bid rigging in § 168b StGB and foresees a custodial sentence of up to three years for acts of collusive tendering. § 292c StGB prohibits collusion during certain auctions, with the possibility of a custodial sentence of up to two years. Both provisions are targeted at natural persons.

96. Austrian unfair competition law can also be relied upon to take action against infringements of Austrian competition law. § 1(1) no 1 of the Unfair Competition Act (UWG) provides that a company that gains a competitive advantage by breaking the law can be served a cease-and-desist order and, where it does so intentionally, the claimant can be awarded damages. This rule also applies to cases in which competition law is infringed by a company. The Supreme Court has stated, however, that – as is the case for any other infringements of the law that are deemed relevant under unfair competition law – § 1(1) no 1 UWG only applies to infringements of the KartG where the infringed competition law provision cannot be interpreted in a way that makes the behaviour complained about appear legal in the eyes of the defendant.[129] Claims based on unfair competition law need to be asserted before the competent civil courts, not the Cartel Court. While the UWG is primarily enforced through claims by competitors, the Federal Competition Authority is one of the statutory parties given the power to enforce this law.[130]

§5. Tests of Illegality

I. Per Se Prohibitions and Naked Restraints

97. Just like Article 101(1) TFEU, § 1(1) KartG prohibits agreements between undertakings, decisions of associations of undertakings and concerted practices that have the object or effect of preventing, restricting or distorting competition. Thereby, the Austrian provision relies on the object/effect distinction that is also known under EU competition law. Where an agreement has the object of restricting competition, its anti-competitive effect does not need to be assessed.[131] Where, however, an agreement does not have the object of restricting competition, its (potential) anti-competitive effect needs to be shown.[132]

98. No matter whether an agreement, decision or concerted practice has the object or effect of restricting competition, in both cases, the behaviour under scrutiny is capable of escaping antitrust liability if the conditions of § 2 KartG (under EU law: Article 101(3) TFEU) are fulfilled. Theoretically, Austrian competition law therefore does not know any per se restrictions that would be unworthy of exemption. This equally applies to horizontal and vertical restrictions. There are certain types of agreements, however, that will find it difficult to be exempted. For instance, the *de minimis* exemption in § 2(2) no 1 KartG only applies where the agreement in

129. OGH 14.7.2009, 4 Ob 60/09s – *Anwaltssoftware*.
130. *See* § 14 UWG.
131. CJEU Joined Cases 56 & 58/64 *Consten and Grundig v. Commission*, ECLI:EU:C:1966:41.
132. CJEU Case 56/65 *Société Technique Minière v. Maschinenbau Ulm*, ECLI:EU:C:1966:38.

question does not aim at fixing selling prices, restricting production or distribution, or sharing markets. These hardcore cartels are thought to be detrimental to a competitive market even where the companies participating in the cartel have no market power. It is difficult to fathom circumstances under which such cartels would fulfil all the cumulative requirements for individual exemption under § 2(1) KartG. Hardcore cartels therefore closely resemble a per se restriction.

II. Balancing Tests

99. Austrian competition law – just like EU competition law – is primarily based upon provisions that require the competition authorities and courts to carry out balancing exercises in order to assess whether a certain commercial behaviour is indeed anti-competitive or not. However, this does not amount to a rule of reason as it is applied under US antitrust law. Indeed, the Supreme Cartel Court has followed the CJEU in holding that it is not necessary to carry out a competitive assessment of the pro- and anti-competitive effects of an agreement and subsequently weigh those against each other.[133]

100. As mentioned in the previous section, under § 2(1) KartG – which mirrors Article 101(3) TFEU – efficiencies brought about by an agreement can be taken into account in the form of a legal exemption from the cartel prohibition. This allows for some balancing of pro- and anti-competitive effects.

101. The ancillary restraints doctrine (on this, *see* § 261 of this monograph) allows for a balancing exercise where a restriction of competition is necessary and ancillary to a main agreement that is not anti-competitive.

III. Merger Tests

102. As briefly mentioned above (§ 91 of this monograph), Austrian merger control now relies on the SIEC test, which also includes anti-competitive effects other than dominance. On this, *see* below (§ 371 of this monograph).

133. KOG 20.12.2004, 16 Ok 17/04 – *Wärmedämmverbundsysteme*.

Chapter 4. Overview of Main Notions

103. Austrian competition law relies on a range of notions that are relevant beyond a single provision of the KartG or the WettbG. These include the notion of an undertaking, the relevant market, the different forms of a dominant position, agreements and concerted practices, the restriction of competition, the abuse of a dominant position, concentrations, and joint ventures.

§1. UNDERTAKING

104. The text of § 1(1) KartG prohibits agreements 'between entrepreneurs' ('zwischen Unternehmern') rather than 'between undertakings' ('zwischen Unternehmen'), as the otherwise identical Article 101(1) TFEU does. Similarly, the wording of § 4(1) KartG speaks of a dominant 'entrepreneur' ('Unternehmer') rather than of a dominant undertaking ('Unternehmen'; Article 102 TFEU). This difference between the wording of the KartG and the TFEU is due to Austrian legal terminology in commercial law, which is very much focused on entrepreneurs. The Supreme Cartel Court has held, however, that this different wording is of no substantive relevance,[134] which is why the following concentrates on the notion of an undertaking.

105. Under Austrian commercial law, a company is understood to be 'any permanent organisation of independent economic activity, even if it is not for profit' (§ 1(2) UGB).[135] This definition is not adopted in Austrian competition law, however. While the Cartel Act originally did not contain a definition of what it considered to constitute an undertaking,[136] the amendment of 2021 introduced such a definition in the provisions on fines. It now states that '[a]ny entity that engages in an economic activity, regardless of its legal form and how it is financed, shall be deemed to be an undertaking' (§ 29(2) KartG). Austrian competition law relies on a broad functional notion of an undertaking that is in line with the European notion of an undertaking for the purposes of competition law.[137]

106. The Supreme Cartel Court has stated that the:

> notion of 'undertaking' [for the purposes of competition law] shall mean any independent and not purely private and non-professional activity carried out by a person in the production or distribution of goods or commercial services. A functional approach is taken, based on the nature of the activity being carried out rather than on the characteristics of the person carrying it out. In order to

---

134. KOG 8.10.2015, 16 Ok 3/15z – *VAMED/NRZ Rosenhügel*.
135. Unternehmensgesetzbuch (UGB; Commercial Law Act), dRGBl 1897/219 as amended.
136. *See* KOG 14.6.2004, 16 Ok 5/04 – *Gebietskrankenkasse II*.
137. For § 1(1) KartG and Art. 101(1) TFEU, *see* KOG 4.10.2010, 16 Ok 6/10 – *Holzhandel I*.

fulfil the functional concept of an undertaking, it is sufficient that economic services are offered or provided for remuneration.[138]

107. The Supreme Cartel Court has emphasised that the economic approach foreseen in § 20 KartG also requires the adoption of a functional understanding of the notion of an undertaking.[139]

108. What is decisive in order to be qualified as an undertaking is the carrying out of a commercial activity.[140] As under EU competition law, the notion of an undertaking is relative, meaning that one and the same company may be regarded as an undertaking for the purposes of competition law for some parts of its business, while not constituting an undertaking for others, such as in the case of social security bodies that primarily fulfil a public function.[141]

109. Austria follows the single economic entity doctrine: where undertakings belong to a group of companies that is controlled by a parent company, these undertakings together form one single undertaking for the purposes of Austrian competition law.[142] For this reason, a parent company may also be fined for the competition law infringement of its daughter companies, unless it can prove that its daughter company operates independently on the market.[143] To that effect, the parent company's turnover can even be included when calculating the fine for breaching Austrian competition law.

110. In 2011, the Supreme Cartel Court made a reference for a preliminary ruling to the Court of Justice of the European Union in the *Compass-Datenbank* case. It asked the CJEU whether a public authority that collects company data for inclusion in the public company register and offers access to that register against a fee is to be regarded as an undertaking for the purposes of Article 102 TFEU. The CJEU answered that 'a data collection activity in relation to undertakings, on the basis of a statutory obligation on those undertakings to disclose the data and powers of enforcement related thereto, falls within the exercise of public powers. As a result, such an activity is not an economic activity'.[144] Thus, due to a lack of private sector activity, the public authority charged with implementing the Austrian company register was not regarded as an undertaking within the meaning of that provision. As a consequence, the applicant could not sue the Federal Republic of Austria for an infringement of Article 102 TFEU in this case.[145]

138. KOG 8.10.2015, 16 Ok 3/15z – *VAMED/NRZ Rosenhügel* (own translation); *see also* RIS-Justiz RS0130406.
139. KOG 17.12.2008, 16 Ok 12/08 – *Private Equity-Ausnahme*; *see also* RIS-Justiz RS0124391.
140. KOG 17.12.2008, 16 Ok 12/08 – *Private Equity-Ausnahme.*
141. KOG 15.12.2003, 16 Ok 12/03 – *Gebietskrankenkasse I.*
142. KOG 15.5.2000, 16 Ok 1/00 – *Mobilfunktelefone.*
143. KOG 8.10.2015, 16 Ok 2/15b & 16 Ok 8/15k – *Spar.*
144. CJEU Case C-138/11 *Compass-Datenbank GmbH v. Republik Österreich*, ECLI:EU:C:2012:449, para. 40.
145. KOG 11.10.2012, 16 Ok 4/12 – *Firmenbuch II.*

111. In another case, the city of Vienna was considered to constitute an undertaking for the purposes of competition law when it permitted the setting-up of newspaper stands on properties administered by the city, even if this was done through an administrative order.[146]

112. In a case involving regional health insurance funds, the Supreme Cartel Court held that competition law did not apply to these because they did not constitute undertakings within the meaning of the KartG. The regional health insurance funds were public bodies whose economic activity exclusively had a social function and was based on the principle of solidarity.[147] This is in line with the CJEU's case law.[148]

§2. Relevant Market

113. The entire system of Austrian competition law is based on the notion of a relevant market, as can be seen throughout the legal provisions. Austrian competition law does not contain a full-fledged definition of what constitutes a relevant market as such, but §§ 21 and 23 KartG already include the main parameters upon which a market definition exercise needs to be based.[149] On market definition and its importance for competition law, the Supreme Cartel Court has stated the following:

> The market is the key fundamental concept of competition law. From an economic perspective, it is the economic place of exchange, defined by the market participants that face each other as suppliers and buyers of goods or services with opposing economic interests. In terms of competition law, markets are economic facts. Therefore, the question of market definition is a question of fact as far as it concerns the determination of objectively verifiable criteria for definition, it is a question of law as far as it concerns an assessment of the method on which the market definition is based. The task of market delineation in the assessment of competition cases is to identify competitive relationships. The purpose of defining a market in both its product and geographic dimension is to determine which competing undertakings are able to constrain the behaviour of the participating companies and prevent them from escaping effective competitive pressure.[150]

146. KOG 11.6.2015, 16 Ok 8/14h – *Verteilerboxen in U-Bahn-Stationen II.*
147. KOG 14.6.2004, 16 Ok 5/04 – *Gebietskrankenkasse II.*
148. *See also* Claudine Vartian, 'Austria' para. 3-037, in: Ioannis Kokkoris (ed.), *Competition Cases from the European Union: The Ultimate Guide to Leading Cases from the EU, Member States and EFTA* (2d ed., Sweet & Maxwell 2010).
149. KOG 17.12.2008, 16 Ok 15/08 – *Gratiswochenzeitung.* On market definition in the case law, *see* RIS-Justiz RS0124671.
150. KOG 11.6.2015, 16 Ok 8/14h – *Verteilerboxen in U-Bahn-Stationen II* (own translation; references to further case law in the quote omitted).

114. Market delineation therefore wants to capture the competitive relationships that are present on a given market. The relevant market is delineated both in its product dimension and in its geographic dimension. In order to gauge the competitive restraints at work, the Supreme Cartel Court holds that it is also relevant whom a market participant regards as their competitor.[151]

115. Market definition is a fact-intense enterprise and cannot be carried out in the abstract. Under Austrian competition law, as is also highlighted by the quote above, it is recognised that the delineation of a relevant market is a question of fact insofar as it concerns the determination of objectively verifiable criteria. It is a question of law, however, where it concerns the methods being used to delineate the relevant market.[152]

116. The Austrian approach to defining relevant antitrust product markets is commonly known as the 'Bedarfsmarktkonzept'[153] and is best translated as a market concept based on the substitutability of demand. In the section on joint provisions, § 23 KartG states that '[u]nder this Federal Act, all goods (services) that under specific market conditions satisfy the same needs shall be deemed to be specific goods (services)'. This provision is seen as an expression of the 'Bedarfsmarktkonzept'.[154] It requires that the opposite market side regards goods or services as interchangeable based on their characteristics, price or intended use.[155] § 21 KartG foresees that in the application of the Cartel Act, market shares are calculated for a specific type of goods or services as defined in § 23 KartG.

117. While the 'Bedarfsmarktkonzept' is heavily based on demand-side substitutability, supply-side substitutability may also be taken into account, in line with the established approach under EU competition law.[156] This includes a supplier's possibility to change production ('Angebotsumstellungsflexibilität' or supply substitution), even if this possibility is not put into action.[157] In a number of cases involving the distribution of movies to cinemas, the Supreme Cartel Court held that a promising movie ('blockbuster') constituted its own narrow relevant antitrust market, as it was not interchangeable with other movies. This led to the finding of a monopoly position. The market share of the film distribution company on the whole film distribution market was not regarded as relevant in this respect.[158]

---

151. KOG 2.12.2013, 16 Ok 6/12 – *BWB/Wiener Wohnen*; KOG 17.12.2008, 16 Ok 15/08 – *Gratiswochenzeitung*.
152. RIS-Justiz RS0124421; KOG 12.7.2018, 16 Ok 1/18k – *Fachverband Reisebüros/Lufthansa*.
153. For example, *see* KOG 21.12.2016, 16 Ok 11/16b – *Novomatic/Casinos Austria II*; KOG 8.10.2015, 16 Ok 6/15s – *Radiusklausel V*; KOG 11.6.2015, 16 Ok 8/14h – *Verteilerboxen in U-Bahn-Stationen II*; KOG 1.7.2002, 16 Ok 5/02 – *Village Cinemas*; KOG 17.12.2001, 16 Ok 9/01 – *W-Beteiligungsgesellschaft I*.
154. KOG 8.10.2015, 16 Ok 6/15s – *Radiusklausel V*.
155. *See* KOG 2.12.2013, 16 Ok 6/12 – *BWB/Wiener Wohnen*; OGH 22.6.1999, 4 Ob 90/99k – *Jahresbonus*.
156. KOG 12.7.2018, 16 Ok 1/18k – *Fachverband Reisebüros/Lufthansa*.
157. KOG 2.12.2013, 16 Ok 6/12 – *BWB/Wiener Wohnen*.
158. KOG 16.7.2008, 16 Ok 6/08 – *Asterix bei den Olympischen Spielen*; KOG 4.4.2005, 16 Ok 20/04 – *Multiplex I*; KOG 1.7.2002, 16 Ok 5/02 – *Village Cinemas*.

118. In practice, the European Commission's Market Definition Notice is frequently referred to. While its first edition dated from 1997,[159] it was newly issued in 2024 and now contains much more detail, particularly as concerns digital markets and ecosystems.[160] While the Supreme Cartel Court regards the SSNIP[161] test that is contained in that Notice as one suitable method for delineating the relevant market, other methods are seen as adequate as well.[162] It has also been warned that the SSNIP test may not be applied mechanically.[163] In particular, the cellophane fallacy of applying a hypothetical price increase to a price that is already raised above the competitive level is routinely acknowledged by Austrian courts.[164]

119. The geographic market limits the relevant product market to those market participants who are competitors within a territory in which conditions of competition are sufficiently homogeneous.[165] For instance, in cases involving radius clauses in contracts concluded by shopping centres, the Supreme Cartel Court has emphasised that the geographical market for the shopping centres and shopping streets in question covered catchment areas that could be reached in a driving time of up to ninety minutes.[166] In a case on the distribution of newspapers in the vicinity of public transport, the Supreme Cartel Court discussed how the parties' market shares varied considerably when comparing Vienna and the whole federal territory, an indication that for the geographic market definition, the conditions of competition in Vienna and elsewhere might not be sufficiently homogeneous to warrant a single relevant geographic market.[167]

120. A temporal relevant market can be delineated where there are seasonal fluctuations for a given product.

159. European Commission, Commission Notice on the definition of relevant market for the purposes of Community competition law (Market Definition Notice 1997) [1997] OJ C372/5.
160. European Commission, Commission Notice on the definition of relevant market for the purposes of Union competition law (Market Definition Notice 2024) [2024] OJ C1645.
161. SSNIP stands for small but significant non-transitory increase in price, meaning a price increase in the range of 5–10% under the Market Definition Notice 1997, para. 17.
162. For instance, *see* KOG 12.7.2018, 16 Ok 1/18k – *Fachverband Reisebüros/Lufthansa*. Also *see* KOG 12.12.2011, 16 Ok 8/10 – *Radiusklausel IV* and the debate that ensued on the issue of market definition in that case in the Austrian Competition Journal: Marcus Lindner, 'Die Rechtsfrage "Methode zur Marktabgrenzung": Die generelle Eignung des SSNIP-Tests unter Artikel 101 und 102 AEUV? Die Fälle Radiusklausel IV (25 Kt 35, 36/08; 16 Ok 8/10) und Flüssiggas (29 Kt 23, 24/09)' (2012) *Österreichische Zeitschrift für Kartellrecht* 73; Gerhard Clemenz, 'Paradoxe Ansichten zum SSNIP-Test' (2015) *Österreichische Zeitschrift für Kartellrecht* 58.
163. KOG 25.3.2009, 16 Ok 14/08 – *Radiusklausel II*.
164. For example, *see* KOG 25.3.2009, 16 Ok 14/08 – *Radiusklausel II*; KOG 8.10.2015, 16 Ok 6/15s – *Radiusklausel V*.
165. KOG 16.7.2008, 16 Ok 4/08 – *Radreisen*; OGH 30.6.1998, 4 Ob 165/98p – *Reparatur von Leasingfahrzeugen*.
166. KOG 25.3.2009, 16 Ok 1/09 – *Radiusklausel III*.
167. KOG 11.6.2015, 16 Ok 8/14h – *Verteilerboxen in U-Bahn-Stationen II*. On this *see also* Astrid Ablasser-Neuhuber, Florian Neumayr, Gerhard Fussenegger & Sebastian Reiter, 'Austria' § 2.04[2], in: Frank L. Fine (ed.), *European Competition Laws*, vol 1 (loose-leaf, Matthew Bender Elite Products, release 21-11/2022).

§3. Dominant Position

121. In order to establish an undertaking's dominant position, the relevant market first needs to be delineated (*see* §§ 113 ff. above). Then, the undertaking's degree of market power or dominance on that relevant market is determined.[168]

122. The concept of a dominant market position is defined in § 4 KartG, in the context of the rules on the abuse of a dominant position. Austrian competition law knows single and collective dominance (§ 4 KartG) as well as relative market power (§ 4a KartG). While the first two concepts are very similar to single and collective dominance as known under EU competition law – albeit with lower market share thresholds – the concept of relative market power is one that is distinctive of Austrian competition law.

123. § 4(1) KartG contains a qualitative definition of single dominance. It states that an undertaking is dominant if it is exposed to no or only insignificant competition, or if it holds a predominant market position in relation to its competitors. In order to determine the latter, the provision considers that a number of factors are relevant: the undertaking's financial strength, its relations to other undertakings, its opportunities to access supply and sales markets, and other circumstances that restrict market entry for other undertakings. The 2021 amendment introduced three further factors to consider when establishing whether a company is dominant, namely the significance of its intermediary services for other undertakings' access to supply and sales markets, its access to competition-relevant data, and the benefits derived from network effects. These three factors aim at better taking into account characteristics that are relevant for market power in dynamic, digital market environments.

124. In the case law, reference is regularly made to the CJEU's qualitative definition of dominance as:

> a position of economic strength enjoyed by an undertaking which enables it to prevent effective competition being maintained on the relevant market by giving it the power to behave to an appreciable extent independently of its competitors, customers and ultimately of its consumers.[169]

125. § 4(2) KartG quantifies single dominance by providing market share levels that reverse the burden of proof for the question of dominance. For single dominance, the burden of proof is reversed:

168. KOG 25.3.2009, 16 Ok 14/08 – *Radiusklausel II.*
169. For the CJEU quote, *see, e.g.*, CJEU Case 27/76 *United Brands v. Commission*, ECLI:EU:C:1978:22, para. 65. For Austrian cases resting thereon, *see, e.g.*, KOG 16.7.2008, 16 Ok 4/08 – *Radreisen*; KOG 27.2.2006, 16 Ok 46/05 – *Styria Media AG.*

- if the undertaking has a market share of at least 30% on the relevant market;
- if it has a market share of over 5% on a relevant market on which it has no more than two competitors; or
- if it has a market share of over 5% on the relevant market and is one of the four biggest undertakings on this market, where these four biggest undertakings have a combined market share of at least 80%.

Where the burden of proof is reversed, it is for the party that is presumed to be dominant to prove that despite fulfilling these market share criteria, it is not in fact dominant on the relevant market.

126. Where an undertaking is the only one to offer certain goods or services on a relevant market, it is a monopolist and dominance is generally assumed.[170]

127. § 4(1a) KartG sets out that two or more companies are collectively dominant if there is no substantial competition between them and if, together, they fulfil the conditions set out in § 4(1) KartG (on these, *see* above). To quantify this provision, § 4(2a) KartG reverses the burden of proof for the question of collective dominance if, together, a number of undertakings have a market share of at least 50% on the relevant market and there are only three or fewer undertakings active on that market; or if the undertakings have a market share of at least two-thirds of the relevant market and there are only five or fewer undertakings active on that market.

128. Apart from single and collective dominance, Austrian competition law also knows another type of dominance, namely relative market power as set out in § 4a KartG.[171] Such a predominant market position in relation to a company's purchasers or suppliers exists if a company's business partners (be they purchasers or suppliers) depend on maintaining business relations with the company in a predominant market position in order to avoid serious economic disadvantages.

129. The 2021 amendment introduced a specific rule for relative market power in the digital sphere into § 4a KartG. It provides that where an undertaking acts as an intermediary on a multisided digital market, it is considered to be dominant if the purchasers of its intermediary services depend on establishing business relations with it in order to avoid serious economic disadvantages. Intermediary services to which said provision applies can, for instance, include marketplace services. While § 4a KartG traditionally only applied when a business relationship had already been established, this new addition to the provision recognises that in the digital sphere, some companies may never be able to enter competition if they cannot establish a business relationship with the predominant platform.

170. KOG 16.7.2008, 16 Ok 6/08 – *Asterix bei den Olympischen Spielen*; KOG 12.7.2018, 16 Ok 1/18k – *Fachverband Reisebüros/Lufthansa*.

171. Before the 2021 amendment, this provision was contained in § 4(3) KartG.

130. In the case law, relative market power has been relied upon in cases involving multiplex movie theatres, i.e., movie theatres with more than eight auditoriums, and their dependence on movie distribution companies.[172] Other cases involved car dealers and their dependence on the respective car manufacturers whose vehicles they were selling.[173] The Supreme Cartel Court has emphasised that in order to assess an undertaking's relative market power, one must appraise the possible alternative sources of supply for purchasers or alternative outlets for suppliers on the relevant market. It must also be assessed whether existing alternatives are available on economically reasonable terms. Even where relative market power is found, however, there may be objective grounds upon which the dominant undertaking may rely in order to refuse to enter into a business relationship with another undertaking.[174]

131. While the Supreme Cartel Court has held that Article 102 TFEU already encompasses the relative market power envisaged by § 4a KartG,[175] this remains questionable as the case law referred to by the Court to support this argument concerned cases in which the essential trading partners held high market shares on the relevant market.[176] § 4a KartG, however, does not require a strong market position on any relevant market but looks at the particular business relationship between the parties involved. It may therefore be seen as a competition rule on unilateral conduct that is stricter than what is foreseen under Article 102 TFEU, something that is expressly allowed under Article 3(2) of Regulation 1/2003.[177]

132. Within the realm of merger control, these definitions of dominance are of direct relevance, as § 12(1) no 2 KartG foresees that the Cartel Court shall prohibit a merger where the concentration would either create or strengthen a dominant position within the meaning of § 4 KartG. § 4a KartG plays no role in merger control.

§4. Agreements and Concerted Practices

133. § 1(1) KartG provides that certain agreements between undertakings, decisions by associations of undertakings and concerted practices are prohibited. This terminology mirrors the one found in Article 101(1) TFEU. Under Austrian competition law, these notions are also interpreted in line with European case law (on

172. KOG 16.7.2008, 16 Ok 6/08 – *Asterix bei den Olympischen Spielen*; KOG 4.4.2005, 16 Ok 20/04 – *Multiplex I*; KOG 1.7.2002, 16 Ok 5/02 – *Village Cinemas*; OGH 9.9.1997, 4 Ob 214/97t – *Filmverleihgeschäft I.*
173. OGH 20.10.2009, 4 Ob 119/09t – *Suzuki*; OGH 15.10.2002, 4 Ob 187/02g – *Alfa Romeo*; KOG 17.2.2021, 16 Ok 4/20d – *Peugeot.*
174. KOG 26.6.2014, 16 Ok 12/13 – *Sports Direct/Asics.* On this case, *see* Wolfgang Schuhmacher, 'Zum Kontrahierungszwang nach NahVG und Kartellrecht' (2014) *Wirtschaftsrechtliche Blätter* 655.
175. KOG 12.7.2018, 16 Ok 1/18k – *Fachverband Reisebüros/Lufthansa.*
176. CJEU Case 85/76 *Hoffmann-La Roche v. Commission*, ECLI:EU:C:1979:36, para. 4; GC Case T-219/99 *British Airways v. Commission*, ECLI:EU:T:2003:343.
177. In this sense, *see also* KG 6.12.2017, 27 Kt 13/16p – *Fachverband Reisebüros/Lufthansa.*

the difference between the term entrepreneur as used in the Austrian provisions and the notion of an undertaking, *see* already above at §§ 104 ff.).[178]

134. The notion of an agreement is interpreted broadly. To be caught out as an agreement under § 1(1) KartG, it is not necessary that the undertakings involved enter into a legally binding contract.[179] The Supreme Cartel Court has held that an agreement within the meaning of that provision requires the parties' concurrence of wills to act in a certain way on the market. The agreement itself may be concluded explicitly, but it may also be implied, and it can be concluded in writing or in any other form.[180]

135. An agreement within the meaning of § 1(1) KartG does not need to consist of a single act but may also consist of several acts or of continuous conduct that together form(s) part of an overall plan.[181] Even where an undertaking only participates in some aspects of an anti-competitive agreement, it will be liable for the entire cartel activity if it is aware of the overall plan.[182] In addition, as under EU competition law, it is of no relevance whether a company voluntarily enters into an anti-competitive agreement with others, or whether it is coerced into doing so, e.g., through economic pressure.[183]

136. As under European competition law, it is not required that a company is active on the relevant market on which an anti-competitive agreement is implemented. For instance, a company that helps stabilise a cartel or a consulting company may become liable under competition law when they support their clients' cartel activities.[184]

137. The second option under § 1(1) KartG, the decision by an association of undertakings, includes any type of decision by an agglomeration of companies. It is of no relevance how the association of undertakings is organised, e.g., as a corporation, an association under the Associations Act,[185] or any other affiliation such as a representation of interests that is foreseen by law.[186] In Austria, the latter applies

178. *See* KOG 12.12.2011, 16 Ok 8/10 – *Radiusklausel IV*; Axel Reidlinger & Isabella Hartung, *Das österreichische Kartellrecht: Ein Handbuch für Praktiker* 51 (5th ed., Linde 2024).
179. KOG 8.10.2015, 16 Ok 2/15b & 16 Ok 8/15k – *Spar*.
180. KOG 25.3.2009, 16 Ok 1/09 – *Radiusklausel III*; KOG 12.12.2011, 16 Ok 8/10 – *Radiusklausel IV*; KOG 7.11.2013, 16 Ok 7/13 – *Sägeindustrie (Hausdurchsuchung)*.
181. KOG 8.10.2015, 16 Ok 2/15b & 16 Ok 8/15k – *Spar*; with reference to CJEU Case C-105/04 P *Nederlanske Federatieve Vereeniging voor de Groothandel op Elektrotechnisch Gebied v. Commission*, ECLI:EU:C:2006:592, para. 110.
182. KOG 31.3.2016, 16 Ok 7/15p – *BWB/Kühne + Nagel*.
183. KOG 12.12.2011, 16 Ok 8/10 – *Radiusklausel IV*.
184. KOG 19.4.2010, 16 Ok 2/10 – *Feuerwehrfahrzeuge II*, with reference to GC Case T-99/04 *AC-Treuhand v. Commission*, ECLI:EU:T:2008:256, para. 146; KOG 31.3.2016, 16 Ok 7/15p – *BWB/Kühne + Nagel*, with reference to CJEU Case C-194/14 P *AC-Treuhand v. Commission*, ECLI:EU:C:2015:717, para. 35.
185. Vereinsgesetz 2002 (Associations Act), BGBl I 2002/66 as amended.
186. KOG 23.6.1997, 16 Ok 14/97 – *Preisliste 2*.

to different kinds of chambers, such as the Notaries' Chamber, the Bar Association, the Chamber of Physicians or the Chamber of Commerce.

138. Concerted practices are equally caught out under § 1(1) KartG. The Supreme Cartel Court regards concerted practices as a fallback option if neither an agreement between undertakings nor a decision by an association of undertakings can be established.[187] The finding of concerted practices requires that one can establish that companies cooperated deliberately and intentionally with the aim of substituting the risks of competition with their practical cooperation, but without reaching the stage of concluding an agreement proper within the meaning of § 1(1) KartG.[188] At the same time, concerted practices may neither be accidental nor simply market-driven behaviour by the undertakings concerned.[189] As the Supreme (Cartel) Court has stated on numerous occasions in the case law just cited, concerted practices can frequently only be established through circumstantial evidence.

§5. Restriction of Competition

139. Under § 1(1) KartG, a restriction of competition can consist in the prevention, restriction or distortion of competition. § 1(2) KartG lists various types of agreements that are considered to constitute a restriction of competition, such as price-fixing, market sharing or tying. These instances will be further discussed below (*see* §§ 258 ff. of this monograph).

140. On a more general level, Austrian competition law considers that a restriction of competition lies in a reduction of an undertaking's freedom of commercial action,[190] similar to Germany.[191] As such, the Supreme Cartel Court has held that it will also find a restriction of competition where the freedom of action that is relevant for competition is impaired for one or several of the undertakings involved in an anti-competitive agreement, decision or concerted practice.[192]

141. Just like Article 101 TFEU, Austrian competition law prohibits both horizontal and vertical agreements that restrict competition. While horizontal agreements are concluded between undertakings that are active at the same level of the economy, vertical agreements are concluded between undertakings at different levels of the economy. In addition, the Supreme Cartel Court has held that Article 101 TFEU (and, by extension, § 1(1) KartG) protects actual as well as potential competition.[193]

187. KOG 17.12.1997, 16 Ok 21/97 – *Preisliste 1*; KOG 23.6.1997, 16 Ok 14/97 – *Preisliste 2.*
188. OGH 30.6.1998, 4 Ob 165/98p – *Reparatur von Leasingfahrzeugen.*
189. KOG 9.10.2000, 16 Ok 7/00 – *Zonentarifsystem.*
190. KOG 1.12.2009, 16 Ok 10/09 – *Pressegrosso II.*
191. *See* Florian Wagner-von Papp, *Competition Law in Germany* para. 233 (International Encyclopaedia of Competition Law, Wolters Kluwer 2013).
192. KOG 26.6.2006, 16 Ok 51/05 – *Asphaltmischanlage II.*
193. KOG 6.9.2017, 16 Ok 10/16f – *BWB/Semperit.*

142. The restriction of competition may either constitute the very object of an agreement between two or more undertakings, of a decision by an association of undertakings or of concerted practices among two or more undertakings, or it may result from such actions ('effect'). This system of restrictions of competition, of course, is closely modelled upon Article 101 TFEU. The object or effect of an anti-competitive agreement are alternatives and under § 1(1) KartG, either is sufficient to find an infringement.[194] While Austrian competition law used to grant certain privileges to cartels by effect, this is no longer the case.[195]

143. Based on the case law of the CJEU, the Supreme Cartel Court holds that in order to decide whether competition is restricted by object, one needs to assess the content of an agreement that is thought to restrict competition, its objectives as well as its economic and legal context. In addition, one should take into account the nature of the products (goods or services). The undertakings' intention, however, is not part of the legal test for finding a restriction of competition by object.[196]

144. Where an agreement, decision or concerted practice does not have the object of restricting competition, its effects need to be assessed. To do so, the Supreme Cartel Court has emphasised that one must engage in a counterfactual analysis by considering what competition would look like without the agreement. Both actual and potential effects may be considered in this analysis. In analysing the effects on competition, the Court will assess the negative effects on prices, production, innovation, choice and quality.[197]

§6. Monopolisation and Abuse of Dominance

145. As under EU competition law, an undertaking's unilateral conduct may be prohibited when it constitutes the abuse of a dominant market position. In order to apply the provision on abuse of dominance, a company must already be dominant at the time of engaging in said behaviour (on dominance, *see* above at §§ 121 ff. of this monograph). The monopolisation of a market by a previously non-dominant undertaking is not prohibited under Austrian competition law but may be addressed in merger situations.

146. Based on the case law of the CJEU, the Supreme Cartel Court does not require a causal relationship between the undertaking's dominant position and its

194. KOG 26.6.2006, 16 Ok 51/05 – *Asphaltmischanlage II.*
195. *See* § 18 KartG 1988, BGBl 1988/600 (no longer in force).
196. KOG 6.9.2017, 16 Ok 10/16f – *BWB/Semperit*; with reference to CJEU Case C-67/13 P *Groupement des Cartes Bancaires*, ECLI:EU:C:2014:2204, para. 52; CJEU Case C-172/14 *ING Pensii*, ECLI:EU:C:2015:484, paras 31 ff.; CJEU Case C-32/11 *Allianz Hungária*, ECLI:EU:C:2013:160, para. 43.
197. KOG 26.6.2006, 16 Ok 51/05 – *Asphaltmischanlage II*; KOG 23.6.2003, 16 Ok 4/03 – *K-Hit-Radio*.

abusive conduct.[198] Instead, the Supreme Cartel Court has held that in the case of an exclusionary abuse, 'it is only necessary that the means [of competition] in question are different from those of normal competition based on the performance of the market participants and that they are capable of further impairing competition; it is not necessary that the means in question are those resulting from the dominant position of the undertaking'.[199]

147. § 5(1) KartG prohibits the abuse of a dominant position and provides a list of abusive behaviour. This list, however, is not exhaustive. The individual abuses under § 5(1) KartG are discussed below (*see* §§ 319 ff. of this monograph).

148. § 6 KartG prohibits dominant undertakings from engaging in retaliatory measures when being accused of an abuse of a dominant position.

149. Based on the supremacy of EU law, the Supreme Cartel Court has held that where Article 102 TFEU finds an abuse of a dominant position, this must also be the case under § 5 KartG.[200]

150. Conduct that constitutes an abuse of a dominant position under § 5 KartG is considered to be unlawful. A legal act affected by such unlawful conduct is rendered null and void under Austrian civil law, even without a prior finding of an infringement by the Cartel Court.[201]

151. According to the long-standing case law of the Supreme Cartel Court,

> any conduct by an undertaking in a dominant position that may affect the structure of a market on which competition is already weakened precisely because of the presence of said undertaking, and which prevents the maintenance of the degree of competition still existing on the market or the development of that competition by using means which depart from the means of normal competition between goods or services on the basis of the performance of the operators on the market, is abusive.[202]

152. Both under Article 102 TFEU and under § 5(1) KartG, an abuse of dominance is held to exist where the dominant undertaking's conduct restricts effective

198. RIS-Justiz RS0115793; e.g., *see* cases KOG 5.9.2001, 16 Ok 3/01 – *Hausbrieffachanlagen*; KOG 17.11.2003, 16 Ok 11/03 – *Schnurlostelefon*.
199. RIS-Justiz RS0115793 (own translation).
200. KOG 15.5.2000, 16 Ok 4/00 – *Hauszustellungssystem III*. This argument was the basis for the request for a preliminary ruling that the Supreme Cartel Court referred to the CJEU in that case; *see* KOG 9.12.1996, 16 Ok 9/96 – *Hauszustellungssystem I*; CJEU Case C-7/97 *Oscar Bronner v. Mediaprint*, ECLI:EU:C:1998:569.
201. Allgemeines Bürgerliches Gesetzbuch (ABGB; General Civil Code), JGS 1811/946 as amended, § 879(1); OGH 15.10.2002, 4 Ob 187/02g – *Alfa Romeo*.
202. RIS-Justiz RS0063530 (own translation), e.g., in cases KOG 27.6.2013, 16 Ok 7/12 – *Taxi-App*; KOG 8.10.2015, 16 Ok 9/15g – *Verpackungen II*; OGH 26.4.2017, 1 Ob 39/17t – *Eintrittskarten*; KOG 12.3.2020, 16 Ok 1/20p – *Simulcrypt-Vereinbarung*. On the latter case, *see* 'Zum Vorliegen eines kartellrechtlichen Preismissbrauchs' (2020) *Wirtschaftsrechtliche Blätter* 289.

and undistorted competition on the market.[203] It is not necessary to establish a subjective side when it comes to § 5(1) KartG.[204]

§7. Concentrations

153. The aim of Austrian merger control is to assess whether an undertaking's external growth ('concentration') that involves at least two undertakings may harm competition on the market.[205] Merger control should help maintain a market structure that is conducive to effective competition, with many independent market participants.[206] § 7(1) KartG establishes several very detailed alternatives of what constitutes a concentration within the meaning of the Act. This allows the KartG to encompass a wide range of changes of control that may have an impact on competition on the market. The alternatives foreseen by § 7(1) KartG are:

1. the acquisition of an undertaking, as a whole or of a substantial part of it, by an undertaking, especially by way of merger or conversion;
2. the acquisition by an undertaking of rights in the business of another undertaking by means of operational lease or management agreements;
3. the direct or indirect acquisition of shares in an undertaking by another undertaking if as a result, the participation held after the acquisition is or exceeds 25%, or is or exceeds 50%;
4. as a result, at least half of the management or members of the supervisory boards of two or more undertakings are identical;
5. any other connection of undertakings which allows one undertaking to have a direct or indirect dominant influence over another undertaking.

154. § 7(1) KartG thus requires that at least two previously independent undertakings are parties to a transaction through which one of them becomes attributable to a new economic entity. The notion of undertaking needs to be understood in a functional sense (*see* above, §§ 104 ff. of this monograph). It does not matter whether Austrian commercial law considers a business to constitute an undertaking, but only whether it constitutes one under the competition law provisions. This may also include shareholders of corporations that exercise control over a business.

155. A concentration may occur through an asset or a share deal. What matters under Austrian merger control is not whether control within the meaning of corporate law or takeover law is established. Instead, an autonomous concept of control exists for competition law purposes, which focuses on the ability of a company to

203. KOG 12.7.2018, 16 Ok 1/18k – *Fachverband Reisebüros/Lufthansa*; with reference to GC Case T-321/05 *Astra Zeneca v. Commission*, ECLI:EU:T:2010:266; CJEU Case 322/81 *Michelin v. Commission (Michelin I)*, ECLI:EU:C:1983:313.

204. KOG 8.10.2015, 16 Ok 9/15g – *Verpackungen II.*

205. RIS-Justiz RS0121884; e.g., in case KOG 12.10.2016, 16 Ok 9/16h – *Novomatic/Casinos Austria I.*

206. KOG 10.3.2003, 16 Ok 20/02 – *Postbus*; also cited in KOG 27.1.2014, 16 Ok 11/13 – *Morawa/Pressegroßvertrieb.*

assert its own competitive interests in the target company, relating to issues such as competitive position, investment decisions, or decisions on production and distribution.[207] Corporate law may, however, indicate under which circumstances control is established for a certain type of company. Therefore, based on Austrian corporate law, a share deal that leads to the holding of at least 50% of shares after the transaction suffices to establish positive control within the meaning of competition law, thereby fulfilling the notion of a concentration. Similarly, the holding of at least 25% of shares after the transaction suffices to establish negative control within the meaning of competition law and triggers the merger control regime. It may also suffice that control over an undertaking is possible, even if that control is not actually exercised.[208]

156. Corporate restructuring within a group of companies is not deemed to constitute a merger within the meaning of Austrian merger control (§ 7(4) KartG). What constitutes a group of companies is determined by § 15 of the Stock Corporation Act[209] and § 115 of the Limited Liability Company Act.[210]

157. According to the Supreme Cartel Court, the acquisition of an undertaking that has seized operations may constitute a concentration within the meaning of the KartG as long as the acquisition confers the (former) undertaking's market share on the acquirer.[211] A concentration was also deemed to have occurred in a case in which a supermarket rented a space in a mall that had previously been rented to another supermarket, although the space was not identical to the one previously rented out, and no supermarket was operated in the mall for eleven months.[212]

158. § 8(1) KartG defines what constitutes a media concentration for the purposes of Austrian merger control. A concentration is a media merger if at least two of the undertakings concerned are:

- media companies;
- media services;
- media support companies; or
- undertakings that (in-)directly hold a share of at least 25% in a media company, media service or media support company.

It is also a media merger if only one of the merging undertakings is a company listed in § 8(1) KartG, but a media company, media service or media support company (in-)directly holds at least 25% in a further company part to the merger (§ 8(3) KartG).

---

207. KG 17.12.2004, 26 Kt 358/04 – *Gewista.*
208. KOG 21.3.2007, 16 Ok 1/07 – *Haftungsverbund III.*
209. Aktiengesetz (AktG), BGBl 1965/98 as amended.
210. GmbH-Gesetz (GmbHG), RGBl 1906/58 as amended.
211. KOG 4.10.2010, 16 Ok 6/10 – *Holzhandel I*, § 3.4.
212. KOG 30.11.2023, 16 Ok 4/23h – *Rewe.*

159. While the terms media company and media service are based on the definitions in § 1(1) no 6 and 7 of the Austrian Media Act,[213] § 8(2) KartG autonomously defines media support companies as publishing companies, printing plants and companies in the pre-press business, undertakings procuring or placing advertising requests, wholesalers of media products and film distributors.

§8. Joint Ventures

160. According to § 7(2) KartG, a joint venture constitutes a concentration within the meaning of Austrian merger control if it fulfils all the functions of an independent economic entity on a lasting basis. A joint venture can only be found where it is jointly controlled by at least two undertakings. The Supreme Cartel Court has held that in order to come under the provision of § 7(2) KartG, a new and independent market participant must be created.[214] Where undertakings acquire joint control over another undertaking, a concentration within the meaning of § 7(1) no 3 KartG may be at stake.

161. As § 7(2) KartG is practically identical to the wording found in Article 3(4) EUMR, the case law on the EUMR can generally be relied upon for joint ventures under Austrian merger control.[215]

213. Mediengesetz, BGBl 1981/314 as amended.

214. KOG 16.12.2002, 16 Ok 9/02 – *O-GmbH & Co KG*; KOG 17.12.2008, 16 Ok 12/08 – *Private Equity-Ausnahme*. Note that this constitutes a difference from EU merger control; European Commission, Consolidated Jurisdictional Notice under Council Regulation (EC) No 139/2004 on the control of concentrations between undertakings [2008] OJ C95/1, paras 106 ff.

215. KG 19.9.2013, 25 Kt 33, 34/13 – *Morawa/Pressegroßvertrieb*; confirmed in KOG 27.1.2014, 16 Ok 11/13 – *Morawa/Pressegroßvertrieb*. On this, *see* Johannes P. Gruber, *Österreichisches Kartellrecht* § 7 KartG 2005, E 265 (3d ed., Manz 2020).

Chapter 5. Consequences of Violations and Enforcement Institutions

162. Austrian competition law is mainly enforced through public authorities, but there is also considerable scope for private enforcement. While the main avenue of enforcement leads both public and private parties to the Cartel Court, other options include damages claims and injunctions obtained by private parties in civil courts.

§1. Public Enforcement

163. Austrian competition law knows two official parties: the Federal Competition Authority and the Federal Cartel Prosecutor. The reason for this duplication of enforcement efforts lies in a political compromise: while the Federal Competition Authority is an independent authority set up at the Ministry for Economic Affairs, the Federal Cartel Prosecutor directly reports to the Ministry of Justice.[216] The two official parties are always party to competition law proceedings before the Cartel Court and the Supreme Cartel Court, even in cases in which neither of the two made the application initiating the case (§ 40 KartG). This shows that both official parties are tasked with the preservation or restoration of competition in Austria, also giving them an active role to play in competition law proceedings that were initiated by private parties.

I. Competition Authorities

164. The Austrian Federal Competition Authority ('Bundeswettbewerbsbehörde' or BWB) is the primary administrative competition authority enforcing Austrian competition law and was first set up in 2002, with the entering into force of the WettbG (Wettbewerbsgesetz or Competition Act). It was set up in order to ensure well-working competition and to prevent restrictions of competition in individual cases, as well as to apply the provisions of the KartG in compliance with EU law and together with the regulators (§ 1(1) WettbG).

165. The second official party in competition law matters is the Federal Cartel Prosecutor ('Bundeskartellanwalt'). This institution was equally set up in 2002 and is regulated in §§ 75 to 82 KartG. The Federal Cartel Prosecutor is meant to represent the public interest in competition law matters before the (Supreme) Cartel Court (§ 75(1) KartG). The Supreme Cartel Court has ruled that, in substantive terms, the Federal Cartel Prosecutor acts as a trustee of the interests that it is legally tasked to protect.[217]

216. *See* on this Stefan Melichar, 'Die Reform des Kartellrechts als Lehrstück über politische Erbpachten und blinde Flecken' *Wiener Zeitung* (11.8.2008).
217. KOG 8.10.2015, 16 Ok 2/15b & 16 Ok 8/15k – *Spar*.

166. Regulation 1/2003 foresees that every Member State of the European Union needs to nominate a 'competent competition authority' for the purposes of applying Articles 101 and 102 TFEU. As neither of the two official parties has decisional powers, in Austria it is the Cartel Court that takes on the role of 'competent competition authority' for the adoption of decisions in competition law matters, while the Federal Cartel Prosecutor takes on the role of 'competent competition authority' within the meaning of Regulation 1/2003 for applications to the Cartel Court (§ 83 KartG). Nevertheless, according to § 3 WettbG, the Federal Competition Authority as an administrative authority is responsible for carrying out the European competition law provisions and for collaborating with the European Commission and other national competition authorities in the framework of the European Competition Network. The Federal Competition Authority can give statements to the European Commission and other national competition authorities of the EU Member States where this facilitates the application of Regulation 1/2003 on the enforcement of Articles 101 and 102 TFEU.

A. *Formation, Composition*

167. The Federal Competition Authority is Austria's main national competition authority. The Director General for Competition heads the Federal Competition Authority and is appointed by the Federal President for a five-year term; the appointment is renewable (§ 6 WettbG). The Director General is proposed by the Federal Government, and any such proposal is preceded by a vacancy notice to invite applications. § 7 WettbG lays down the conditions for appointment. The Director General's deputy is the Head of Office. The Director General adopts rules of procedure.

168. The current Director General of the Federal Competition Authority is Natalie Harsdorf-Borsch, and her interim deputy is Martin Janda.[218] About fifty employees were employed by the Federal Competition Authority on 31 December 2023;[219] in 2024, a further eighteen new positions were going to be filled by the authority.[220]

169. The Federal Competition Authority is a monocratic authority; i.e., the Director General is responsible for the authority carrying out its assigned tasks (§ 2 WettbG) and for taking the required decisions, including giving instructions to the authority's employees. In doing so, the Director General is independent and not bound by any instructions (§ 1(3) WettbG). This ensures the authority's autonomy vis-à-vis the Ministry of Economic Affairs.

---

218. Bundeswettbewerbsbehörde, 'Allocation of Tasks and Staff' (30.7.2024) https://www.bwb.gv.at/fileadmin/user_upload/Geschaeftseinteilung_Englische_UEbersetzung_30.7.2024.pdf last accessed 8.8.2024.
219. Bundeswettbewerbsbehörde, 'Tätigkeitsbericht 2023' (June 2024) https://www.bwb.gv.at/fileadmin/user_upload/2406_BWB_Taetigkeitsbericht2023_barrierefreiFINAL.pdf last accessed 8.8.2024.
220. Viktoria H.S.E. Robertson, 'Fünf Fragen an Natalie Harsdorf-Borsch' (2024) *Wirtschaft und Wettbewerb* 60.

170. As per § 75(1) KartG, a Federal Cartel Prosecutor is appointed to represent the public interest in competition law matters before the (Supreme) Cartel Court. The Federal Cartel Prosecutor directly reports to the Federal Minister of Justice and is not independent but bound by the Minister's instructions (§ 75(2) KartG). The Federal Cartel Prosecutor and its deputy or deputies are appointed by the Federal President for a five-year term, an appointment which is renewable (§ 76 KartG). While the Federal Cartel Prosecutor is proposed by the Federal Government, its Deputy is proposed by the Federal Minister of Justice. Before any such proposal is made, however, a vacancy notice is published to invite general applications.

171. The current Federal Cartel Prosecutor is Heinz Ludwig Majer, and his deputies are Gustav Stifter and Verena Strasser.[221]

172. § 81 KartG contains provisions on the cooperation between the Federal Cartel Prosecutor and the Federal Competition Authority. Before the Federal Cartel Prosecutor files a request for a merger review, the Federal Competition Authority must be given a chance to express its opinion on the matter. Importantly, the Federal Cartel Prosecutor can request information from the Federal Competition Authority, access its files and ask it to carry out investigations. In turn, the Federal Competition Authority can request information or statements from the Federal Cartel Prosecutor as well as access the Federal Cartel Prosecutor's files (§ 10(1) and (3) WettbG).

173. In merger proceedings, the Competition Commission (*see* §§ 178 ff. of this monograph) can access the merger notification documents held by the Federal Competition Authority in order to make a recommendation on whether or not the Federal Competition Authority should request a review of the notified merger by the Cartel Court (§ 17(2) WettbG).

B. Investigating Powers

174. § 2(1) WettbG lays down the duties of the Federal Competition Authority as a competition authority and the powers it is granted in order to perform these duties. These enforcement powers include investigative powers that are further detailed in §§ 11 (investigations), 11a (request of information and submission of documents) and 12 (search of premises) WettbG. On these, *see* §§ 407 ff. of this monograph.

175. If so requested by the Federal Competition Authority, law enforcement officials assist the latter when carrying out investigations and searching business premises (§ 14(1) WettbG). With particular reference to e-discovery, § 14(2) WettbG stipulates that law enforcement officials may also assist the Federal Competition Authority when electronically securing documents.

221. Österreichische Justiz, 'Bundeskartellanwalt' www.justiz.gv.at/bundeskartellanwalt last accessed 8.8.2024.

176. The Federal Cartel Prosecutor has no investigative powers. Instead, it can ask the Federal Competition Authority to carry out investigations (§ 81(3) no 1 KartG).

C. Adjudicating Powers (Ascertaining and Sanctioning)

177. Neither the Federal Competition Authority nor the Federal Cartel Prosecutor has decisional powers as regards competition law matters. Instead, they must make an application to the Cartel Court in order to enforce the competition law provisions. On possible applications to the Cartel Court, *see* § 36 KartG and §§ 478 ff. of this monograph.

178. When making requests for information or for the submission of a document, however, the Federal Competition Authority has the power to adopt an administrative decision ('Bescheid') that requires the addressee to produce the required information or document (§ 11a(3) WettbG). If the addressee does not comply with the decision, it can be fined (§ 11a(5) WettbG). For further details, *see* §§ 410 ff. of this monograph.

D. Other Institutional Tasks (Consultancy to Parliament/Government)

179. The Competition Commission ('Wettbewerbskommission', §§ 16 ff. WettbG) is an advisory body established at the Federal Competition Authority. Upon request by the Federal Competition Authority or the Ministry for Economic Affairs, the Competition Commission submits expert opinions on general competition issues and issues recommendations on notified mergers (§ 17 WettbG). The Competition Commission also submits annual recommendations to the Federal Competition Authority regarding its priority-setting for the upcoming calendar year (§ 16(1) WettbG).

180. The Competition Commission consists of eight members and eight substitute members with expertise in the wider field of competition law (economics, business administration, social policy, technology and commercial law). The members elect a chairperson and secretary among themselves. Appointments to the Competition Commission are renewable and are made by the Federal Minister of the Economy, upon nomination by the Austrian Chamber of Commerce, the Federal Chamber of Labour, the Austrian Trade Union Federation and the Standing Committee of the Presidents of the Austrian Chambers of Agriculture (§ 16(3) WettbG). In carrying out their duties, the members of the Commission are not bound by any instructions and are sworn to official secrecy ('Amtsverschwiegenheit'; § 16(5) WettbG). The Cartel Court's and Supreme Cartel Court's expert lay judges may not be appointed to the Competition Commission (§ 16(2) WettbG).

181. The Federal Competition Authority is required to publish an annual report on its activities (§ 2(4) WettbG). The Federal Minister for Economic Affairs hears the Competition Commission on this report and then submits it to the National Assembly, which is one of the two chambers of the Austrian Parliament. The Competition Commission's recommendations on merger examinations shall be contained in that report (§ 17(5) WettbG; *see* § 592 of this monograph).

182. On the international level, the Federal Competition Authority has concluded several bilateral and multilateral cooperation agreements with other national competition authorities. It is a member of the European Competition Network (ECN) and the International Competition Network (ICN) as well as of the International League of Competition Law (LIDC) and the European Law Institute (ELI). The Federal Competition Authority cooperates with the Organisation for Economic Co-operation and Development (OECD) and the United Nations Conference on Trade and Development (UNCTAD).[222]

II. Government Direct Enforcement Activities

183. As discussed above, there are two competition authorities in Austria, the Federal Competition Authority and the Federal Cartel Prosecutor. While the Federal Competition Authority is set up at the Ministry for Economic Affairs, its Director General is independent and not bound by any instructions (§ 1(3) WettbG). The Federal Cartel Prosecutor, however, directly reports to the Ministry of Justice (§ 75(2) KartG) and is not independent but bound by the Minister's instructions.

184. Based on § 36(4) no 3 KartG, the Austrian Chamber of Commerce, the Federal Chamber of Labour and the Standing Committee of Presidents of the Chambers of Agriculture may also make applications to the Cartel Court, although they may not request the imposition of fines or the review of a merger. While these are not direct enforcement activities by the government, they constitute a type of quasi-public enforcement.

III. Other Administrative Agencies Applying Competition Rules

185. At the federal level, there are the following sector-specific regulators:[223] the Telecoms-Control Commission (Telekom-Control Kommission or TCK),[224] the Post-Control Commission (Post-Control Kommission or PCK)[225] and the Austrian

222. On this, *see* Bundeswettbewerbsbehörde, 'International Cooperation' https://www.bwb.gv.at/en/international_cooperation/ last accessed 8.8.2024; *see also* Bundeswettbewerbsbehörde, 'Tätigkeitsbericht 2023' 17 ff. (June 2024).
223. For an overview of the Austrian regulatory landscape, *see also* Katja Tautscher, Martin Abram & Bernhard Wychera, 'Austria' 43 ff., in: Marjorie Holmes & Lesley Davey (eds), *A Practical Guide to National Competition Rules Across Europe* (Kluwer Law International 2007).
224. Telekommunikationsgesetz 2003 (TKG; Telecommunications Act), BGBl I 2003/70 as amended, § 116.
225. Postmarktgesetz (Post Market Act), BGBl I 2009/123 as amended, § 39.

Communications Authority (Kommunikationsbehörde Austria or KommAustria)[226] are all established at the Austrian Regulatory Authority for Broadcasting and Telecommunications (Rundfunk und Telekom Regulierungs-GmbH or RTR-GmbH), which acts as head office for these three regulators.[227] Furthermore, there is an energy regulator (E-Control)[228] and a regulator for railway tracks (Schienen-Control Kommission).[229]

186. Sector-specific regulators, such as those set out in the previous paragraph, apply their respective sector-specific rules. In case of certain suspected breaches of these rules, the sector-specific regulators can request that the Cartel Court impose a fine or issue a search warrant.[230] This can lead to a parallel application of the KartG and the sector-specific rules (on this, *see* already § 62 of this monograph).[231]

187. In addition, § 36(4) no 2 KartG foresees that sector-specific regulators that are established by a Federal Act can make applications related to breaches of the KartG to the Cartel Court.[232] However, as specified above, the sector-specific regulators cannot apply for the imposition of fines or the review of mergers under the KartG, as this is the prerogative of the Federal Competition Authority and the Federal Cartel Prosecutor.

IV. The Cartel Courts

188. For both private and public enforcement under the KartG, the Cartel Court and the Supreme Cartel Court are the decision-making instances. The Cartel Court is the first instance, while the Supreme Cartel Court decides on appeals of the Cartel Court's decisions.

189. The Cartel Court can only decide based on an application (§ 36 KartG). Applications can be made by the two official parties, sector-specific regulators or certain private parties. Such applications can ask the Cartel Court to decide on the termination of an infringement, to make commitments binding on a party, to issue a declaratory decision on a past infringement or to impose interlocutory injunctions (§§ 26, 27, 28, 48 KartG). The two official parties can also apply for the imposition of a fine or penalty payments, for the finding that an undertaking enjoys a dominant position on a multisided digital market, and for the legal scrutiny of a merger (§§

226. KommAustria-Gesetz (Austrian Communications Authority Act), BGBl I 2001/32 as amended, § 1(1); Audiovisuelle Mediendienste-Gesetz (Audiovisual Media Services Act), BGBl I 2001/84 as amended, § 66; Privatradiogesetz (Private Radio Act), BGBl I 2001/20 as amended, § 31(2).
227. § 5 KommAustria-Gesetz; § 116(2) Telekommunikationsgesetz; § 39(2) Postmarktgesetz.
228. Energie-Control-Gesetz (Energy Control Act), BGBl I 2010/110 as amended, § 2.
229. Eisenbahngesetz (Railway Act), BGBl 1957/60 as amended, § 76.
230. For example, *see* § 111 Telekommunikationsgesetz; § 56 Postmarktgesetz; § 24(2) and (5) Energie-Control-Gesetz.
231. To that effect, *see also* § 11(7) and § 67(1) Audiovisuelle Mediendienste-Gesetz; § 29(1) Privatradiogesetz; § 21(3) Energie-Control-Gesetz; §§ 53f(2) and 74(4) Eisenbahngesetz.
232. *See also* § 127 Telekommunikationsgesetz.

12, 28a, 29, 35 KartG). Furthermore, the Federal Competition Authority alone can apply for the Cartel Court to issue a search warrant (§ 12 WettbG).

190. For the proceedings before the Cartel Court, *see* §§ 468–547 of this monograph; for the appellate proceedings before the Supreme Cartel Court, *see* §§ 625–633 of this monograph.

V. Administrative and Other Fines

191. In Austria, the administrative competition authorities have no decisional powers regarding the termination of infringements, the finding of infringements and the declaration making an undertaking's commitments binding. They cannot impose administrative fines based on competition law infringements, either.

192. The only exception is the case in which the Federal Competition Authority adopts an administrative decision ('Bescheid') ordering the submission of information or documents. An addressee not complying with that administrative decision is liable to pay a fine of up to 1% of their total turnover in the preceding business year (§ 11a(5) WettbG). Should the Federal Competition Authority merely request information or documents without adopting a formal decision, then the person providing wrong or misleading information can be punished with an administrative fine of up to 0.5% of their total turnover in the preceding business year (§ 11a(5) WettbG).

193. While the Federal Competition Authority cannot decide on fines against infringers of competition law, it can make an application to the Cartel Court to do so. For this reason, the Cartel Court is identified as a 'competent competition authority' within the meaning of Regulation 1/2003 (§ 83 KartG). On fines imposed by the Cartel Court, *see* §§ 520 ff. of this monograph.

194. The Federal Competition Authority also plays a central role in the Austrian leniency programme (*see* §§ 451 ff. below). In addition, it can make use of the settlement procedure (*see* §§ 463 ff. of this monograph).

VI. Administrative Injunctions and Other Restrictive Orders

195. As the Federal Competition Authority does not take any administrative decisions in the course of competition investigations that it carries out – apart from the ones detailed above (*see* § 11a(3) WettbG) – it does not adopt any administrative injunctions or other restrictive orders either. However, as an official party, it can request that the Cartel Court impose certain fines or periodic penalty payments in the event that an undertaking does not comply with the standstill obligation under the merger control regime or with competition law-related decisions. In addition, in the course of an investigation or when requesting that the Cartel Court terminate a company's competition law infringement, the official party making such a request can ask the Court to grant an interlocutory injunction (§ 48 KartG). The official parties can also request the imposition of fines and periodic penalty payments. On these instruments, *see* §§ 486 ff. of this monograph.

VII. Interim Measures

196. Where the need for interim measures arises in the course of an investigation carried out by the Federal Competition Authority or when one of the official parties makes an application for enforcement to the Cartel Court, either official party can apply for such an interim measure with the Cartel Court (§ 48 KartG; on this, *see* §§ 496 ff. of this monograph).

197. Private parties can equally apply for an interlocutory injunction when making an application to the Cartel Court. In the *ASFINAG* case, the applicant was granted an interlocutory injunction that granted it access to the respondent's webshop to buy digital toll products until the final decision becomes binding. While the initial injunction's phrasing was very wide, it was subsequently narrowed down, limiting the applicant's access to the webshop to those instances in which it acquired digital toll products for its own use or for the commercial resale of digital toll products to consumers, if the latter had a validity period of less than eighteen days from the date of purchase.[233]

§2. Civil Enforcement

198. Private enforcement of Austrian competition law can take two main forms: first of all, private parties can make an application to the Cartel Court if they have a legal or economic interest in the Court's decision (§ 36(4) no 4 KartG). An application by a private party cannot, however, request the imposition of periodic penalty payments or fines, or the review of a merger.

199. The second form of private enforcement is the claim for damages in civil courts that are competent to hear private damages claims. This type of private enforcement is at issue in the present chapter.

200. A further type of private enforcement can be seen in competition law being used as a shield, e.g., by invoking the nullity of a contractual provision based on the latter's breach of competition law (§§ 1(3) and 17(3) KartG; § 879(3) ABGB).

233. KOG 12.10.202, 16 Ok 1/21i – *ASFINAG*. On this case, *see* Axel Reidlinger, 'Wann gilt ein Kontrahierungszwang für Marktbeherrscher? Markierungen im Dschungel anlässlich der KOG-Entscheidung 16 Ok 1/21i' (2022) *Österreichische Zeitschrift für Kartellrecht* 12.

I. Competent Civil Courts

201. Where a private party makes an application to the Cartel Court, for instance, requesting injunctive relief (§ 48 KartG), the termination of an infringement (§ 26 KartG), or the finding that an infringement was committed in the past (§ 28 KartG), the Cartel Court has exclusive jurisdiction over such applications. In their applications, parties can rely on the Austrian provisions (Part I of the KartG) as well as on the European provisions of Articles 101 and 102 TFEU (§ 83(1) KartG). Where an appeal to a decision of the Cartel Court is lodged, this is heard by the Supreme Cartel Court, which forms part of Austria's Supreme Court (§ 58(2) KartG).

202. Where a private party brings a damages action that is based on an infringement of the competition rules, the competent civil court is the court that, based on Austrian jurisdictional rules, is competent to hear such a damages case.

203. If the infringement of competition law giving rise to the claim for damages took place among undertakings within the realm of a specific company-related business transaction, the commercial courts are competent to hear such a claim (§ 51(1) no 1 of the Jurisdictional Norm or JN).[234] In addition, under § 51(2) no 10 JN, claims based on unfair competition law are also heard by the commercial courts, irrespective of the value of the claim.[235] In this respect, damages claims based on unfair competition law and on competition law are treated the same, leading to the competence of commercial courts where a claim arises between companies.

204. Where a damages claim based on the infringement of the competition law provisions is brought by a so-called qualified entity under the new regime for representative actions, which Austria introduced in 2024 to implement Directive 2020/1828,[236] the Commercial Court of Vienna has exclusive jurisdiction for such claims.[237]

205. Where commercial courts have no jurisdiction, for instance because a claim is brought by an individual consumer, a claim for damages will be heard by the general civil courts. Where damages up to the amount of EUR 15,000 are claimed, the competent court is the District Court for civil litigation (§ 49(1) JN; 'Bezirksgericht'). An appeal of the District Court's judgment will be heard by the Regional Court (§ 3 JN; 'Landesgericht'). Claims exceeding the amount of EUR 15,000 are heard by the Regional Court for civil litigation (§ 50 JN; 'Landesgericht'). An appeal of the Regional Court's judgment will be heard by the Higher Regional Court (§ 4 JN; 'Oberlandesgericht').

---

234. Jurisdiktionsnorm (JN; Jurisdictional Norm), RGBl 1895/111 as amended.
235. This may become relevant because an intentional breach of competition rules with the aim of getting ahead of competitors can be sanctioned under § 1 UWG; OGH 17.3.1998, 4 Ob 62/98s – *Servicegutscheine*.
236. Directive (EU) 2020/1828 of the European Parliament and of the Council of 25 November 2020 on representative actions for the protection of the collective interests of consumers [2020] OJ L409/1.
237. § 630 ZPO.

206. In exceptional cases, and limited to points of law, an appeals decision – either by the Regional Court or by the Higher Regional Court – can be further appealed before the Supreme Court (this appeal is called 'Revision', §§ 3, 4 JN). As a rule, the existence of a significant legal question, i.e., a question which is of considerable importance for maintaining legal unity, legal certainty or legal development, is required in order to bring an appeal before the Supreme Court (§ 502(1) of the Code of Civil Procedure).[238]

207. In terms of territorial jurisdiction,[239] Article 7 no 2 of Regulation 1215/2012[240] states that in matters relating to tort, delict or quasi-delict, a person domiciled in a Member State may be sued in another Member State in the courts of the place where the harmful event occurred or may occur. In this respect, the CJEU has held that where a damages claim results from a cartel, the injured party can choose to either sue the cartelist at the place of the causal event, i.e., the place of the conclusion of the cartel, or at the place where the damage occurred, i.e., the place of the injured party's registered office or place of residence.[241] Similarly, Austria's Supreme Court has held that for the purposes of competition law damages, the place where the harmful event occurs may be the place where the damage caused by the cartel occurs. This can be the place of residence or the place of the registered office of the injured party.[242]

II. Sanctions

208. Private enforcement actions can be brought before the Cartel Court in order to obtain a decision requiring the defendant to terminate an infringement (§ 26 KartG), finding that an infringement occurred in the past (§ 28 KartG), or to obtain an interlocutory injunction (§ 48 KartG).[243] They can be brought before civil courts to be awarded damages for the infringement of competition law (§§ 37a ff. KartG). The following provides an overview of the relief that private parties can seek before the Cartel Court or before competent civil courts, namely nullity, damages and interim measures.

238. Zivilprozessordnung (ZPO; Code of Civil Procedure), RGBl 1895/113 as amended.
239. For more detail on this, *see* Michael Brand, *Schadenersatz im Kartellrecht: Praxishandbuch Private Enforcement* 304 ff. (Linde 2017).
240. Regulation (EU) No 1215/2012 of the European Parliament and of the Council of 12 December 2012 on jurisdiction and the recognition and enforcement of judgments in civil and commercial matters [2012] OJ L351/1.
241. CJEU Case C-352/13 *CDC Hydrogen Peroxide v. Akzo Nobel*, ECLI:EU:C:2015:335, paras 34–56.
242. OGH 30.8.2016, 4 Ob 120/16z – *Libormanipulation*.
243. On the practical difficulties for private parties to obtain an interlocutory injunction, *see* Anna Wolf-Posch & Caroline Liertzer, 'Die Gewährung des rechtlichen Gehörs im kartellgerichtlichen Provisorialverfahren' (2014) *Österreichische Zeitschrift für Kartellrecht* 213.

A. Nullity

209. European competition law provides in Article 101(2) TFEU that an agreement or decision that breaches Article 101(1) TFEU is null and void. The civil sanction of nullity foreseen in European competition law is directly applicable.[244] Austrian case law has acknowledged that the nullity foreseen in Article 101(2) TFEU is absolute, i.e., neither the parties to the agreement nor any third parties can invoke the void provision. This also implies that the nullity applies ex tunc, i.e., from the outset.[245] Based on the case law of the CJEU, the nullity foreseen in Article 101(2) TFEU only applies to those parts of the agreement that are directly affected by the prohibition in Article 101(1) TFEU or that cannot be severed from the latter.[246] If other parts of the agreement do not contravene Article 101(1) TFEU and can be severed from those parts that are anti-competitive, then they remain valid.[247] This is a question of fact that needs to be assessed on a case-by-case basis and with a view to objectively assessing the stand-alone nature of the remaining agreement.[248]

210. The same is true for Austrian competition law:[249] based on § 1(3) KartG, any agreements or decisions that are forbidden under § 1(1) KartG are automatically void and the European principles outlined above apply. At the same time, EU law does not provide for all civil law consequences related to conduct that infringes competition law. The question of whether a transaction needs to be reversed following the nullity of an agreement must therefore be answered based on national law.[250] The Supreme Court has found that the reversal of a transaction needs to be based on § 877 ABGB,[251] which foresees claims based on the law of unjust enrichment.[252]

211. Article 102 TFEU does not provide for the nullity of agreements or decisions upon which the abuse of a dominant position is based. However, Austrian civil law leads to the nullity of agreements or parts of agreements that infringe Article 102 TFEU or § 5(1) KartG: § 879(1) ABGB foresees the nullity of agreements that violate a legal prohibition or that are contrary to common decency. Article 102 TFEU and § 5 KartG are understood to constitute such legal prohibitions that want to protect a party against the abuse of power. As this provision is contained in the General Civil Code rather than in the KartG, however, the Cartel Court cannot rule

244. OGH 25.10.2000, 3 Ob 296/99x – *Discothèque*.
245. OGH 16.11.2009, 9 ObA 59/09f – *Tankstellenpächter I*.
246. CJEU Case 56/65 *Société Technique Minière v. Maschinenbau Ulm*, ECLI:EU:C:1966:38, p. 304. For Austria, *see also* OGH 22.2.2001, 6 Ob 322/00x – *Tankstellenbelieferungsübereinkommen*.
247. OGH 18.2.2015, 2 Ob 22/14w – *Mengenreduktionsklausel (Erdgas)*.
248. OGH 25.10.2000, 3 Ob 296/99x – *Discothèque*.
249. OGH 13.3.2012, 10 Ob 10/12m – *Bierbezugsvertrag III*.
250. OGH 13.3.2012, 10 Ob 10/12m – *Bierbezugsvertrag III*.
251. Allgemeines Bürgerliches Gesetzbuch (ABGB; General Civil Code), JGS 1811/946 as amended.
252. OGH 13.3.2012, 10 Ob 10/12m – *Bierbezugsvertrag III*.

on the nullity of agreements contravening Article 102 TFEU or § 5 KartG.[253] In some cases, the victim of an abuse of a dominant position might actually benefit from being able to invoke an agreement that is found to be void based on § 879(1) ABGB. In such a case, it has been argued that the nullity should not apply.[254]

212. A further sanction of nullity is foreseen in the context of the standstill obligation in merger proceedings: § 17(3) KartG provides that any contracts in violation of the standstill obligation are ineffective. Contrary to the nullity foreseen in Article 101(2) TFEU and § 1(3) KartG, the nullity provided for in § 17(3) KartG is only of a pending nature; if the merger is allowed to go ahead or the official parties do not apply for a review by the Cartel Court, then the contracts concerned retroactively become legally binding.[255] The practical implications of § 17(3) KartG are still being debated in Austria.[256]

B. Damages

213. Two landmark preliminary rulings at the European level – *Courage v. Crehan* (2001)[257] and *Manfredi* (2006)[258] – established that victims of an infringement of competition law have to be able to bring private claims for damages in the EU Member States, based on the principles of effectiveness and equivalence. This has been acknowledged by the Austrian Supreme (Cartel) Court.[259] At the same time, the Supreme Court has underlined that the general requirements for bringing a civil claim for damages also apply to competition law-based actions for damages, whether under national or EU competition law. These general requirements foresee that all of the following conditions are met, cumulatively:

a. an infringement of competition law has occurred;
b. the claimant is affected by the infringement;
c. damage;
d. causality and imputability between the infringement and the damage; and
e. fault.[260]

214. The Supreme Court has highlighted that national competition law provisions as well as EU competition law provisions have the dual purpose of protecting

253. Axel Reidlinger & Isabella Hartung, *Das österreichische Kartellrecht: Ein Handbuch für Praktiker* 174 f. (5th ed., Linde 2024).
254. On this issue, *see* Diana Holzinger, *Marktmissbrauch und Nichtigkeit: Vertragsnichtigkeit bei Verstößen gegen das Marktmissbrauchsverbot* (Manz 2012).
255. KG 12.9.2018, 25 Kt 6/18x – *BWB/TCH*.
256. Axel Reidlinger & Isabella Hartung, *Das österreichische Kartellrecht: Ein Handbuch für Praktiker* 246 f. (5th ed., Linde 2024).
257. CJEU Case C-453/99 *Courage v. Bernard Crehan*, ECLI:EU:C:2001:465.
258. CJEU Joined Cases C-295 to C-298/04 *Vincenzo Manfredi v. Lloyd Adriatico Assicurazioni and others*, ECLI:EU:C:2006:461.
259. OGH 2.8.2012, 4 Ob 46/12m – *Bankomatvertrag IV*; KOG 8.10.2008, 16 Ok 8/08 – *Aufzugs- und Fahrtreppenkartell II*.
260. OGH 2.8.2012, 4 Ob 46/12m – *Bankomatvertrag IV*.

competition and preventing market participants from overreaching by harming the other market side through cartels. As such, the competition law provisions are understood to constitute special norms that protect against the abuse of power within the meaning of § 1311 ABGB (so-called Schutzgesetze).[261]

215. Further preliminary rulings on the EU level – *Pfleiderer* (2011),[262] *Donau Chemie* (2013)[263] and *Kone v. ÖBB-Infrastruktur* (2014)[264] – clarified important aspects of damages actions for the breach of competition law that also apply to Austria, such as the standing of parties, causality and access to the file. In addition, Regulation 1/2003 on the enforcement of EU competition law made Articles 101 and 102 TFEU directly enforceable in the Member States[265] and thereby opened up greater possibilities for damages actions.

216. In 2013, the Austrian legislator followed a step taken by the German legislator and for the first time introduced a provision foreseeing damages for the infringement of competition law into the KartG.[266] This single provision was § 37a KartG. In its four paragraphs, it contained rules on the payment of damages for competition law infringements and the payment of interest, the suspension of proceedings while a case is ongoing before the Cartel Court, the European Commission or a competition authority, the binding nature of certain final decisions on the civil court dealing with the damages claim, and limitation periods.

217. The European Directive on damages claims for the infringement of competition law (2014)[267] provided an important impetus for EU Member States to enact more detailed legislation for damages actions based on competition law breaches. In the summer of 2017, the Directive led to significant changes in the Austrian KartG: while the KartG had previously only contained the single provision on cartel damages discussed above, the amendment of 2017[268] introduced thirteen new provisions solely dedicated to damages for infringements of competition law: §§ 37a to 37m KartG in Chapter 5 of the KartG.

218. Recently, further preliminary rulings from the CJEU have clarified this area of EU (competition) law with respect to standing, jurisdiction clauses, jurisdiction, limitation periods, liability for subsidiaries and liability for acquired companies:

261. OGH 14.2.2012, 5 Ob 39/11p – *Aufzugs- und Fahrtreppenkartell IV*; OGH 2.8.2012, 4 Ob 46/12m – *Bankomatvertrag IV*.
262. CJEU Case C-360/09 *Pfleiderer v. Bundeskartellamt*, ECLI:EU:C:2011:389.
263. CJEU Case C-536/11 *Bundeswettbewerbsbehörde v. Donau Chemie*, ECLI:EU:C:2013:366.
264. CJEU Case C-557/12 *Kone and others v. ÖBB-Infrastruktur*, ECLI:EU:C:2014:1317.
265. Article 1 of Regulation 1/2003; Georg-Klaus de Bronett, *Europäisches Kartellverfahrensrecht: Kommentar zur VO 1/2003* Art. 1, para. 5 (2d ed., Carl Heymanns 2012).
266. For the legislative materials of this provision, *see* 1804 der Beilagen XXIV. GP (Erläuterungen zur Regierungsvorlage), p. 10 f.; for the amendment *see* Kartell- und Wettbewerbsrechts-Änderungsgesetz 2012 (KaWeRÄG 2012), BGBl I 2013/13.
267. Directive 2014/104/EU of the European Parliament and of the Council of 26 November 2014 on certain rules governing actions for damages under national law for infringements of the competition law provisions of the Member States and of the European Union [2014] OJ L349/1.
268. Kartell- und Wettbewerbsrechts-Änderungsgesetz 2017 (KaWeRÄG 2017), BGBl I 2017/56.

Apple Sales International (2018),[269] *Cogeco* (2019),[270] *Skanska* (2019),[271] *Tibor-Trans* (2019)[272] and *Otis* (2019),[273] *Wikingerhof v. Booking.com* (2020)[274] as well as *Sumal* (2021).[275]

219. It is worth pointing out that several of the references for a preliminary ruling in the area of damages claims were made by Austrian courts: *Donau Chemie* was a request for a preliminary ruling from the Higher Regional Court Vienna that revolved around national rules on access to file, while *Kone* was a request for a preliminary ruling from the Austrian Supreme Court that dealt with the question of umbrella pricing. *Otis* was equally sent to Luxembourg by the Austrian Supreme Court and dealt with a public body's right to claim damages, even if it was not active on the market on which the cartel operated.

1. Implementation of Directive 2014/104/EU

220. Chapter 5 of the KartG as it is currently in force applies to civil liability for harm caused by an infringement of national or EU competition law and claims for damages for such infringements (§ 37a(1) KartG). It constitutes the Austrian implementing measure for Directive 2014/104/EU (§ 37a(2) KartG). The new rules apply to harm that occurred after 26 December 2016 (for the temporal application, *see* § 86(9) KartG).

221. § 37b no 1 KartG sets out the types of infringements that Chapter 5 applies to, namely infringements of § 1 KartG (cartel prohibition), § 5 KartG (abuse of a dominant position), § 6 KartG (prohibition of retaliatory measures), Article 101 TFEU (anti-competitive agreements) and Article 102 TFEU (abuse of a dominant position) as well as the national laws of other EU or EEA Member States that pursue the same objective as Articles 101 and 102 TFEU. Only the infringements listed in § 37b no 1 KartG benefit from the detailed rules in Chapter 5 of the KartG. While Germany made its specific competition law-related rules for claiming damages applicable to infringements of the Digital Markets Act,[276] no such rule has been implemented in Austria.

222. Due to the scope of application that § 37b no 1 KartG foresees, several rules found in the KartG are not subject to these detailed rules when they are being infringed, although they are included in the rules on fines in § 29 KartG. This includes the prohibition on providing incorrect or misleading information when

---

269. CJEU Case C-595/17 *Apple Sales International*, ECLI:EU:C:2018:854.
270. CJEU Case C-637/17 *Cogeco Communications v. Sport TV Portugal*, ECLI:EU:C:2019:263.
271. CJEU Case C-724/17 *Skanska Industrial Solutions*, ECLI:EU:C:2019:204.
272. CJEU Case C-451/18 *Tibor-Trans*, ECLI:EU:C:2019:635.
273. CJEU Case C-435/18 *Otis v. Land Oberösterreich*, ECLI:EU:C:2019:1069.
274. CJEU Case C-59/19 *Wikingerhof v. Booking.com*, ECLI:EU:C:2020:950.
275. CJEU Case C-882/19 *Sumal v. Mercedes Benz Trucks España*, ECLI:EU:C:2021:800.
276. § 33(1) GWB.

notifying a merger (§ 9 KartG), non-compliance with subsequent measures in merger proceedings (§ 16 KartG), the infringement of the standstill obligation (§ 17 KartG), non-compliance with binding commitments (§ 27 KartG), and non-compliance with decisions of the Cartel Court (§ 19(3) KartG). Should any of these infringements lead to harm that can be asserted through civil liability, then the respective provisions of the KartG must be relied upon as special norms that protect against the abuse of power within the meaning of § 1311 ABGB ('Schutzgesetze'), in which case the burden of proof is reversed (§ 1298 ABGB) and the claimant does not need to prove the defendant's fault.[277]

223. The civil courts of the Member States are competent to determine whether or not an infringement of competition law that may give rise to civil liability has taken place.[278] When doing so, however, they must take into account any (pending) European Commission decision in a specific case and may not issue conflicting decisions (*see* Article 16(1) of Regulation 1/2003). This only applies to the Commission's infringement decisions under Article 7 of Regulation 1/2003, but not to commitment decisions (Article 9 of Regulation 1/2003) or interim measures (Article 8 of Regulation 1/2003; these should lead a national court to stay its proceedings or to refer a question to the CJEU).[279]

224. Another possibility regarding the question of whether an infringement took place in the past is provided for in § 28(1a) no 2 KartG: where a party intends to claim damages for an infringement, this intention represents a legitimate interest for asking the Cartel Court to make a finding that an infringement existed in the past, even where that infringement has already been brought to an end. Such a decision is then binding before the civil courts (§ 37i(2) KartG). Another court or competition authority's finding that no competition law infringement was committed is not binding for the damages proceedings, however.[280]

225. Based on § 190(1) of the Code of Civil Procedure,[281] a civil court can also stay a case before it – e.g., a case on damages due to a competition law infringement – if the outcome of another civil or administrative case is decisive for its own case. This recently occurred in a damages action for the breach of § 5 KartG against the Austrian general importer of new vehicles and original spare parts of a specific brand.[282]

---

277. OGH 2.8.2012, 4 Ob 46/12m – *Bankomatvertrag IV*; Michael Brand, *Schadenersatz im Kartellrecht: Praxishandbuch Private Enforcement* 24 f., 239 (Linde 2017).
278. On this, *see* already OGH 22.2.2001, 6 Ob 322/00x – *Tankstellenbelieferungsübereinkommen*; OGH 8.10.2008, 16 Ok 8/08 – *Aufzugs- und Fahrtreppenkartell II*.
279. Georg-Klaus de Bronett, *Europäisches Kartellverfahrensrecht: Kommentar zur VO 1/2003* Art. 16, paras 6–9 (2d ed., Carl Heymanns 2012).
280. Michael Brand, *Schadenersatz im Kartellrecht: Praxishandbuch Private Enforcement* 293 (Linde 2017).
281. Zivilprozessordnung (ZPO; Code of Civil Procedure), RGBl 1895/113 as amended.
282. OGH 12.8.2020, 4 Ob 117/20i – *Verfahrensunterbrechung*.

2. Causality in Damages Claims for Competition Law Infringements

226. Under Austrian law, § 1295 ABGB emphasises that anybody who causes injury to another person through their fault is liable for damages. § 37c(1) KartG clarifies that anybody who culpably commits an infringement of competition law is liable for damages. The reversal of the burden of proof (§ 1298 ABGB) applies in this case. While claims for damages are typically brought against undertakings in the form of legal persons, it is also possible that such a claim be brought against a natural person who has acted on behalf of said legal person. The Supreme Court has ruled that, for such a claim to be successful, the undertaking's competition law infringement must be directly attributable to the natural person acting in their capacity as the company's manager, for instance. This will be the case where the manager himself committed the competition law infringement, was actively involved in it or did not stop the infringement despite knowing (or negligently not knowing) of it.[283]

227. Questions of causality and adequacy can be not only complex but also decisive in cases on damages for competition law infringements. The KartG therefore establishes the presumption that a cartel between competitors causes harm (§ 37c(2) KartG). However, the presumption of harm is rebuttable, as is also foreseen in § 270 of the Code of Civil Procedure. In addition, the presumption does not extend to anti-competitive agreements between non-competitors or to abuses of a dominant position.

228. The question of causality was central to a preliminary reference that the Austrian Supreme Court made to the CJEU in 2012: in *Kone v. ÖBB-Infrastruktur*, the Supreme Court wanted to know whether Article 101 TFEU and the principle of effectiveness established by the CJEU required that any person could claim damages from members of a cartel, even if the loss the claimant wanted to assert against cartel members had been caused by a company that was not a member of the cartel but had raised its own prices against the background of the increased prices that the cartel had led to (umbrella pricing).[284] The CJEU answered that Union law and its principle of effectiveness required that umbrella pricing claims could be brought by injured parties,[285] thereby extending the notion of causality that Austrian law had relied on up until that point.

229. The later *Otis* case (2019) again extended the Austrian notion of causality: in that case, the Federal State of Upper Austria had acted as a funding body by granting loans to buyers of housing. Upper Austria wanted to recover damages from the members of the elevator cartel. The loans granted by Upper Austria represented a percentage of the housing costs, which would have been lower without the cartel

283. OGH 14.2.2012, 5 Ob 39/11p – *Aufzugs- und Fahrtreppenkartell IV*.
284. Case C-557/12 *Kone and others v. ÖBB-Infrastruktur*, ECLI:EU:C:2014:1317, para. 17.
285. Case C-557/12 *Kone and others v. ÖBB-Infrastruktur*, ECLI:EU:C:2014:1317, para. 37. On this case, *see* Isabella Hartung & Maximilian Mertel, 'Also sprach der EuGH zu "Umbrella Claims"' (2014) *Österreichische Zeitschrift für Kartellrecht* 163.

agreement. Upper Austria claimed that its loss consisted in those amounts of funding that it was not able to profitably invest, and which would have been lower absent the elevator cartel.[286] Upper Austria was not active on the market for elevators that were affected by the cartel, neither as a supplier nor as a customer. The CJEU replied that in such a case, the members of the cartel may still be ordered to pay compensation for the losses suffered by the funding body.[287] Under the traditional Austrian interpretation, this would not have fulfilled the criterion of causality.

3. Right to Full Compensation

230. § 37d KartG provides the victim's right to full compensation, which includes loss of profit. The party liable to pay damages also needs to pay interest from the moment the harm occurred. This provision is significant as in some cases, the interest that accumulates over the years reaches the amount of the initial damages. While Directive 2014/104/EU provides that Member States must foresee full compensation – including interest – for victims of competition law infringements, it does not provide the level of interest or whether this includes compound interest, i.e., interest that accrues on interest.[288] In terms of the amount of damages to be paid, this can make an important difference. § 37d KartG also references § 1333 ABGB, a provision in general civil law that provides that the debtor must pay default interest to the creditor based on § 1000(1) ABGB. § 1000(1) ABGB, however, sets the statutory interest rate at 4% per annum – unless specific legislation foresees a different interest rate. According to that provision, the payment of interest is mandatory even if the debtor has not actually benefitted from or is not responsible for the delay.

231. The Austrian Commercial Code (Unternehmensgesetzbuch or UGB) in § 456 UGB foresees a higher statutory interest rate for commercial transactions.[289] For this higher interest rate to apply, the damages sought must be classified as contractual damages between commercial parties. Where both the debtor and the creditor are parties to a contractual relationship and the damages claim arises from this relationship, the higher interest rate applies. According to § 456 UGB, the debtor must pay interest amounting to 9.2% above the base rate, although it may never go below zero even if the base rate is negative. Depending on the level of the base rate,

286. Case C-435/18 *Otis v. Land Oberösterreich*, ECLI:EU:C:2019:1069, para. 19.
287. Case C-435/18 *Otis v. Land Oberösterreich*, ECLI:EU:C:2019:1069, para. 34. On this case, *see* Isabelle Innerhofer & Sebastian Hinterdorfer, 'Jedermann ist Jedermann – Aktivlegitimation bei Kartellschadenersatz (Otis ua C-435/18)' (2020) *Österreichische Zeitschrift für Kartellrecht* 20.
288. On this and the Austrian rules on interest in damages claims for competition law infringements prior to the implementation of the Damages Directive, *see* Viktoria H.S.E. Robertson, 'Austria' 31, in: Giorgio Monti (ed.), *EU Law and Interest on Damages for Infringements of Competition Law: A Comparative Report* (EUI Law Working Paper 2016/11). *See also* Viktoria H.S.E. Robertson, 'Der Zinsanspruch beim kartellrechtlichen Schadenersatz: § 37a Kartellgesetz und die Richtlinie 2014/104/EU' (2016) *Österreichische Blätter für Gewerblichen Rechtsschutz und Urheberrecht* 156; Michael Brand, 'Der Zinssatz bei Schadenersatz wegen Kartellrechtverletzungen' (2024) *Österreichische Zeitschrift für Kartellrecht* 123.
289. Unternehmensgesetzbuch (Commercial Code), dRGBl 1897/219 as amended.

this may be higher or lower than 4%. Where a damages claim among business partners is purely based on tort, however, the general statutory interest rate applies.[290]

232. § 1000(2) ABGB sets the rate of compound interest at 4% per annum, irrespective of whether a higher statutory interest rate applies for single interest.

4. Joint and Severable Liability and Passing-On

233. Undertakings that have jointly infringed competition law are jointly and severally liable for the arising harm (§ 37e KartG).[291] Nevertheless, an undertaking may only be liable for harm arising to its own direct and indirect purchasers or suppliers if it satisfies the following conditions laid down in § 37e(2) KartG: first of all, the undertaking must be a small- or medium-sized enterprise according to set criteria, its market share on the relevant market was below 5%, and unlimited liability would irretrievably jeopardise its economic viability and cause its assets to lose all their value. Second, the undertaking has not spearheaded the infringement, has not coerced other undertakings to participate in the infringement and has not previously been found to have infringed competition law.

234. Successful leniency applicants also benefit from this limited liability (§ 37e(3) KartG), unless the injured parties would otherwise be unable to obtain full compensation from the other liable parties.

235. Where a defendant invokes the defence that the claimant passed on the overcharge resulting from an infringement of competition law (passing-on), § 37f(1) KartG provides that it is upon the defendant to prove this. Even if this defence is successful, however, the claimant may claim compensation for loss of profits. Where an indirect purchaser claims compensation, they must prove that the overcharge was passed on to them (§ 37f(2) KartG). § 37f(3) KartG provides under which circumstances such proof is deemed successful. These provisions also apply, *mutatis mutandis*, to harm that results from prices that are too low (§ 37f(5) KartG).

5. Limitation Periods

236. Limitation periods for damages claims are set out in § 37h KartG.[292] The provision foresees that the limitation period does not begin to run before the infringement of competition law has ceased. Where an infringement is qualified as

290. Wilma Dehn, 'Das Zinsenrechts-Änderungsgesetz' (2002) *Österreichisches Recht der Wirtschaft* 514, 515.

291. On that provision, *see* Isabelle Innerhofer & Nathalie Jeneral, 'Die neue Solidarhaftung bei kartellrechtlichen Kronzeugen' (2016) *Österreichische Zeitschrift für Kartellrecht* 209.

292. On the new rules on limitation periods for competition law damages claims, *see also* Jörg Zehetner & Konstantin Köck, 'Neue Verjährungsregeln im Kartellschadenersatzrecht' (2017) *Österreichische Zeitschrift für Kartellrecht* 68.

a single and continuous infringement, this may mean that the statute of limitations can be prolonged for a considerable amount of time. Furthermore, § 37h(1) KartG provides for two different types of limitation periods: a relative one and an absolute one. The relative limitation period starts to run from the time the injured party has gained knowledge (or is reasonably expected to have gained knowledge) of

a. the identity of the infringer;
b. the harm;
c. the conduct causing the harm; and
d. the fact that such conduct represents an infringement of competition law.

These are cumulative conditions that need to be fulfilled before the limitation period of five years starts to run.

237. The Supreme Court has held that the facts need to be known to such an extent that the claimant could claim damages with a prospect of success. Newspaper reports about an ongoing antitrust investigation were not regarded as sufficient for this purpose.[293]

238. The law also foresees an absolute limitation period of ten years, irrespective of the conditions set out for the relative limitation period being fulfilled.

239. § 37h(2) KartG provides scenarios under which the limitation period for bringing actions for damages shall be suspended. In the case of ongoing antitrust investigations or proceedings, the suspension of the limitation period ends one year after the infringement decision has become final or the proceedings or investigations are terminated. After the suspension has ended, the limitation period continues to run its remaining course. § 37h KartG applies to claims that were not yet time-barred on 26 December 2016 (*see* § 86(9) KartG), unless the rules previously applicable were more favourable for the claimant.

240. An important rule for victims of competition law infringements is contained in § 37i KartG, namely the effects of proceedings before a competition authority.[294] First of all, a legal dispute on compensation for a competition law infringement can be suspended while proceedings on the competition law infringement are ongoing before a competition authority – which, in Austria, includes the Cartel Court (§ 37i(1) KartG). More importantly, however, a court deciding on damages for a competition law infringement is bound by any final decision issued by a competition authority or by a court that decided on the decision of a competition

293. OGH 2.8.2012, 4 Ob 46/21m – *Bankomatvertrag IV*; *see also* established case law at RIS-Justiz RS0034524 and RIS-Justiz RS0034327.

294. A similar provision was already contained in then-§ 37a(2) and (3) KartG before the 2017 amendment.

authority (§ 37i(2) KartG). This rule extends to decisions by any competition authority or court in the world and therefore greatly facilitates follow-on damages claims.[295]

6. Disclosure of Evidence

241. Of similar importance for claimants is the disclosure of evidence, on which §§ 37j and 37k KartG contain a number of rules. The law regards it as sufficient to substantiate the claim for damages based on a competition law infringement so that it contains all such facts and evidence as are reasonably available to the claimant. In addition, the facts and evidence provided must sufficiently support the plausibility of the claim for damages (§ 37j(1) KartG). The claimant may also ask the court to order the defendant or a third party to disclose evidence under their control (§ 37j(2) KartG). In deciding on whether to grant the disclosure of evidence, the court must take into account a number of considerations as per § 37j(4) KartG. However, an undertaking's interest in avoiding actions for damages following on from an infringement of competition law is explicitly barred from being considered a legitimate interest that warrants protection (§ 37j(5) KartG).

242. Concerning disclosure and use of evidence included in the files of courts or authorities, § 37k(1) KartG foresees that disclosure of these files can be ordered if such evidence cannot otherwise be reasonably obtained by the parties concerned or by a third party concerned. Leniency statements as well as settlement submissions, however, are both exempt from the disclosure of evidence (§ 37k(4) KartG). Where the submission of evidence contained in a competition authority's files cannot be ordered, it is not admissible as evidence in any type of court proceedings and its use is subject to penalties of up to EUR 100,000 (§ 37a(3) KartG).

243. There currently is a preliminary reference pending before the CJEU on the issue of disclosure of evidence. The reference was lodged by the Higher Regional Court Vienna in January 2023. It concerns the relationship between access to leniency statements and settlement submissions on the one hand, and criminal proceedings on the other hand. While the Public Prosecutor's Office was conducting criminal investigations against around 860 persons accused of bid rigging in the construction cartel case, the Federal Competition Authority accepted leniency applications by two undertakings, leading to two reduced fines by the Cartel Court. Upon request by the Public Prosecutor's Office in the context of mutual assistance, the Federal Competition Authority transmitted the leniency statements and settlement submissions to the latter. The Public Prosecutor's Office added these to its file and requested the police conduct additional investigations based on them. The two undertakings objected to this, leading to a case before the Regional Court for Criminal Matters in Vienna. As the Court rejected the undertakings' objection, the case

295. Michael Brand, *Schadenersatz im Kartellrecht: Praxishandbuch Private Enforcement* 293 (Linde 2017).

came before the Higher Regional Court for Criminal Matters, which made the referral now before the CJEU. The referring court intends to ascertain whether the mutual assistance which the Federal Competition Authority and the Public Prosecutor's Office are required to afford each other under Austrian law can effectively undermine the protection that EU law affords to leniency statements and settlement submissions.[296] Conflicting interests arise because parties and victims have access to the criminal file, which now contains the leniency statements and settlement submissions. This may in turn jeopardise both the leniency programme and the settlement procedure, both of which are important pillars of public antitrust enforcement.

244. § 13a WettbG sets out that evidence held by the Federal Competition Authority can be obtained through the order of a national court if a party or a third party cannot otherwise obtain such evidence with reasonable effort. In addition, the Federal Competition Authority must have already brought its own proceedings in that matter to an end, either by decision or in another way. The damages claim must therefore constitute a follow-on action. Where all these conditions are satisfied, the Federal Competition Authority may disclose three categories of evidence:

1. information compiled by a natural or legal person specifically for proceedings before the competition authority;
2. information the Federal Competition Authority has compiled and transmitted to the parties in the course of its investigations; and
3. settlement submissions that have been withdrawn.

Internal documents of the Federal Competition Authority and its correspondence with other competition authorities or law enforcement authorities may not be disclosed at any time (*see also* § 37k(3) KartG). This provision was amended in line with Directive 2014/104/EU.[297]

7. Further Issues on Damages Claims

245. § 37g KartG provides rules on the effect of consensual dispute resolution. It states that where an infringer settles with an injured party, that settlement counts towards any damages the settling infringer may be found to be liable for. The provision also provides rules on how shared liability and settled claims interact.

246. Upon request by a national court, and if the Federal Competition Authority deems that this is appropriate, the Federal Competition Authority may give a statement in proceedings concerning damages for the infringement of competition law (§ 13b WettbG). In addition, the Cartel Court, the Federal Cartel Prosecutor and the

296. CJEU Case C-2/23 *FL und KM Baugesellschaft and S* (pending) [2023] OJ C127/17.
297. For the legislative materials of this provision, *see* 1804 der Beilagen XXIV. GP (Erläuterungen zur Regierungsvorlage), p. 19.

Federal Competition Authority may assist a court in fixing the amount of compensation for damages, if so requested by that court (§ 37l KartG).

247. So far, a limited number of cases on damages have been decided in Austria. The very first such case involved a follow-on claim in the driving school cartel that had been condemned by the Cartel Court.[298] In that case, damages of EUR 174.40 and interest of 4% per annum were awarded to the claimant by the District Court and later confirmed by the Regional Court.[299] Further cases followed from the lifts and elevators cartel: in *Kone*, the Austrian Railways brought an umbrella pricing claim against members of the elevator cartel, in which the Austrian Supreme Court sent the case back to the lower court for establishing additional facts.[300] More recently, the Federal State of Upper Austria asked for damages from the members of the elevator cartel, which the Supreme Court, following a preliminary ruling of the CJEU in that case, held it could generally ask for; the case was also sent back to the lower court.[301] The European trucks cartel led to a number of damages claims, many of which were settled out of court. In the construction cartel cases, damages claims are expected to be brought shortly.[302]

C. *Interim Measures*

248. Interim measures in civil enforcement actions generally follow the rules of the Execution Act.[303]

249. If an infringement of competition law is relied upon in a case involving unfair competition law (on this possibility, *see* § 96 of this monograph), an interlocutory injunction may also be sought before the ordinary courts (§ 24 UWG).[304] The Supreme Court considers that whenever main proceedings are taking place before the Cartel Court, it is the latter which must issue interlocutory injunctions related to the case.[305]

298. KG 28.10.2005, 25 Kt 34, 253, 36, 42, 249, 250, 30, 32, 29, 35, 251, 252/05 – *Grazer Fahrschulen.*
299. BG Graz-Ost, 4 C 463/06h; LG Graz, 17 R 91/07p.
300. OGH 29.10.2014, 7 Ob 121/14s – *Kone v. ÖBB.*
301. Case C-435/18 *Otis v. Land Oberösterreich*, ECLI:EU:C:2019:1069; OGH 21.10.2020, 9 Ob 86/19s – *Otis.*
302. *E.g., see* Österreichischer Gemeindebund, 'Das österreichische Baukartell – Schadenersatzansprüche der Gemeinden' (4.10.2022) https://gemeindebund.at/das-oesterreichische-baukartell-schadenersatzansprueche-der-gemeinden/ last accessed 8.8.2024.
303. §§ 378 ff. Exekutionsordnung (EO; Execution Act), RGBl 1896/79 as amended. On this area of the law, *see* Bernhard König, *Einstweilige Verfügungen im Zivilverfahren: Handbuch für die Praxis* (5th ed., Manz 2017).
304. For instance, *see* the interlocutory injunctions granted in cases based on unfair competition law (§ 1 UWG) in combination with a competition law infringement: OGH 14.7.2009, 4 Ob 60/09s – *Anwaltssoftware*; OGH 22.6.1999, 4 Ob 90/99k – *Jahresbonus.*
305. KOG 16.7.2008, 16 Ok 3/08 – *Sägerundholz I.*

§3. Criminal Enforcement

250. In Austria, only very few aspects of competition law are criminalised today. Up until July 2002, heads of companies could be dealt custodial sentences or fines for breaches of competition law (*see* §§ 129–141 KartG 1988).[306] These sanctions were rarely enforced, however, and have since been replaced with purely monetary fines to be paid by the company.[307] Criminal enforcement of competition law remains available under the Criminal Code (StGB), albeit to a very limited degree (*see* below).

I. Criminal Sanctions for Antitrust Violations

251. § 168b StGB prohibits bid rigging, i.e., agreements restricting competition in procurement procedures. The provision applies to anyone who submits an application to participate in a procurement procedure, submits a tender or conducts negotiations that are based on an illegal agreement that is aimed at inducing the contracting party to accept a particular tender. The punishment foreseen in § 168b(1) StGB is a custodial sentence of up to three years. If the party voluntarily prevents the contracting party from accepting the rigged bid or prevents the contracting party from its performance, then no penalty is imposed (§ 168b(2) StGB).

252. The so-called construction cartel ('Baukartell') that the Federal Competition Authority uncovered remains the largest case (or rather: collection of successive cases) on bid rigging to date and has required close cooperation between the Federal Competition Authority and prosecutors.[308]

253. § 292c StGB prohibits collusion during certain auctions.[309] This provision entered into force on 1 January 2016.[310] It foresees the possibility of a custodial sentence of up to two years for anyone who demands, accepts or requests someone to promise an advantage in exchange for not appearing at an auction and acting as a co-bidder, or to bid only up to a certain price or in a certain way. The advantage can accrue to the natural person under scrutiny or a third party.

254. The Law on the Responsibility of Associations,[311] applicable since 2006, foresees that companies can be penalised for actions that are punishable under the Austrian Criminal Code, such as the ones set out above. In a recent case, the

306. Kartellgesetz 1988, BGBl 1988/600 (no longer in force).
307. Axel Reidlinger & Isabella Hartung, *Das österreichische Kartellrecht: Ein Handbuch für Praktiker* 292 (5th ed., Linde 2024).
308. On this cooperation, *see also* Bundeswettbewerbsbehörde,'FAQ Baukartell – Ermittlungen der Bundeswettbewerbsbehörde' (June 2024) https://www.bwb.gv.at/fileadmin/user_upload/FAQ_Baukartell_Juni_2024_V2_final1.pdf last accessed 8.8.2024.
309. *See* Judith Feldner & Dieter Thalhammer, *Die Hausdurchsuchung im Kartellrecht* para. 96 (Manz 2016).
310. *See* BGBl I 2015/112.
311. Verbandsverantwortlichkeitsgesetz, BGBl I 2005/151 as amended.

Supreme Cartel Court held that the principle of *ne bis in idem* does not apply in cases where a company is subject to fines under the KartG and also prosecuted under the rules of the Criminal Code, but that the criminal sanction should be considered when imposing the competition law fine.[312]

II. Other Application of Criminal Law to Relevant Conduct

255. Fraud under § 146 StGB may be committed in the competitive process where a natural person deceives someone about facts and thereby causes them to erroneously hold a belief that leads them to dispose of their assets in a damaging way. Depending on the gravity of the committed fraud, possible penalties include a custodial sentence of several months to several years or a monetary fine (*see* §§ 147, 148 StGB for aggravated and professional fraud).

256. In addition to the relevant provisions outlined in the previous section, there is also the possibility that certain other provisions contained in the Criminal Code may apply to behaviour that constitutes an abuse of a dominant position, for instance, relating to excessive prices or unfair trading conditions.[313]

III. Role of Prosecutors

257. The Central Public Prosecutor's Office for the Prosecution of White-Collar Crime and Corruption (Wirtschafts- und Korruptionsstaatsanwaltschaft, WKStA) is in charge of investigating bid rigging (§ 168b StGB) and bringing such cases before the competent criminal court (§ 20a(1) no 5 StPO). Other cases are investigated by the Public Prosecutor's Office and brought before the competent criminal court.

258. § 209b StPO provides special rules on the withdrawal from prosecution for cooperation with the Public Prosecutor's Office in connection with competition law infringements for leniency applicants. This provision needs to be seen together with leniency applications under § 11b WettbG, which it also references. It intends to provide criminal immunity for those natural persons who are instrumental in uncovering a cartel under the leniency procedures available before the Federal Competition Authority, the European Commission or the competition authorities of other Member States.

259. Under § 209b(1) StPO, the Federal Cartel Prosecutor can ask the Public Prosecutor's Office to refrain from prosecuting an individual (natural person) if that

312. On this, *see* KOG 17.5.2024, 16 Ok 5/23f – *Meinungsforschungskartell*; Axel Reidlinger & Isabella Hartung, *Das österreichische Kartellrecht: Ein Handbuch für Praktiker* 292 f. (5th ed., Linde 2024).

313. For example, *see* Severin Glaser & Ursula Pirko, 'Missbrauch einer marktbeherrschenden Stellung aus strafrechtlicher Sicht' (2010) *Österreichische Zeitschrift für Kartellrecht* 20 (part I), 59 (part II).

individual was instrumental in a company's leniency application (§ 11b(1) no 3 WettbG). This lies within the Federal Cartel Prosecutor's discretion. However, if the Federal Cartel Prosecutor decides to make such an application, then the Public Prosecutor's Office must discontinue its investigations against the natural person in question (§ 209b(2) StPO), provided that said natural person has disclosed to the Office as well as to the court all their knowledge about their own actions and other facts that are relevant in order to clarify any criminal actions. The discontinuation of investigations is subject to subsequent prosecution.

260. The Austrian Ministry of Justice issued a Handbook on the Leniency Rules in January 2017.[314] In that comprehensive Handbook, it also sets out how to apply § 209b StPO.

IV. Competent Criminal Courts

261. Depending on the maximum sanctions foreseen by the Criminal Code, the District Courts (§ 30 StPO) or the Regional Courts (§ 31 StPO) are the competent criminal courts to hear a case. In the case of bid rigging, the accused or the WKStA can request that the case be heard by a special chamber of the Regional Criminal Court Vienna as the competent criminal court (*see also* § 32a(1) StPO).

314. Bundesministerium für Justiz, 'Handbuch zur Kronzeugenregelung: §§ 209a, 209b StPO in der Fassung des Strafprozessrechtsänderungsgesetzes II 2016' (1.1.2017). For the competition law-related sections, *see* pp. 24–30. A new version of the handbook is currently in preparation.

Part II. Application of the Prohibitions

Chapter 1. Restrictive Agreements

262. § 1 KartG on anti-competitive agreements states:

> § 1. (1) Any agreements between undertakings,[315] decisions of associations of undertakings and concerted practices which have as their object or effect the prevention, restriction or distortion of competition (cartels) shall be prohibited.
>
> (2) Pursuant to para. 1, it shall particularly be prohibited to:
> 1. directly or indirectly fix purchase and selling prices or any other trading conditions;
> 2. limit or control production, markets, technical development or investments;
> 3. share markets or sources of supply;
> 4. apply dissimilar conditions to equivalent transactions with other trading partners, thereby placing them at a competitive disadvantage;
> 5. make the conclusion of contracts subject to acceptance by the other contract parties of supplementary obligations which, by their nature or according to commercial usage, have no connection with the subject of such contracts.
>
> (3) Any agreements and decisions prohibited pursuant to para. 1 shall be automatically void.
>
> (4) Any recommendations to maintain certain prices, price limits, calculation guidelines, trade margins and discounts which aim at or result in the restriction of competition shall be equivalent to a cartel under para. 1 ('recommendation cartels'). This shall not apply to recommendations which explicitly state to be non-binding and which are not or shall not be enforced by exerting economic or social pressure.

263. The Supreme Cartel Court has emphasised that § 1(1) KartG is identical to the first sentence of Article 101(1) TFEU, apart from the requirement of an effect

315. The original German text speaks of agreements between 'Unternehmern' (i.e., entrepreneurs) rather than between undertakings. This is due to Austrian legal terminology in commercial law, and the Supreme Cartel Court has found that it is not of relevance, *see* KOG 8.10.2015, 16 Ok 3/15z – *VAMED/NRZ Rosenhügel*; *see* § 103 of this monograph above.

on trade between Member States. The list of anti-competitive agreements in § 1(2) KartG also conforms to the list contained in Article 101(1) TFEU.[316] § 1(3) KartG declares anti-competitive agreements null and void and is the mirror provision of Article 101(2) TFEU. This, of course, is no coincidence, for the Austrian legislator found that a harmonious interpretation of Austrian competition law in line with EU competition law would be beneficial. Where a case may affect trade between Member States, national rules on anti-competitive agreements may not prohibit agreements that are allowed under Article 101(1) TFEU or that fulfil the conditions of individual or block exemption under Article 101(3) TFEU (Article 3(2) of Regulation 1/2003). Where no such effect on trade between Member States arises, however, national legislation has greater leeway. Nevertheless, national rules tend to stay in line with Article 101 TFEU, as it is hardly recommendable to foresee different national rules for agreements that may have an effect on trade between Member States and those that may not.

264. Against this background, it becomes clear why Austrian case law frequently relies on European case law even where there is no effect on intra-EU trade. In the following, the sole aim is to discuss Austrian cases on restrictive agreements as decided by the Cartel Court and the Supreme Cartel Court. However, the reader should keep in mind that the European case law on anti-competitive agreements and European Commission block exemption regulations are often the basis for the Austrian case law and should therefore be consulted in parallel (on this, *see* the forthcoming IEL monograph on Competition Law in the European Union).

265. The ancillary restraints doctrine is applied under § 1 KartG. Under that doctrine, an anti-competitive restraint that is ancillary to a main agreement that is not anti-competitive is not prohibited under § 1 KartG if that restraint is required for the implementation of the main agreement. However, the ancillary restraint may not go beyond what is necessary. This is to be determined on an objective rather than a subjective basis. What is decisive is the objective of the main agreement.[317] On the ancillary restraints doctrine, particularly on agreements that may be concluded within the context of concentrations, also *see* the European Commission's notice of 2005.[318] The Austrian practice may be somewhat stricter than the European approach to ancillary restraints.[319]

---

316. KOG 26.6.2006, 16 Ok 51/05 – *Asphaltmischanlage II*.
317. *See* KOG 6.9.2017, 16 Ok 10/16f – *BWB/Semperit*; KOG 9.12.1996, 16 Ok 3/96 – *Kiesabbau*; KOG 14.12.1993, Okt 6/93 – *Transportbeton*.
318. European Commission, Commission Notice on restrictions directly related and necessary to concentrations [2005] OJ C56/24, esp para. 13.
319. Astrid Ablasser-Neuhuber, Florian Neumayr, Gerhard Fussenegger & Sebastian Reiter, 'Austria' § 2.02[1][b][xii], in: Frank L. Fine (ed.), *European Competition Laws*, vol 1 (loose-leaf, Matthew Bender Elite Products, release 21-11/2022).

§1. HORIZONTAL AGREEMENTS

266. The Supreme Cartel Court has emphasised that neither Article 101 TFEU nor § 1 KartG differentiates between horizontal and vertical agreements. The provisions equally apply to both. However, because of the different competitive effects that emanate from horizontal and vertical agreements, it can be useful to differentiate between the two types of agreements.[320] Where defendants operate at the same stage of the economy for the purpose of an agreement, it should be assessed whether horizontal restrictions of competition exist among them.[321]

267. The leniency programme under § 11b WettbG (*see* §§ 452–463) is open to all types of anti-competitive agreements under § 1 KartG. However, in practice, it particularly targets the uncovering of anti-competitive horizontal agreements.

I. Cartels

268. In § 1(2) nos 1, 2 and 3 KartG, the KartG lists those types of behaviour that are typically understood to constitute a cartel: price-fixing, the limitation of production or innovation, and the allocation of markets. These are generally understood to constitute hardcore restrictions under the European Commission's *De Minimis* Notice[322] and cannot benefit from the Austrian *de minimis* rules (*see* §§ 63–64 of this monograph).

A. *Price-Fixing*

269. § 1(2) no 1 KartG prohibits the direct or indirect fixing of purchase or selling prices. Price-fixing needs to be understood broadly and can concern purchase prices, selling prices, price increases, rebates or price components, price intervals, minimum prices, margins, credit terms and target prices.[323] In one instance, the Supreme Cartel Court held that an agreement on a fixed cost for the collection of batteries among suppliers of batteries had the aim of aligning this cost factor and could have a price-unifying effect, and therefore came under the prohibition of § 1(2) no 1 KartG.[324] In another case, the Supreme Cartel Court warned that standard prices that were issued by an association of undertakings could deteriorate competition, as such standard prices allow all market participants to predict their

320. KOG 6.9.2017, 16 Ok 10/16f – *BWB/Semperit*.
321. KOG 23.6.2003, 16 Ok 4/03 – *K-Hit-Radio*.
322. European Commission, Notice on agreements of minor importance which do not appreciably restrict competition under Article 101(1) of the Treaty on the Functioning of the European Union (*De Minimis* Notice) [2014] OJ L291/1, para. 13.
323. KOG 8.10.2015, 16 Ok 2/15b & 16 Ok 8/15k – *Spar*; Axel Reidlinger & Isabella Hartung, *Das österreichische Kartellrecht: Ein Handbuch für Praktiker* 100 f. (5th ed., Linde 2024).
324. KOG 9.12.1996, 16 Ok 11/96 – *UFS-Sammelsystem*.

competitors' pricing policies.[325] An agreement on a package price for airport transfers has also been held to constitute price-fixing.[326]

270. As price-fixing is understood to constitute a restriction of competition by object, its effects on the market do not need to be assessed.[327]

271. In a case involving driving schools from the city of Graz, six driving schools were found to have fixed prices for driving lessons. The driving schools argued that this was necessary as a countermeasure to ruinous price competition, an argument that was not accepted by the Cartel Court.[328]

272. According to the Supreme Cartel Court, the fixing of maximum prices does not usually come within the prohibition on price-fixing, as such an agreement can be seen as ancillary to another agreement that, in itself, is not restrictive of competition.[329]

273. Hub and spoke cartels have also come under scrutiny in Austria: in such a scenario, anti-competitive agreements are concluded between a supplier and several retailers (i.e., at the vertical level), effectively leading to anti-competitive effects among retailers (i.e., at the horizontal level). As the Supreme Cartel Court emphasised in the *Spar* case (2015), hub and spoke cartels that assign the task of price moderation to a supplier are caught by § 1(2) no 1 KartG.[330]

274. While prices and price-fixing are, of course, frequently at the centre of antitrust investigations, other trading conditions may just as well be directly or indirectly fixed among competitors. In the *Haftungsverbund* case (2007), the Supreme Cartel Court dealt with agreements among a number of savings banks that concerned both prices and other trading conditions.[331] In that case, however, it found that the agreements in question did not limit the participating savings banks' trading potential as regards the banking services concerned to such a degree that competition was excluded.

275. On § 1(4) KartG, which prohibits 'recommendation cartels' in both horizontal and vertical settings, *see* below at §§ 298 ff. of this monograph.

325. KOG 20.12.2005, 16 Ok 45/05 – *Honorarordnung der Baumeister.*
326. KOG 15.5.2000, 16 Ok 2/00 – *Flughafenfunktaxizentrale.*
327. KOG 8.10.2008, 16 Ok 5/08 – *Aufzugs- und Fahrtreppenkartell I.*
328. KG 28.10.2005, KG 25 Kt 34, 253, 36, 42, 249, 250, 30, 32, 29, 35, 251, 252/05 – *Grazer Fahrschulen.* For a summary of this unpublished case, *see* Claudine Vartian, 'Austria' paras 3-021–3-023, in: Ioannis Kokkoris (ed.), *Competition Cases from the European Union: The Ultimate Guide to Leading Cases from the EU, Member States and EFTA* (2d ed., Sweet & Maxwell 2010).
329. KOG 9.12.1996, 16 Ok 5/96 – *UFH-System II.*
330. KOG 8.10.2015, 16 Ok 2/15b & 16 Ok 8/15k – *Spar.*
331. KOG 21.3.2007, 16 Ok 12/06 – *Haftungsverbund II.*

276. While § 1(2) no 1 KartG prohibits price-fixing, under § 1(2) no 4 KartG – and also § 5(1) no 3 KartG (§§ 336 ff. of this monograph) – it is prohibited to apply dissimilar conditions to equivalent transactions with other trading partners. This can also involve price discrimination.

277. In one well-reported case on the fixing of deposit and lending rates by Austrian banks, it was the European Commission that pursued the case. While the banks disputed that their agreement had an effect on trade between Member States, the CJEU found that 'the "Lombard network" impeded free access to the Austrian market so that the cartel was liable to have a cross-border effect'.[332]

B. Market/Client Allocation

278. § 1(2) no 3 KartG prohibits the sharing of markets and of sources of supply. The market allocation targeted by this prohibition can occur based on geographical areas (territorial allocation) or based on types of customers (customer allocation).

279. In the elevator cartel, the Supreme Cartel Court held that where competitors allocate customers or orders, in addition to coordinating price increases, this constituted a restriction of competition by object.[333] The manifold anti-competitive behaviour in this case led to a considerable cumulative fine.

280. A special type of market allocation can be seen in collusive tendering (bid rigging), whereby competitors coordinate their offers in the time leading up to a public tender in order to ensure that a specific bidder wins the contract. Collusive tendering is also prohibited under criminal law (*see* § 168b StGB; discussed in § 247 of this monograph). Collusive tendering was at issue in the case of *Wiener Wohnen* (2013), in which the Federal Competition Authority accused a number of undertakings of bid rigging. The Supreme Cartel Court, however, agreed with the Cartel Court that the primarily small undertakings active on the relevant market of plumbing services needed to enter into working groups in order to be able to take part in the tender. This led to an exemption under § 2(2) no 1 KartG, as the provision at the time did not state that hardcore cartels could not be exempted under it (the provision has since been amended to that effect).[334]

281. In recent years, the Federal Competition Authority has repeatedly brought cases on collusive tendering before the Cartel Court, most notably in cases involving

332. CJEU Joined Cases C-125/07 P, C-133/07 P, C-135/07 P & C-137/07 P *Erste Group Bank & others v, Commission ('Lombard Club')*, ECLI:EU:C:2009:576, para. 41.
333. KOG 8.10.2008, 16 Ok 5/08 – *Aufzugs- und Fahrtreppenkartell I.*
334. KOG 2.12.2013, 16 Ok 6/12 – *BWB/Wiener Wohnen.*

the drywall cartel (2017).[335] In one of these cases on collusive tendering, the defendant repeatedly prepared offer calculations for competitors that were higher than the defendant's own offer. The competitors then submitted these prepared offers, resulting in the defendant obtaining the contract. At the same time, competitors also sent higher cover offers to the defendant, which the defendant then submitted, with the competitors obtaining the contract. The Cartel Court agreed with the Federal Competition Authority that this repeatedly used system had the object of restricting competition; the effects of this system therefore did not have to be assessed.[336] In that case, one of the undertakings that participated in the collusive tendering scheme applied for leniency with the Federal Competition Authority in 2015 and was subsequently granted immunity from fines.[337]

282. The construction cartel, which involved bid rigging between all major construction companies in Austria from 2006 to 2017, has led to numerous cases before the Cartel Court since 2021 and continues to do so. It involved several dozen construction companies in the whole of Austria, and investigations remain ongoing. So far, twelve cases against construction companies have been concluded in which the undertakings were required to pay fines between EUR 1.1 million and EUR 62.35 million.[338] A further four cases are currently ongoing before the Cartel Court.[339] The case also led to multiple leniency applications and settlements. Together, the construction cartel cases are the largest competition law case Austria has ever seen. The complexity of the cases is due to the fact that bid rigging is also sanctioned by criminal law, leading to parallel investigations and proceedings both under competition law and under criminal law.

C. Production/Innovation Limitation

283. § 1(2) no 2 KartG forbids agreements that limit or control production, markets, technical development or investments. The Supreme Cartel Court has held that

335. For example, *see* KG 26.1.2017, 27 Kt 12/16 – *BWB/Wagner & Jüptner (Trockenbau)*; KG 27.6.2017, 128 Kt 1/17t – *BWB/Tüchler (Trockenbau)*; KG 22.9.2017, 128 Kt 3/17m – *BWB/E+H Trockenbau*; KG 9.11.2017, 24 Kt 7/16h – *BWB/3P Trockenbau*.

336. KG 26.1.2017, 27 Kt 12/16 – *BWB/Wagner & Jüptner (Trockenbau)*.

337. Therefore, the Federal Competition Authority did not apply for a fine to be imposed on the undertaking, but only for a declaration by the Cartel Court that the infringement had existed; KG 29.6.2017, 26 Kt 10/16i – *Akustik-Blasch*.

338. *See*, for instance, KG 21.10.2021, 27 Kt 12/21y – *STRABAG* (EUR 45.37 million); KG 17.2.2022, 26 Kt 5/21m – *PORR* (EUR 62.35 million); KG 27.3.2023, 25 Kt 10/22s – *Swietelsky* (EUR 27.15 million). One leniency applicant was not required to pay a fine; *see* KG 20.6.2023, 127 Kt 3/23p – *Kostmann*. The *STRABAG* decision was subsequently annulled and the Cartel Court was asked to reopen the case, as it emerged that the leniency applicant had not fully disclosed all required information; see KOG 25.5.2023, 16 Ok 8/22w – *STRABAG*.

339. *See* Bundeswettbewerbsbehörde,' FAQ Baukartell – Ermittlungen der Bundeswettbewerbsbehörde' pp. 8-9 (June 2024) https://www.bwb.gv.at/fileadmin/user_upload/FAQ_Baukartell_Juni_2024_V2_final1.pdf last accessed 8.8.2024.

an agreement between competitors not to compete with each other, for instance, by not producing or selling goods on the relevant product market, was anti-competitive.[340]

D. Group Boycott

284. While group boycotts can constitute anti-competitive agreements within the meaning of § 1(1) KartG, they are usually caught out under the provisions of the Unfair Competition Act or § 5 KartG (abuse of a dominant position).[341] In one instance, the Federal Competition Authority brought three cases before the Cartel Court because three well-known breweries had agreed among each other not to supply cash and carry markets with draught beer (group boycott). This was seen as an anti-competitive agreement within the meaning of § 1 KartG and Article 101 TFEU.[342]

E. Collusion on Other Objects

285. § 1(1) KartG generally prohibits anti-competitive agreements, decisions by associations of undertakings and concerted practices. Although § 1(2) KartG provides an exemplary list of types of behaviour that are regarded as anti-competitive under that provision, further categories of anti-competitive restrictions may be developed in the case law.

II. Information Exchange Practices

286. The exchange of information will usually form part of many types of anti-competitive agreements, such as price-fixing or market allocation. In addition, however, pure information exchanges can also be prohibited under the competition law provisions. The Supreme Cartel Court has held that a pure information exchange is anti-competitive when competitors exchange information on circumstances that are significant for competition and that are not generally and readily available. In particular, the information exchange may be anti-competitive where it eliminates the uncertainty about competitors' future behaviour on the market.[343]

340. KOG 26.2.1996, 16 Ok 13/95 – *Wettbewerbsverbote*. On non-compete clauses among competitors, *see also* KOG 21.3.2007, 16 Ok 12/06 – *Haftungsverbund II*.
341. On this, *see* Astrid Ablasser-Neuhuber, Florian Neumayr, Gerhard Fussenegger & Sebastian Reiter, 'Austria' § 2.02[1][b][vi], in: Frank L. Fine (ed.), *European Competition Laws*, vol 1 (loose-leaf, Matthew Bender Elite Products, release 21-11/2022).
342. Bundeswettbewerbsbehörde, 'BWB/FD-212 Bierbrauer' (10.4.2012) https://www.bwb.gv.at/kartelle_marktmachtmissbrauch/entscheidungen/detail/bwbfd-212-bierbrauer last accessed 8.8.2024.
343. KOG 21.3.2007, 16 Ok 12/06 – *Haftungsverbund II*.

III. Cooperation Agreements

A. Research and Development

287. The general prohibition of § 1(1) KartG applies to research and development agreements. On research and development, the European Commission's block exemption regulation 2023/1066[344] can be relied upon, even though – as explained above (§ 30 of this monograph) – there only is a legal basis for applying this block exemption regulation where a case has at least a potential effect on trade between Member States (Article 288 TFEU).

B. Specialisation

288. The general prohibition of § 1(1) KartG applies to specialisation agreements. For specialisation agreements, the European Commission's block exemption regulation 2023/1067[345] is relied upon in practice.

C. Standardisation

289. The general prohibition of § 1(1) KartG applies to standardisation agreements. The European Commission's Guidelines on Horizontal Co-operation (2023)[346] contain guidance on standardisation agreements that is also taken into account in Austria.

D. Joint Production

290. The general prohibition of § 1(1) KartG applies to joint production agreements. Joint production agreements are covered by the European Commission's block exemption regulation 2023/1067.[347] The European Commission's Guidelines on Horizontal Co-operation (2023)[348] contain guidance on joint production that is also taken into account in Austria.

---

344. Commission Regulation (EU) 2023/1066 of 1 June 2023 on the application of Article 101(3) of the Treaty on the Functioning of the European Union to certain categories of research and development agreements [2023] OJ L143/9.
345. Commission Regulation (EU) 2023/1067 of 1 June 2023 on the application of Article 101(3) of the Treaty on the Functioning of the European Union to certain categories of specialisation agreements [2023] OJ L143/20.
346. European Commission, Guidelines on the applicability of Article 101 of the Treaty on the Functioning of the European Union to horizontal co-operation agreements [2023] OJ C259/1, paras 436 ff.
347. Commission Regulation (EU) 2023/1067 of 1 June 2023 on the application of Article 101(3) of the Treaty on the Functioning of the European Union to certain categories of specialisation agreements [2023] OJ L143/20, Art. 1(1)(c).
348. European Commission, Guidelines on the applicability of Article 101 of the Treaty on the Functioning of the European Union to horizontal co-operation agreements [2023] OJ C259/1, paras 172 ff.

291. In 2003, the Cartel Court had to rule on a payment transaction company that was jointly set up by three major banks. In that case, the Court accepted that such a production joint venture – that was not regarded as fully functional by the banks – could be economically justified.[349]

292. In *Asphaltmischanlage II* (2006), the Supreme Cartel Court had to rule on the joint production of asphalt mixture by a company in which undertakings held stakes that were active in the same geographic market and that were competitors in the downstream market of road construction. It held that joint production as such did not constitute an anti-competitive agreement by object. In the case at hand, however, the road construction companies under investigation offered asphalt mixture at nearly identical prices up to the year 2004, the companies involved were the three biggest road construction companies on the relevant market served by the joint venture, the managers of the joint venture were also active in other asphalt mixture companies, and information exchanges at the joint venture related to costs for the production of asphalt mixture. Taken together, the Supreme Cartel Court viewed the pricing behaviour of the companies involved as evidence of reduced price competition and of anti-competitive coordination of market behaviour through joint production. It therefore regarded the prohibition of § 1(1) KartG as applicable to that case.[350]

E. Joint Purchasing

293. The general prohibition of § 1(1) KartG applies to joint purchasing agreements. The European Commission's Guidelines on Horizontal Co-operation (2023)[351] contain guidance on joint purchasing that is also taken into account in Austria.

F. Joint Selling

294. The general prohibition of § 1(1) KartG applies to joint selling and marketing agreements. Where a joint selling and marketing agreement prevents, restricts or distorts competition, it can come within the scope of § 1(1) KartG, particularly where it limits markets or fixes trading conditions, including prices.[352]

---

349. KG 11.7.2003, 27 Kt 456, 498, 499/02 – *Abwicklung des Zahlungsverkehrs*.
350. KOG 26.6.2006, 16 Ok 51/05 – *Asphaltmischanlage II*. However, the initial decision was quashed on other grounds and the case remanded to the Cartel Court.
351. European Commission, Guidelines on the applicability of Article 101 of the Treaty on the Functioning of the European Union to horizontal co-operation agreements [2023] OJ C259/1, paras 273 ff.
352. Astrid Ablasser-Neuhuber, Florian Neumayr, Gerhard Fussenegger & Sebastian Reiter, 'Austria' § 2.02[1][b][vii], in: Frank L. Fine (ed.), *European Competition Laws*, vol 1 (loose-leaf, Matthew Bender Elite Products, release 21-11/2022).

295. The cooperative privilege ('Genossenschaftsprivileg') of § 2(2) no 3 KartG exempts certain restrictions among a cooperative from this prohibition.[353] The exemption applies to restrictions of competition among the members of a cooperative as well as between the cooperative and its members. To benefit from this exemption, however, the restriction of competition must be necessary in order to fulfil the cooperative's statutory mandate to provide benefits to its members. Joint selling and marketing agreements frequently feature in cooperatives and may be exempted from the prohibition in § 1 KartG if all requirements are fulfilled. No similar exemption can be found at the level of the European Union.[354]

296. The European Commission's Guidelines on Horizontal Co-operation (2023)[355] contain guidance on joint selling that is also taken into account in Austria.

§2. Vertical Agreements

297. Vertical agreements are entered into between undertakings that, for the purpose of the agreement, operate at different levels of the economy. Frequently, these are distribution agreements.[356]

298. Hardcore restrictions, such as those listed in Article 4 of the Vertical Agreements Block Exemption Regulation 2022/720 (VABER), are generally thought to be the most anti-competitive type of vertical agreements.[357] According to this black list, vertical agreements containing any of the following clauses are held to infringe Article 101(1) TFEU and will not be able to benefit from block exemption under the VABER – and frequently, they may also have difficulties being considered for individual exemption under Article 101(3) TFEU:

a. the restriction of the buyer's ability to determine its sale price, without prejudice to the possibility of the supplier to impose a maximum sale price or recommend a sale price, provided that they do not amount to a fixed or minimum sale price as a result of pressure from, or incentives offered by, any of the parties;

353. For the notion of cooperative and its raison d'être, the KartG refers to Gesetz über Erwerbs- und Wirtschaftsgenossenschaften (Act Concerning Commercial and Industrial Cooperatives), RGBl 1873/70 as amended.

354. Axel Reidlinger & Isabella Hartung, *Das österreichische Kartellrecht: Ein Handbuch für Praktiker* 78 (5th ed., Linde 2024).

355. European Commission, Guidelines on the applicability of Article 101 of the Treaty on the Functioning of the European Union to horizontal co-operation agreements [2023] OJ C259/1, paras 317 ff.

356. KOG 1.12.2009, 16 Ok 10/09 – *Pressegrosso II*. For a comprehensive work on the European, German and Austrian law on distribution agreements, *see* Frank Wijckmans, Filip Tuytschaever, Moritz Lorenz & Andreas Zellhofer, *Vertriebsverträge im Kartellrecht: Deutsche, österreichische und unionsweite Rechtspraxis vertikaler Vereinbarungen* (C.H. Beck 2019).

357. Commission Regulation (EU) 2022/720 of 10 May 2022 on the application of Article 101(3) of the Treaty on the Functioning of the European Union to categories of vertical agreements and concerted practices (VABER) [2022] OJ L134/4.

b. where the supplier operates an exclusive distribution system, the restriction of the territory into which, or of the customers to whom, the exclusive distributor may actively or passively sell the contract goods or services, except:
   i. the restriction of active sales by the exclusive distributor and its direct customers, into a territory or to a customer group reserved to the supplier or allocated by the supplier exclusively to a maximum of five other exclusive distributors;
   ii. the restriction of active or passive sales by the exclusive distributor and its customers to unauthorised distributors located in a territory where the supplier operates a selective distribution system for the contract goods or services;
   iii. the restriction of the exclusive distributor's place of establishment;
   iv. the restriction of active or passive sales to end users by an exclusive distributor operating at the wholesale level of trade;
   v. the restriction of the exclusive distributor's ability to actively or passively sell components, supplied for the purposes of incorporation, to customers who would use them to manufacture the same type of goods as those produced by the supplier;

c. where the supplier operates a selective distribution system,
   i. the restriction of the territory into which, or of the customers to whom, the members of the selective distribution system may actively or passively sell the contract goods or services, except:
      1. the restriction of active sales by the members of the selective distribution system and their direct customers, into a territory or to a customer group reserved to the supplier or allocated by the supplier exclusively to a maximum of five exclusive distributors;
      2. the restriction of active or passive sales by the members of the selective distribution system and their customers to unauthorised distributors located within the territory where the selective distribution system is operated;
      3. the restriction of the place of establishment of the members of the selective distribution system;
      4. the restriction of active or passive sales to end users by members of the selective distribution system operating at the wholesale level of trade;
      5. the restriction of the ability to actively or passively sell components, supplied for the purposes of incorporation, to customers who would use them to manufacture the same type of goods as those produced by the supplier;
   ii. the restriction of cross-supplies between the members of the selective distribution system operating at the same or different levels of trade;
   iii. the restriction of active or passive sales to end users by members of the selective distribution system operating at the retail level of trade, without prejudice to points (c)(i)(1) and (3);

d. where the supplier operates neither an exclusive distribution system nor a selective distribution system, the restriction of the territory into which, or of the customers to whom, the buyer may actively or passively sell the contract goods or services, except:
   i. the restriction of active sales by the buyer and its direct customers into a territory or to a customer group reserved to the supplier or allocated by the supplier exclusively to a maximum of five exclusive distributors;
   ii. the restriction of active or passive sales by the buyer and its customers to unauthorised distributors located in a territory where the supplier operates a selective distribution system for the contract goods or services;
   iii. the restriction of the buyer's place of establishment;
   iv. the restriction of active or passive sales to end users by a buyer operating at the wholesale level of trade;
   v. the restriction of the buyer's ability to actively or passively sell components, supplied for the purposes of incorporation, to customers who would use them to manufacture the same type of goods as those produced by the supplier;
e. the prevention of the effective use of the internet by the buyer or its customers to sell the contract goods or services, as it restricts the territory into which or the customers to whom the contract goods or services may be sold within the meaning of points (b), (c) or (d), without prejudice to the possibility of imposing on the buyer:
   i. other restrictions of online sales; or
   ii. restrictions of online advertising that do not have the object of preventing the use of an entire online advertising channel;
f. the restriction, agreed between a supplier of components and a buyer who incorporates those components, of the supplier's ability to sell the components as spare parts to end users or to repairers, wholesalers or other service providers not entrusted by the buyer with the repair or servicing of its goods.

299. The Supreme Cartel Court has emphasised that the VABER can, among other indicators, be relied upon in order to identify vertical restrictions of competition by object.[358]

I. Vertical Price-Fixing

300. In practical terms, enforcement by the Federal Competition Authority has been particularly active in the area of vertical price-fixing. This type of enforcement is based on § 1(2) no 1 KartG, which prohibits not only horizontal but also vertical price-fixing. At the European level, vertical price-fixing is black-listed in

358. KOG 1.12.2009, 16 Ok 10/09 – *Pressegrosso II* (still with reference to the previously applicable VABER 2790/99). *See* Commission Regulation (EC) No 2790/1999 of 22 December 1999 on the application of Article 81(3) of the Treaty to categories of vertical agreements and concerted practices [1999] OJ L336/21 (no longer in force).

Article 4(a) VABER, and the European Commission's Vertical Guidelines contain guidance on dealing with resale price restrictions.[359]

301. In 2014, the Federal Competition Authority published a Standpoint on Resale Price Maintenance, setting out its view as to vertical price-fixing and emphasising that vertical price-fixing constitutes a restriction of competition by object.[360] In that Standpoint, the Federal Competition Authority clearly stresses that in order not to be caught out under competition law, a recommended retail price must be purely non-binding, meaning that it must not be enforced through any economic or social pressure.[361] A non-binding recommended retail price is block exempted under the VABER (*see* Article 4(a) VABER) where the parties to the agreement do not exceed a 30% market share on their respective markets (Article 3(1) VABER). Where the market share threshold of the VABER is exceeded by any undertaking party to the vertical agreement, however, Austria adopts a strict view on recommended retail prices.[362] For instance, the Cartel Court has emphasised in *Benetton* (2002) that where all retailers of a certain product (tacitly) comply with the retail price recommended by the producer, and where this behaviour effectively leads to a uniform price on the market, this may very well be qualified as an anti-competitive restriction under the Austrian view – perhaps not as an agreement, but as a concerted practice.[363]

302. § 1(4) KartG prohibits 'recommendation cartels' whereby certain prices, price limits, calculation guidelines, trade margins and discounts are 'recommended' unless said recommendation is in fact explicitly non-binding and not enforced by exerting economic or social pressure.[364] § 1(4) KartG only applies where § 1(1) KartG – for lack of an agreement – cannot be applied.[365] The type of anti-competitive conduct envisaged by this provision can be of a horizontal or a vertical nature. While a price recommendation is typically a one-sided expression of will that leaves the other party free to set its price,[366] the Supreme Court has emphasised that the undertaking making the recommendation thereby shows an interest in the other party complying with this recommendation. Due to the retailers' dependence on the supplier, they may be inclined to set prices in the recommended way, thus amounting to a possibly anti-competitive practice that the legislator has prohibited under § 1(4) KartG.[367]

---

359. European Commission, Guidelines on Vertical Restraints [2022] OJ C248/1, paras 185 ff.
360. Bundeswettbewerbsbehörde, 'Standpoint on Resale Price Maintenance' (July 2014).
361. *Ibid.*, 9–10.
362. Axel Reidlinger & Isabella Hartung, *Das österreichische Kartellrecht: Ein Handbuch für Praktiker* 82 (5th ed., Linde 2024).
363. *See* on this KG 19.12.2002, 26 Kt 369, 370/96-74 – *Benetton* (speaking of a 'behavioural cartel'), with reference to KOG 23.6.1997, 16 Ok 14/97 – *Preisliste 2*; KOG 17.12.1997, 16 Ok 21/97 – *Preisliste 1*.
364. On this, *see also* KOG 5.9.2001, 16 Ok 5/01 – *E. L. Depotkosmetik*.
365. 926 der Beilagen XXII. GP (Erläuterungen zur Regierungsvorlage), p. 4.
366. *See* OGH 11.3.1965, 9 Os 85/64 – *Strumpfverkaufsautomaten*.
367. OGH 29.3.1967, 9 Os 66/66 – *Haushaltsgeräte*.

303. The Federal Competition Authority has already brought an important number of cases on vertical price-fixing before the Cartel Court. For instance, in 2013, the Cartel Court fined Philips Austria because of vertical price-fixing with the retail sector involving consumer lifestyle products (e.g., kitchen appliances and personal care appliances).[368] This case had come to the Federal Competition Authority's attention because of online retailers' complaints.[369] Also in 2013, the Cartel Court fined REWE, which owns major Austrian supermarket chains (Billa, Billa Plus) as well as a drug store chain (Bipa), EUR 20.8 million for vertically agreeing on retail prices and promotion periods with suppliers, especially from the beer and dairy industry.[370] And the Austrian supermarket chain Spar was fined EUR 30 million in 2015[371] and an additional EUR 10.2 million in 2016,[372] in both cases for anti-competitive agreements spanning over a decade in which the food retailer fixed retail prices with suppliers for product categories such as dairy products, beer, non-alcoholic beverages and flour.

304. In April 2020, the Cartel Court fined Specialized Europe EUR 378,000 for retail price maintenance as well as for restricting the online sale and distribution of its bicycles over the course of nearly six years.[373] Similarly, the headphone producer Bose was fined EUR 650,000 for vertically agreeing on retail prices in the area of consumer electronics over the course of 3.5 years.[374] In June 2020, the Cartel Court fined Zodiac Pool Care Europe EUR 294,000 for resale price agreements with retailers and wholesalers on the Austrian market for automatic pool cleaning equipment.[375] The Federal Competition Authority also uncovered vertical price-fixing in the area of school bags, leading the Cartel Court to impose a fine of EUR 3.4 million on the company Fond of, the manufacturer of the popular 'Ergobag' and 'Satch' school bags, in 2021.[376] In addition, three retailers received fines.[377]

305. The cases mentioned in this section demonstrate that vertical price-fixing continues to be a pervasive practice in Austria that is actively pursued by the Federal Competition Authority and strictly enforced by the Cartel Court. In fact, of the eighty-five decisions that the Cartel Court issued on anti-competitive agreements between 2012 and 2022, fifty concerned vertical price-fixing.[378]

---

368. KG 26.3.2013, 29 Kt 26/13-6 – *Philips Austria.*
369. Bundeswettbewerbsbehörde, 'BWB/K-285 Elektronikbranche' (26.3.2013) https://www.bwb.gv.at/kartelle_marktmachtmissbrauch/entscheidungen/detail/bwbk-285-elektronikbranche last accessed 8.8.2024.
370. KG 13.5.2013, 25 Kt 29/13 – *BWB/REWE.*
371. KOG 8.10.2015, 16 Ok 2/15b & 16 Ok 8/15k – *Spar.*
372. KG 30.6.2016, 29 Kt 10/16m– *BWB/Spar (Brauereiprodukte).*
373. KG 8.4.2020, 128 Kt 2/19t – *Specialized Europe.*
374. KG 14.6.2019, 24 Kt 7/19p – *Bose.*
375. KG 26.6.2020, 25 Kt 3/20h – *Zodiac Pool Cleaning Europe.*
376. KG 15.7.2021, 24 Kt 5/21d – *Fond of.* The fine was reduced due to leniency.
377. KG 12.5.2022, 24 Kt 1/22k – *Kastner & Öhler*; KG 1.7.2022, 25 Kt 4/22h – *Thalia*; KG 5.12.2022, 25 Kt 8/22x – *Georg Hausmann KG.*
378. *See* Jan Amthauer, Jürgen Fleiß, Franziska Guggi & Viktoria H.S.E. Robertson, 'Detecting resale price maintenance for competition law purposes: Proof-of-concept study using web scraped data' (2023) 51 *Computer Law & Security Review* 105901, p. 3-4.

306. There is one important exemption for vertical price-fixing in Austrian competition law: § 2(2) no 2 KartG contains an exemption for resale price maintenance between a final seller of books, art prints, sheet music, magazines and newspapers and the publisher setting the sales price. The exemption equally covers resale price maintenance between newspaper and magazine publishers on the one hand and undertakings that obtain newspapers or magazines with an option of returning them and selling them with the same option to the final seller (press wholesalers) on the other hand. This system of fixed book prices ('Buchpreisbindung') is only allowed, however, insofar as the resale price maintenance is required to guarantee a nationwide and non-discriminatory distribution of a range of newspapers and magazines by stationary retail trade. The system of fixed book prices has a long tradition in Austria and beyond, dating back to the nineteenth century.[379] As it concerns a hardcore restriction, this exemption needs to be interpreted narrowly.[380]

307. In a case decided in 2013, the Cartel Court underlined that while the system of fixed book prices could infringe Article 101(1) TFEU, it could be exempted under Article 101(3) TFEU.[381] In that decision, it emphasised the particularities of media markets and their importance for free speech. The Cartel Court held that benefits within the meaning of Article 101(3) TFEU could not only accrue to customers through lower prices but also from a diverse range of available titles and their ubiquity. As the Austrian legislator has noted, however, this assessment is restricted to the Austrian perspective and may be decided differently where a cross-border dimension is at stake.[382] The similar German provision on fixed book prices ('Sammelrevers') has led to an investigation by the European Commission concerning the conformity of this system of fixed book prices with EU competition law, which was ended following commitments offered by the undertakings involved.[383]

II. Distribution

A. *Exclusive Distributorship*

308. In an exclusive distribution agreement, the supplier only authorises one (exclusive) distributor to distribute its goods or services in a particular area or to a particular customer group. Exclusive distribution can take several forms. Where absolute territorial or customer protection is granted to an exclusive distributor, this will usually infringe competition law. For instance, in *Semperit*, the Supreme Cartel

379. *See* OGH 2.4.1985, 4 Ob 395/84 – *Baedeker's Reiseführer*.
380. Alexander Hiersche & Maximilian Mertel, '§ 12 KartG' para. 38, in: Alexander Egger & Natalie Harsdorf-Borsch (eds), *Kartellrecht – Kommentar* (Linde 2022).
381. KG 20.3.2013, 26 Kt 17, 18, 27, 28/07 – *Preisbindung*.
382. 1522 der Beilagen XXV. GP (Erläuterungen zur Regierungsvorlage), p. 3.
383. *See* European Commission, Cases COMP/34.657 *Sammelrevers* & COMP/35.245–35.251 *Einzelreverse* [2000] OJ C162/25; European Commission, Case COMP/37.906 *Internetbuchhandel* Commission Decision of 22 March 2002.

Court took issue with undertakings that jointly produced and distributed a product and agreed that one of them should be the sole distributor for the European Union.[384]

309. The VABER[385] as well as the European Commission's Vertical Guidelines[386] contain relevant guidance on exclusive distribution.

310. The ancillary restraints doctrine can also apply to vertical restraints contained in distribution agreements.[387]

B. Exclusive Dealing

311. Where exclusive dealing is understood as a distribution agreement through which the supplier ensures that the distributor (almost) only sells the supplier's products, this is referred to as single branding in Europe. The Vertical Guidelines contain guidance on this type of vertical restraint.[388] They also provide guidance on exclusive supply, whereby the supplier is obliged to (almost) only sell to one buyer.[389]

C. Selective Distribution

312. In a selective distribution agreement, the supplier only supplies its goods or services to distributors that fulfil certain requirements. These requirements can be of a qualitative or quantitative nature, or consist of a combination of the two.

313. The criteria for the admissibility of a selective distribution system that the CJEU has developed in its long-standing jurisprudence are also of relevance under Austrian competition law.[390] The more lenient rules on selective distribution contained in the VABER[391] are also of utmost relevance for Austrian competition law practice, at least for vertical agreements in which none of the business partners involved has any significant market power. The European Commission's Vertical Guidelines[392] also contain pertinent information on selective distribution.

384. *See* KOG 6.9.2017, 16 Ok 10/16f – *BWB/Semperit.*
385. *See* the black-listed provisions in Art. 4(b)VABER.
386. European Commission, Guidelines on Vertical Restraints [2022] OJ C248/1, paras 117 ff.
387. KOG 5.9.2001, 16 Ok 4/01 – *Steinbruch.*
388. European Commission, Guidelines on Vertical Restraints [2022] OJ C248/1, paras 298 ff.
389. European Commission, Guidelines on Vertical Restraints [2022] OJ C248/1, paras 321 ff.
390. For example, *see* CJEU Case 26/76 *Metro v. Commission*, ECLI:EU:C:1977:167.
391. *See* the black-listed provisions in Art. 4(c) VABER; and the grey-listed provision in Art. 5(1)(c) VABER.
392. European Commission, Guidelines on Vertical Restraints [2022] OJ C248/1, paras 143 ff.

D. *Franchising*

314. In a franchising agreement, the franchisor licences its know-how and certain intellectual property rights to a franchisee. The European Commission's Vertical Guidelines contain pertinent guidance on franchising agreements.[393]

315. In one Austrian case concerning the franchise of a bakery, the franchisor and the franchisees were found to have engaged in anti-competitive resale price maintenance: the franchisor had central control of the cash register system that the franchisees were obliged to use, and thereby controlled the retail prices for baked goods, snacks and drinks sold at the franchise outlets.[394] The franchisor was fined EUR 210,000.

III. Technology Licencing

316. The European Commission's Technology Transfer Block Exemption Regulation (TTBER)[395] as well as its Technology Transfer Guidelines[396] contain valuable guidance on technology licensing that, in practice, is also relevant under Austrian competition law.[397] In a 2003 case involving a refrigerator reprocessing plant, for instance, the Cartel Court referred to the TTBER (in an earlier version) in assessing the case and drew a parallel to Austrian competition law.[398]

A. *Patent Licensing*

317. The general prohibition of § 1(1) KartG applies to patent licensing. The TTBER[399] as well as the European Commission's Technology Transfer Guidelines[400] contain relevant guidance on patent licensing.

393. European Commission, Guidelines on Vertical Restraints [2022] OJ C248/1, paras 165 ff.
394. KG 11.4.2019, 25 Kt 1/19p – *Anker*. On this case, *see* Stefan Ruech, Luca Schicho & Anastasios Xeniadis, 'Aktuelle Judikatur zu vertikalen Preisbindungen in Franchisesystemen' (2020) *Österreichische Zeitschrift für Kartellrecht* 93.
395. Commission Regulation (EU) No 316/2014 of 21 March 2014 on the application of Article 101(3) of the Treaty on the Functioning of the European Union to categories of technology transfer agreements (TTBER) [2014] OJ L93/17. On the TTBER and the Technology Transfer Guidelines, *see* the forthcoming IEL monograph on EU competition law.
396. European Commission, Guidelines on the application of Article 101 of the Treaty on the Functioning of the European Union to technology transfer agreements [2014] OJ C89/3.
397. For a similar conclusion, *see* Astrid Ablasser-Neuhuber, Florian Neumayr, Gerhard Fussenegger & Sebastian Reiter, 'Austria' § 2.03[1][a], in: Frank L. Fine (ed.), *European Competition Laws*, vol 1 (loose-leaf, Matthew Bender Elite Products, release 21-11/2022).
398. KG 1.10.2003, 29 Kt 206/03 – *Kühlgeräteaufbereitungsanlage*.
399. Art. 1(1)(b) TTBER.
400. European Commission, Guidelines on the application of Article 101 of the Treaty on the Functioning of the European Union to technology transfer agreements [2014] OJ C89/3.

B. *Trademark Licensing*

318. The general prohibition of § 1(1) KartG applies to trademark licensing, while the TTBER does not apply to trademark licensing.[401]

C. *Know-How and Trade Secret Licensing*

319. The general prohibition of § 1(1) KartG applies to know-how and trade secret licensing. The TTBER[402] as well as the European Commission's Technology Transfer Guidelines[403] contain relevant guidance on know-how and trade secret licensing.

IV. Further Types of Vertical Agreements

320. Non-compete obligations in the form of radius clauses have come before Austrian courts: the operator of a shopping mall prohibited tenants from also running a shop in another mall within a certain perimeter of its own shopping mall. The Cartel Court did not view this restriction as a restriction by object, and owing to the shopping mall operator's low market share, the provisions were regarded as *de minimis.*[404] Non-compete obligations in vertical relationships that exceed five years are also contained in the grey list of the VABER[405] and discussed in the Vertical Guidelines.[406]

321. Agency agreements may come within the ambit of vertical restraints. Genuine agency agreements will not lead to antitrust responsibility under Article 101(1) TFEU and § 1 KartG, because the genuine agent is seen as part of the principal's business (single economic entity doctrine) and does not bear the business's risk. Where the agent himself bears the commercial risk, however, restrictions that are agreed upon in the agency relationship might come under Article 101 TFEU and § 1 KartG.[407] To assess whether or not one is dealing with a 'genuine' agent within the meaning of competition law, one must assess the extent of the commercial risk that is borne by the agent in relation to the agency activities the agent fulfils, and which go beyond the commercial risk borne by any independent economic activity.[408] In

401. Art. 1(1)(b) TTBER; Guidelines on the application of Article 101 of the Treaty on the Functioning of the European Union to technology transfer agreements [2014] OJ C89/3, para. 47.
402. Art. 1(1)(b) and (i) TTBER.
403. European Commission, Guidelines on the application of Article 101 of the Treaty on the Functioning of the European Union to technology transfer agreements [2014] OJ C89/3, para. 45.
404. KG 23.1.2015, 25 Kt 7/09 – *Radiusklausel*; KOG 8.10.2015, 16 Ok 6/15s – *Radiusklausel V.*
405. Art. 5(1)(a) and (b) VABER.
406. European Commission, Guidelines on Vertical Restraints [2022] OJ C248/1, paras 247 ff.
407. *See* European Commission, Guidelines on Vertical Restraints [2022] OJ C248/1, paras 29 ff.; Bundeswettbewerbsbehörde, 'Standpoint on Resale Price Maintenance' 14; KOG 30.5.2005, 16 Ok 8/05 – *Flugscheinverkauf.*
408. KOG 15.7.2009, 16 Ok 6/09 – *Pressegrosso I*; KOG 1.12.2009, 16 Ok 10/09 – *Pressegrosso II.*

the case of a press wholesaler, the Supreme Cartel Court decided that based on the significant amount of commercial risk borne by the wholesaler – for the transport costs of unsold copies and the credit risk concerning retailers – such a wholesaler could not be viewed as a genuine agent that forms part of the business of press publishers.[409] Article 101(1) TFEU was therefore found to apply. In the case of a petrol station leaseholder, however, the Supreme Court found that the latter bore such a limited commercial risk that it could be qualified as a genuine agent.[410]

322. A type of vertical restraint that is particularly relevant under EU competition law is the restraint on parallel imports, as this will usually be seen as a restraint that hinders the single market objective. In Austria, the Cartel Court recently held that a restriction of cross-border parallel trading – seen in combination with other restrictions, including on online sales – was anti-competitive under § 1 KartG and Article 101 TFEU.[411]

409. KOG 15.7.2009, 16 Ok 6/09 – *Pressegrosso I*; KOG 1.12.2009, 16 Ok 10/09 – *Pressegrosso II.*
410. OGH 16.11.2009, 9 ObA 58/09f – *Tankstellenpächter I.*
411. KG 29.8.2018, 26 Kt 2/18s – *BWB/Devolo Austria.*

Chapter 2. Dominant Undertakings' Prohibited Practices

323. § 5 KartG prohibits the abuse of a dominant market position:

> § 5. (1) The abuse of a dominant position shall be prohibited. In particular, the following shall be deemed to be an abuse:
>
> 1. demanding purchasing or selling prices or other business terms which differ from those which would be very likely to arise if effective competition existed, particularly taking into account the conduct of undertakings in comparable markets where effective competition exists;
> 2. limiting production, markets or technical developments to the detriment of consumers,
> 3. discriminating contract partners in competition by applying dissimilar business terms to equivalent transactions;
> 4. making the conclusion of contracts subject to acceptance by the other contract parties of supplementary obligations, which neither by their nature nor according to commercial usage are related to the subject of the contract;
> 5. selling goods below cost without any objective justification.
>
> (2) In the case of paragraph 1 subparagraph 5, the dominant undertaking shall bear the burden of proof for the rebuttal of the presumption of sales below cost price as well as for providing an objective justification for such sale.

324. It is not prohibited to possess a dominant position. Instead, it is the abuse of said market position that triggers the prohibition contained in § 5 KartG. Nevertheless, § 28a KartG foresees that the two official parties may request the Cartel Court to find that an undertaking has a dominant position in a multisided digital market. In a second step, private applicants as well as the official parties could then rely on such a finding to argue that the platform has committed an abuse related to that dominant position. So far, this provision has not been applied. On this new provision, *see* § 93 of this monograph.

325. The concept of abuse in § 5 KartG is an objective concept; it is irrelevant whether an undertaking (or a manager or employee) intends to abuse that dominant position.[412]

326. Like under EU competition law, there is no need under § 5 KartG to establish causality between an undertaking's dominant position and its abusive behaviour.[413]

412. KOG 11.10.2004, 16 Ok 11/04 – *TikTak Freiminuten*; KOG 19.1.2009, 16 Ok 13/08 – *Telekom 'KombiPaket'*.

413. KOG 5.9.2001, 16 Ok 3/01 – *Hausbrieffachanlagen*; KOG 11.10.2004, 16 Ok 11/04 – *TikTak Freiminuten*; KOG 20.12.2004, 16 Ok 12/04 – *TikTak-Tarife*.

327. As § 5 KartG is nearly identical to Article 102 TFEU, the Supreme (Cartel) Court has emphasised that the Austrian provision should be interpreted against the background of Article 102 TFEU and the case law regarding that provision. In particular, and based on the supremacy of EU law over national law, unilateral behaviour that is prohibited by Article 102 TFEU will not be allowed under Austrian competition law.[414] For this reason, the European provision should be consulted in parallel when applying the Austrian prohibition of abuse of a dominant position (on this, *see* the forthcoming IEL monograph on Competition Law in the European Union).

328. While Regulation 1/2003 ensures that national competition law is neither stricter nor more lenient towards anti-competitive agreements that may affect trade between Member States, it does allow Member States to foresee 'stricter national laws which prohibit or sanction unilateral conduct engaged in by undertakings'.[415]

329. Two main areas can be distinguished where Austrian competition law rules on unilateral conduct are stricter than Article 102 TFEU: first of all, as set out above (§§ 78, 128–131 of this monograph), § 4a KartG foresees that the prohibition on the abuse of a dominant position (§ 5 KartG) applies not only to companies that are held to be dominant in a traditional sense but also to companies that have relative market power, i.e., a predominant market position in relation to their purchasers or suppliers. Such a predominant market position exists where a company's 'purchasers or suppliers depend on maintaining business relations in order to avoid serious economic disadvantages'.

330. Second, the Fair Conditions of Competition Act (FWBG) contains provisions on unilateral conduct that are not tied to the existence of a dominant position. In particular, § 2 FWBG prohibits discriminatory practices and is thus – apart from not requiring the existence of a dominant position – in the tradition of non-discrimination provisions under § 5 KartG and Article 102 TFEU.[416]

331. In a recent investigation of Amazon's business practices vis-à-vis its third-party sellers, the Federal Competition Authority viewed several of these practices as problematic under the rules on abuse of dominance. The investigations were carried out together with the German Federal Competition Office.[417] The problematic practices included account termination, suspension of sellers, transparency issues in terms of conditions, and unfavourable trading conditions for third-party sellers that do not rely on Amazon's 'fulfilled by Amazon' logistics services. These concerns

414. OGH 8.4.2004, 4 Ob 23/08y – *Tageszeitung Ö*; KOG 15.5.2000, 16 Ok 4/00 – *Hauszustellungssystem III*.
415. Article 3(2) of Regulation 1/2003.
416. KOG 25.3.2009, 16 Ok 2, 3/09 – *Sägerundholz II*.
417. Bundeswettbewerbsbehörde, 'Amazon.de Marketplace' https://www.bwb.gv.at/fileadmin/user_upload/Fallbericht_20190911_en.pdf last accessed 8.8.2024; Bundeswettbewerbsbehörde, 'BWB informs: Amazon modifies its terms and conditions' (17.7.2019) https://www.bwb.gv.at/en/news/news_2019/detail/bwb-informs-amazon-modifies-its-terms-and-conditions-1 last accessed 8.8.2024.

were resolved when Amazon agreed to change its terms and conditions,[418] with the result that it adapted them as would have in some respects become necessary under the P2B Regulation that started to apply in July 2020.[419]

§1. Exploitative Practices

332. The Supreme Cartel Court has acknowledged that two types of abuse of a dominant position can be distinguished: exploitative practices that take advantage of customers or suppliers, and exclusionary practices that lead to a restriction of competition and the exclusion of competitors.[420] The following focuses on exploitative abuses of dominance, while §§ 344 ff. will look at exclusionary abuses.

I. Excessive/Unfair Pricing

333. § 5(1) no 1 KartG prohibits a dominant undertaking from demanding prices or trading conditions that differ from those which would be likely to arise if effective competition existed.[421] The provision also provides courts with one possibility on how to ascertain which price or which trading conditions would have arisen in a competitive market, namely by comparing the excessive price or unfair trading condition with those demanded by undertakings in comparable markets where effective competition exists ('Vergleichsmarktkonzept'). Other methods, however, remain available.[422]

334. In *Europay*, the Cartel Court compared the significantly lower transaction fees that the dominant undertaking had to pay to its trading partners, i.e., banks, with those that new competitors were required to pay, and found that the transaction fees for competitors were excessively high in comparison.[423]

335. The Supreme Cartel Court has emphasised that excessive pricing is not limited to a dominant undertaking requiring excessive prices or other unfair trading

418. Bundeskartellamt, 'Case Summary: B2-88/18' (17.7.2019) https://www.bundeskartellamt.de/SharedDocs/Entscheidung/EN/Fallberichte/Missbrauchsaufsicht/2019/B2-88-18.pdf?__blob=publicationFile&v=5 last accessed 8.8.2024; Bundeskartellamt, 'Bundeskartellamt obtains far-reaching improvements in the terms of business for sellers on Amazon's online marketplaces' (17.7.2019) https://www.bundeskartellamt.de/SharedDocs/Meldung/EN/Pressemitteilungen/2019/17_07_2019_Amazon.html last accessed 8.8.2024.

419. Regulation (EU) 2019/1150 of the European Parliament and of the Council of 20 June 2019 on promoting fairness and transparency for business users of online intermediation services (P2B Regulation) [2019] OJ L186/57.

420. KOG 14.6.1993, Okt 3/93 – *Werbung mit Preisherabsetzungen II*; OGH 29.4.2003, 4 Ob 79/03a – *Ö3 Millionengewinnspiel*; OGH 28.1.2009, 9 Ob 66/07g – *Reisen*.

421. The provision was amended in 2013 in order to introduce stricter rules on excessive pricing; *see* 1804 der Beilagen XXIV. GP (Erläuterungen zur Regierungsvorlage), pp. 3, 7.

422. Claudine Vartian & Florian Schuhmacher, '§ 5 KartG' para. 26, in: Alexander Petsche, Franz Urlesberger & Claudine Vartian (eds), *Kartellgesetz 2005* (2d ed., Manz 2016).

423. KOG 12.9.2007, 16 Ok 4/07 – *Bankomatvertrag III*.

conditions during contract negotiations but may also be found where a dominant undertaking refuses to lower prices or adapt contractual conditions.[424]

336. An excessive price will only be found by the Supreme (Cartel) Court where there is a blatant imbalance between costs and revenues,[425] where the hypothetical competitive price is significantly exceeded,[426] or where the price is either significantly or clearly excessive.[427]

337. While cases on excessive prices usually target excessively high prices, excessively low prices are also prohibited under § 5(1) no 1 KartG. In a case involving the sale of stamps to end consumers through private companies in their own name and at their own expense ('Verschleiß'), the Austrian Post unilaterally reduced the commission awarded to such companies ('Verschleißerprovision') by 70%, resulting in said companies no longer being able to cover their costs for the distribution of stamps. Many sales points, however, were dependent on the sale of stamps as the distribution of other products sold at those outlets partially depended on the availability of stamps (compound effect). In addition, these sales outlets were also in competition with the Austrian Post's own distribution of stamps. Against this background, the Supreme Cartel Court regarded the commission as excessively low pricing under Austrian law.[428]

338. The *Wiener Zeitung* case involved the newspaper of the same name which was by law the mandatory publication medium for a number of documents, such as certain companies' annual financial statements. The Supreme Cartel Court had to decide whether it constituted an unfair trading condition when the Wiener Zeitung as a dominant undertaking did not accept the mandatory publication of an annual financial statement in smaller print than 6pt, as this was not easily legible and the law required legibility. The Supreme Cartel Court carried out a weighing of interests and concluded that, in this case, the Wiener Zeitung's behaviour did not amount to the imposition of unfair trading conditions.[429]

339. In order to assess whether a price is excessive, the Supreme Cartel Court takes an overall look at the price rather than focusing on individual components making up the price. In the words of the Court, 'it is not the pricing method but only its result that can, at the end of the day, constitute an abuse of a dominant position'.[430] Similarly, when carrying out a weighing of interests to assess the potential

424. KOG 16.9.2014, 16 Ok 13/13 – *Linz Strom.*
425. OGH 12.4.2000, 4 Ob 62/00x – *Fiat II (SAV).*
426. KOG 16.9.2014, 16 Ok 13/13 – *Linz Strom.*
427. KOG 12.7.2018, 16 Ok 1/18k – *Fachverband Reisebüros/Lufthansa.*
428. KOG 17.11.2003, 16 Ok 14/03 – *Verschleißerprovision.*
429. KOG 15.5.2000, 16 Ok 10/99 – *Wiener Zeitung.*
430. KOG 16.9.2014, 16 Ok 13/13 – *Linz Strom* (author's own translation).

unfairness of contractual clauses, as carried out in the *Wiener Zeitung* case discussed above, the court takes an overall view of the contractual relationship and assesses whether it is a balanced one; certain disadvantageous clauses may be remedied by more advantageous ones.[431]

II. Discrimination

340. § 5(1) no 3 KartG prohibits a dominant undertaking from discriminating against trading partners by applying dissimilar business terms to equivalent transactions. For agreements, such a prohibition is also contained in § 1(2) no 4 KartG.

341. One of the elements of that prohibition is the comparability of trading partners. In *ÖBB/Westbahn II*, the Supreme Cartel Court held that potential customers were not protected by the prohibition of Article 102(c) TFEU – which is identical to § 5(1) no 3 KartG. Instead, potential customers could only rely on a refusal to deal where a trading partner refuses to enter into a business relationship.[432] This has been criticised in the literature as unnecessarily narrowing down non-discrimination.[433]

342. A further element of § 5(1) no 3 KartG is that it only requires the non-discriminatory treatment of trading partners where equivalent transactions are concerned. Where a dominant undertaking enters into a business relationship with a new trading partner and asks for guarantees that extant trading partners do not have to provide, then such behaviour may be in line with § 5(1) no 3 KartG where this practice is neither unusual nor disproportional, taking into account the investment expected from the dominant undertaking.[434]

343. In a case on unaddressed bulk mailings, the Supreme Cartel Court had to decide on the legality of different amounts of rebates that the Austrian Post granted. The Court emphasised that it did not amount to equivalent transactions where one company ordered bulk mailings mainly to distribution areas that are difficult to manage and that do not cover costs because household density is low, while other companies ordered bulk mailings to more balanced distribution areas. The difference in the rebate granted could therefore not come under the prohibition of § 5(1) no 3 KartG.[435]

344. § 2 FWBG, the provision on non-discrimination in the Fair Conditions of Competition Act, prohibits discriminatory practices also for non-dominant undertakings where authorised resellers (‘gewerberechtlich befugte Wiederverkäufer’) are concerned:

431. OGH 27.2.2007, 1 Ob 1/07i – *Kreditkarte*.
432. KOG 11.10.2012, 16 Ok 1/12 – *ÖBB/Westbahn II*.
433. Claudine Vartian & Florian Schuhmacher, ‘§ 5 KartG’ para. 51, in: Alexander Petsche, Franz Urlesberger & Claudine Vartian (eds), *Kartellgesetz 2005* (2d ed., Manz 2016).
434. KOG 10.3.2003, 16 Ok 1/03 – *Belieferung mit Regionaldaten*.
435. KOG 11.10.2004, 16 Ok 9/04 – *Nicht adressierte Massensendungen*.

> § 2. (1) A supplier who grants or offers different conditions to authorised resellers in the same circumstances without objective justification may be sued for a cease-and-desist order.
> (2) Similarly, a reseller may be sued for requesting or accepting objectively unjustified conditions from suppliers.

345. In a number of cases involving saw logs and recycling systems,[436] the Supreme Cartel Court fleshed out this provision. It particularly emphasised the compatibility of § 2 FWBG with Article 102 TFEU and § 5 KartG.

346. § 6 KartG prohibits dominant undertakings from adopting retaliatory measures against undertakings where a case for abusing a dominant position has been brought under § 26 KartG or a complaint has been made to an official party (§ 40 KartG). This type of prohibition also aims at ensuring non-discrimination by dominant undertakings.[437]

347. Non-discrimination is also at the centre of the Federal Competition Authority's 'Fairness catalogue for companies' of 2022, in which it emphasises that discrimination is among the exclusionary practices that both the KartG and the FWBG prohibit.[438]

§2. Exclusionary Practices

I. Predation

348. § 5(1) no 5 KartG prevents dominant undertakings from selling goods below cost price ('Einstandspreis' or acquisition price) without any objective justification. § 5(2) KartG foresees that the dominant undertaking needs to bear the burden of proof for the rebuttal of the presumption of sales below cost price as well as providing an objective justification for such a sale.

349. The Supreme Court has highlighted that § 5(1) no 5 KartG specifically targets cost price ('Einstandspreis') rather than just any price. It is a special case of predatory pricing that only applies to trading companies and only to goods rather than services. For other types of predatory pricing, the Supreme Court applies the general clause in § 5(1) KartG.[439]

---

436. KOG 9.6.2010, 16 Ok 1/10 – *Sägerundholz IV*; KOG 25.3.2009, 16 Ok 2, 3/09 – *Sägerundholz II*; KOG 9.10.2000, 16 Ok 8/00 – *Regionalpartnerverträge*.
437. *See also* Axel Reidlinger & Isabella Hartung, *Das österreichische Kartellrecht: Ein Handbuch für Praktiker* 163 (5th ed., Linde 2024).
438. Bundeswettbewerbsbehörde, 'Fairnesskatalog für Unternehmen – Standpunkt für unternehmerisches Wohlverhalten' (May 2022) https://www.bwb.gv.at/fileadmin/user_upload/_BWB_Fairnesskatalog_.pdf last accessed 8.8.2024.
439. OGH 14.7.2009, 4 Ob 60/09s – *Anwaltssoftware*.

350. In one case on § 5(1) no 5 KartG, an undertaking operated a loyalty points system that allowed customers to obtain certain household goods at a significantly reduced price. That price was, in itself, below cost price. However, the Supreme Court held that it was not unreasonable to assess this case from a broader perspective: customers needed to have spent a considerable amount of money at the undertaking in question in order to obtain enough loyalty points to buy the household goods at the significantly reduced price. When approached from this broader perspective, the price of the household goods sold through the loyalty programme – which, as pointed out above, was below cost price – was offset by the profit margin in the main goods bought by participants in the loyalty programme.[440]

351. Under the general clause of § 5(1) KartG, the Supreme Court had to decide a case about software for lawyers. The dominant undertaking specifically targeted customers of its competitor, the third-largest provider of software for lawyers in Austria, and offered its software to them at a considerably lower price. The Supreme Court found that while the rebate for the software was significant, the software only constituted a part of the services offered by the dominant undertaking. Absent further facts on this, it was not able to determine whether the dominant undertaking was operating profitably.[441]

352. In the eyes of the Supreme Cartel Court, and following on from EU case law, predatory pricing might be at issue where the sales price does not reach the dominant undertaking's own average variable cost. Where prices are above average variable cost, but below average total cost, an abuse may exist where predatory pricing forms part of an overall strategy aimed at excluding a competitor from the market (intent to exclude).[442] The Supreme Cartel Court applied this very reasoning in a case on the recycling of commercial packaging, citing both CJEU case law and the European Commission's soft law guidance. In that case, it was found that an undertaking with a dominant position on the market for the recycling of packaging for households used that position to engage in predatory pricing on the market for the recycling of commercial packaging.[443]

II. Tying

353. § 5(1) no 4 KartG prohibits a dominant undertaking from making the conclusion of a contract subject to acceptance by the other contracting party of supplementary obligations that are not related to the subject of the contract, either by their nature or according to commercial usage. It should be noted that an identical provision is contained in § 1(2) no 5 KartG, which does not require a dominant position.

---

440. OGH 23.3.2011, 4 Ob 34/11w – *Treuebonus*.
441. OGH 14.7.2009, 4 Ob 60/09s – *Anwaltssoftware*.
442. KOG 9.10.2000, 16 Ok 6/00 – *Abonnementpreise*; KOG 16.12.2002, 16 Ok 11/02 – *Red Bull*.
443. KOG 8.10.2015, 16 Ok 9/15g – *Verpackungen II* (relying on the Commission's terminology of long-run average incremental cost – LRAIC – and average avoidable cost – AAC).

354. In its case law, the Supreme Cartel Court has had to deal with the question of whether a dominant telecommunications provider and former state monopolist could legitimately provide end customers that obtained access to its landline network ('access service') with a limited number of free connection services. The dominant undertaking's competitor argued that this constituted anti-competitive tying and, as end customers required the access service, this curtailed their freedom of choice for connection services. The Supreme Cartel Court held that where two complementary services on different relevant markets (access to the landline network; connection services) were offered as a package deal by a dominant undertaking, and where this package deal was the cheapest way for end consumers to obtain the access services from the quasi-monopolistic provider, this came within the prohibition on abusing a dominant position as the dominant undertaking thereby leveraged its market power from the access services market to the connection services market.[444]

355. In another case involving the same Austrian telecommunications provider and former state monopolist, a special offer for cordless phones was at issue. The dominant undertaking offered such phones to existing customers for the price of EUR 49.90 (instead of EUR 99.90). However, two functionalities – call by call (CbC) and carrier preselection (CPS) – could not be obtained with this offer. Both of these functionalities entail that connection services provided by alternative (competing) connection network operators are used by end consumers, rather than the connection services offered by the (dominant) network operator. The special offer ensured that end consumers had to make use of the dominant undertaking's connection services. The Supreme Cartel Court found that the fact that the former state monopolist was not dominant on the market for cordless phones was not relevant. What mattered was that the dominant undertaking tried to cement its market power or exclude competitors on the market on which it was dominant.[445]

356. Where a tie can be objectively justified, it will not infringe § 5(1) no 4 KartG. For instance, in a case involving an exclusive purchasing obligation for liquid gas that was tied to the rental of fuel tanks, the Supreme Cartel Court accepted that safety considerations justified this particular tie.[446] Frequently, however, tying an aftermarket product to a primary product will be held to be abusive.

III. Rebates

357. Based on EU case law, Austrian courts differentiate between permissible quantity rebates and abusive loyalty and target rebates.[447]

444. KOG 11.10.2004, 16 Ok 11/04 – *TikTak Freiminuten*. It can also be questioned whether such a behaviour could amount to a margin squeeze. On that abuse, *see* § 363 of this monograph.
445. KOG 17.11.2003, 16 Ok 11/03 – *Schnurlostelefon*.
446. KOG 1.12.2015, 16 Ok 4/15x – *Flüssiggas III*.
447. Claudine Vartian & Florian Schuhmacher, '§ 5 KartG' para. 75, in: Alexander Petsche, Franz Urlesberger & Claudine Vartian (eds), *Kartellgesetz 2005* (2d ed., Manz 2016).

358. In the case of unaddressed bulk mail already discussed above (§ 339 of this monograph), apart from the issue of discrimination the question of rebates also played a central role. The former monopolist concluded framework agreements that included services that concerned its monopoly as well as services that it had to provide in competition. These framework agreements foresaw the granting of rebates that provided the dominant undertaking with an advantage that its competitors – who were not (also) monopolists – simply could not obtain. The Supreme Cartel Court held that the former monopolist could not grant such rebates that were not commercially explicable.[448]

359. In another case, the producer of clay roof tiles offered an annual bonus of 3% of total net sales to master roofers if the latter agreed to exclusively obtain roof tiles from the dominant undertaking. Against the background of the CJEU's case law on rebates, the Supreme Court viewed the loyalty bonus offered by the dominant undertaking as abusive.[449]

IV. Refusal to Deal

360. Under Austrian competition law, cases of refusal to deal come under § 5(1) no 2 KartG.[450] That provision contains elements of an exclusionary practice as well as of an exploitative practice when it prohibits the limiting of production, markets or technical developments to the detriment of consumers.[451]

361. *Oscar Bronner* was a landmark Austrian case on refusal to deal.[452] In that case, Mediaprint – which is a dominant operator on the Austrian markets for publishing, producing and marketing daily newspapers – operated the only nationwide home-delivery distribution service for subscribers, a service Austrian consumers have become accustomed to. Mediaprint published the Kronen Zeitung, a tabloid with the widest total circulation, advertising revenue and range of influence among all Austrian daily newspapers. Oscar Bronner, who in 1988 started publishing Der Standard, a quality daily newspaper, had asked for access to Mediaprint's home-delivery distribution service and relied on the Austrian equivalent of Article 102 TFEU for that claim. Mediaprint did not want to grant such access. Subsequently, the Cartel Court sent a preliminary reference to Luxembourg, asking the CJEU a number of questions on refusals to deal under Article 102 TFEU. In particular, the Cartel Court asked whether Mediaprint's refusal to deal was abusive in light of the

448. KOG 11.10.2004, 16 Ok 9/04 – *Nicht adressierte Massensendungen.*
449. OGH 22.6.1999, 4 Ob 90/99k – *Jahresbonus.*
450. Claudine Vartian & Florian Schuhmacher, '§ 5 KartG' para. 46, in: Alexander Petsche, Franz Urlesberger & Claudine Vartian (eds), *Kartellgesetz 2005* (2d ed., Manz 2016).
451. Claudine Vartian & Florian Schuhmacher, '§ 5 KartG' para. 39, in: Alexander Petsche, Franz Urlesberger & Claudine Vartian (eds), *Kartellgesetz 2005* (2d ed., Manz 2016).
452. *See* KG 1.7.1996, 26b Kt 630/95 – *Hauszustellungssystem II.*

low circulation of Der Standard, which made it impossible for Oscar Bronner to build up his own home-delivery scheme at a reasonable cost and with a profitable prognosis.[453]

362. In its preliminary ruling, the CJEU held that in order for Mediaprint's refusal to deal to be abusive, the following had to be established: 'that the refusal of the service comprised in home delivery be likely to eliminate all competition in the daily newspaper market on the part of the person requesting the service [i.e., Oscar Bronner]', 'that such refusal be incapable of being objectively justified' and 'that the service in itself be indispensable to carrying on that person's business, in as much as there is no actual or potential substitute in existence for that home-delivery scheme'.[454] On the criterion of indispensability, the CJEU noted that the option of relying on other methods for distributing daily newspapers had to be considered, even if they were less advantageous. The argument that the establishment of a second nationwide home-delivery scheme for daily newspapers was not economically viable was dismissed by the CJEU insofar as it required that the economic viability would have to be shown not for a daily newspaper with low circulation but for a daily newspaper comparable to the one distributed by Mediaprint.[455]

363. Back at the Cartel Court and, subsequently, at the Supreme Cartel Court, the case led to the denial of Oscar Bronner's request for access to Mediaprint's distribution system based on competition law.[456]

364. Similarly, in a case on access to a multi-operator phone directory, the Supreme Court found that the claimant could not rely on the essential facilities doctrine because it could have obtained the required phone numbers from each single telephone service provider at cost-based prices (under the Telecommunications Act) in order to create its own multi-operator phone directory.[457]

365. In a later case, the railway operator Westbahn – which only runs a limited number of lines – asked to be included in the dominant Austrian Railways' electronic timetable information system, as well as in other information systems run by Austrian Railways (*ÖBB/Westbahn II*).[458] In this case, the Supreme Cartel Court granted the claimant's request to be included in the dominant operator's electronic timetable information based on competition law by interlocutory injunction, holding that while Westbahn, as a potential customer of Austrian Railways, could not rely on non-discrimination, it could make a claim under refusal to deal, as Austrian

453. CJEU Case C-7/97 *Oscar Bronner v. Mediaprint*, ECLI:EU:C:1998:569, para. 11.
454. CJEU Case C-7/97 *Oscar Bronner v. Mediaprint*, ECLI:EU:C:1998:569, para. 41.
455. CJEU Case C-7/97 *Oscar Bronner v. Mediaprint*, ECLI:EU:C:1998:569, paras 43–46.
456. KG 25.1.2000, 26b Kt 630/95 – *Hauszustellungssystem II*; KOG 15.5.2000, 16 Ok 4/00 – *Hauszustellungssystem III*.
457. OGH 13.7.2010, 4 Ob 191/09f – *Telefonverzeichnis*.
458. KOG 11.10.2012, 16 Ok 1/12 – *ÖBB/Westbahn II*.

Railways was already including other competitors (e.g., Deutsche Bahn) in its timetable information system and could not provide an objective justification for not also including Westbahn.

366. In a number of early cases involving film distributors, the latter were required to distribute copies of their films to movie theatres because withholding them was considered an anti-competitive refusal to deal.[459]

367. § 4(1) FWBG provides that while companies should remain free to choose their final sellers, they may be required to conclude a contract if their refusal to deal with a final seller threatens local supply or significantly affects the final seller's competitiveness in the goods not supplied. § 4(2) FWBG sets out what it considers to be a threat to local supply, namely a situation in which a substantial number of consumers is not able to obtain the goods necessary to satisfy the needs of daily life at a reasonable cost and time without using a motor vehicle or public transport. This provision also speaks to the geographic specificities of the Austrian territory and the considerable urban sprawl in Austria. According to § 4(3) FWBG, an obligation under paragraph 1 is conditional upon the final seller's counter-performance. In addition, § 4(4) FWBG foresees that no obligation to supply shall be ordered where it is economically unreasonable for the supplier to deliver the goods, or where the supply would be *contra bonos mores.*

V. Price Squeeze

368. Austrian courts were previously sceptical whether a vertically integrated dominant undertaking had to afford companies that were its customers on an upstream market but competitors on a downstream market had the ability to compete with them through its pricing policies (margin squeeze).[460] However, based on case law from the CJEU,[461] this view should be overcome.[462]

VI. Further Abusive Practices

369. It is important to recall that the abuses listed in § 5 KartG are not exhaustive. This was also acknowledged by the Supreme Cartel Court in a recent case, in which it emphasised that abuses that are not listed in § 5 KartG are typically such in which the dominant undertaking uses methods outside of competition on the merits.[463]

---

459. OGH 9.9.1997, 4 Ob 214/97t – *Filmverleihgeschäft I*; KOG 4.4.2005, 16 Ok 20/04 – *Multiplex I*; KOG 16.7.2008, 16 Ok 6/08 – *Asterix bei den Olympischen Spielen.*
460. KG 14.5.2002, 29 Kt 554, 555/00 – *Telekom Austria Wintertarif.*
461. *See* CJEU Case C-280/08 P *Deutsche Telekom v. Commission*, ECLI:EU:C:2010:603; CJEU Case C-295/12 P *Telefónica v. Commission*, ECLI:EU:C:2014:2062.
462. Axel Reidlinger & Isabella Hartung, *Das österreichische Kartellrecht: Ein Handbuch für Praktiker* 135 (4th ed., Linde 2019; not contained in the 5th ed.).
463. KOG 25.5.2023, 16 Ok 6/22a – *AMATIC.*

370. Apart from the cases discussed in the previous sections, the Supreme Cartel Court has dealt with further instances of exclusionary practices. In one case, the two only Viennese radio taxi control centres threatened taxi companies with the termination of their contracts if they collaborated with new entrants, such as app providers that were trying to acquire taxi drivers. While the Federal Competition Authority argued that this type of exclusivity was abusive, the Cartel Court found that the exclusivity clause was not abusive because there was a short termination period of one month foreseen in the contract that the taxi companies could have made use of. In addition, an individual radio contract was concluded for each specific vehicle of a taxi company and could also be terminated for that individual vehicle, meaning that a taxi company would not have to give up its entire contractual relationship with the radio taxi control centres.[464]

371. In a case on exclusivity clauses as an abuse of a dominant position in the healthcare sector, the Cartel Court granted an interlocutory injunction that prevented the dominant undertaking from relying on a multi-supplier clause. That clause foresaw a significant reduction of the contractual fee (of up to 40%) in case the dominant undertaking's contractual parties (i.e., pharmaceutical wholesalers providing information for the dominant undertaking's sales tracking analysis) also provided information to competing information service providers.[465]

372. In a recent case involving the contract terms between individual car dealerships and their reliance on the car manufacturer – in that case: Peugeot – the Cartel Court held in May 2020 that the car manufacturer enjoyed a dominant position vis-à-vis its car dealer (relative market power) and abused that dominant position by engaging in various behaviours: economically forcing the dealer to take part in promotions and thereby restricting its pricing freedom, tying the dealer's bonus payments to customer satisfaction surveys, reducing the dealer's margin if sales targets – that were inflated by Peugeot – were not reached, operating a control system for guarantee and warranty work and hourly rates that did not cover the dealer's costs, and passing on the costs of Peugeot's mystery shopping and audit system to the dealer.[466] On appeal, the Supreme Cartel Court, in a decision of February 2021, largely upheld the Cartel Court's decision.[467] This case provides some important insights into both relative market power in individual business relationships and contractual terms that can lead to an abuse of a dominant position within the framework of a vertical agreement. It was also the first case of a follow-on fine: after the private applicant had won the case, the Federal Competition Authority requested a fine for Peugeot before the Cartel Court.[468]

373. In the A*MATIC* case, the Cartel Court had to decide whether a monopolist for casinos (with a concession by the State) used leveraging so as to combine its

464. KOG 27.6.2013, 16 Ok 7/12 – *Taxi-App*.
465. KG 19.12.2017, 25 Kt 2/17g & 25 Kt 3/17d – *Insight Health/IQVIA*.
466. KG 12.5.2020, 27 Kt 5/18i – *Peugeot*.
467. KOG 17.2.2021, 16 Ok 4/20d – *Peugeot*.
468. Bundeswettbewerbsbehörde, 'Tätigkeitsbericht 2023' p. 53 (June 2024).

casino services with its online gambling services, for which it did not enjoy a monopoly position and thereby extended its market power. It found that this type of behaviour was not anti-competitive leveraging.[469] This was confirmed by the Supreme Cartel Court.[470] In light of the recent *European Superleague* decision of the CJEU, this case may need to be revisited.[471]

469. KG 21.6.2022, 27 Kt 14/21t – *AMATIC/Österreichische Lotterien*. Note that the author provided a legal opinion in that case.
470. KOG 25.5.2023, 16 Ok 6/22a – *AMATIC*.
471. CJEU Case C-333/21 *European Superleague Company*, ECLI:EU:C:2023:1011.

Chapter 3. Concentrations

374. Concentrations need to be notified to the Federal Competition Authority if certain thresholds are surpassed (Phase I; on this *see* already above, §§ 82 ff., 153 ff. of this monograph). Subsequently, a concentration is only assessed by the Cartel Court if either of the official parties (§ 40 KartG) submits an application for review to the Cartel Court (Phase II).

375. In substantive terms, § 12(1) no 2 KartG foresees that the Cartel Court shall prohibit a merger when it is expected that it would create or strengthen a dominant position (lit a) or when it is expected that the merger would otherwise significantly impede effective competition (SIEC; lit b). While obtaining and holding a dominant position through pro-competitive means is therefore not prohibited under Austrian competition law (*see* § 320 of this monograph), the creation or strengthening of such a position through a concentration may well be prohibited. In order to close any possible enforcement gaps that a dominance test entails for merger control, the Austrian legislator decided to introduce the SIEC test in 2021.[472]

376. For the definition of a dominant position, § 12(1) no 2 KartG refers to § 4 KartG – but not to § 4a KartG (relative market power). As § 4(2) KartG contains a rebuttable presumption of dominance starting from certain market share thresholds, it is not surprising that Austrian merger control has also strongly focused on market shares.[473] However, the Supreme Cartel Court indicated that a dominant undertaking's dominance may also be strengthened where the merger would not add further market shares to it,[474] thereby highlighting that the qualitative definition of dominance in § 4(1) KartG must also be considered. In some cases, countervailing buyer power may mean that even high market shares do not necessarily indicate the strengthening of a company's dominance.[475]

377. The law requires a prognosis on how the notified concentration may affect competition in the future.[476] In assessing the concentration's effect on market dominance, the Cartel Court will have regard to changes in market structure, including changes in market shares, financial resources, entry barriers and access to upstream and downstream markets.[477] The weakening of competition following a merger can also strengthen a dominant position.[478] In addition, it is required that a causal relationship can be established between the merger and the creation or strengthening of

472. On this, *see* Stefan Holzweber, Christoph Müller & Christine Dietz, '§ 12 KartG' paras 28 f., in: Stefan Holzweber & Christine Dietz (eds), *Fusionskontolle in Österreich: Kommentar zu §§ 7 – 24 KartG* (LexisNexis 2024).
473. *See* the examples in Astrid Ablasser-Neuhuber, Florian Neumayr, Gerhard Fussenegger & Sebastian Reiter, 'Austria' § 2.07[4][c], in: Frank L. Fine (ed.), *European Competition Laws*, vol 1 (loose-leaf, Matthew Bender Elite Products, release 21-11/2022).
474. KOG 14.2.2005, 16 Ok 1/05 – *Lyocell.*
475. KG 3.3.2008, 29 Kt 129/07 – *Intersnack/Kelly.*
476. KOG 17.12.2008, 16 Ok 15/08 – *Gratiswochenzeitung.*
477. KG 19.4.2017, 26 Kt 13, 14/16 – *Gewista/Ankünder.*
478. KG 28.3.2018, 24 Kt 8/17g & 24 Kt 9/17d – *VTG Rail Assets/CIT Europe.*

the dominant position.[479] To date, no cases have dealt with the SIEC test that has become the substantive test for Austrian merger control, modelled on Article 2(3) EUMR.

378. § 13 KartG contains additional rules for the substantive appraisal of media mergers, especially focused on media pluralism.

379. The merging parties' notification forms the basis of the analysis carried out by the Cartel Court; whether or not the information provided by the notifying parties is correct and complete does not come within the review undertaken by the Cartel Court.[480]

380. The Federal Competition Authority is quite vocal in the area of competition policy and merger control. In November 2019, following a heated European debate about the prohibited merger of *Siemens/Alstom*[481] and the need to strengthen European champions in the face of extra-EU takeovers,[482] the Federal Competition Authority published a Position Paper on European champions underlining how the construct of European champions could not be clearly defined and that the concept would ultimately harm consumers. The Federal Competition Authority also emphasised that, eventually, any 'European champion' would be beaten by competition from outside the EU if European companies did not keep up with competition.[483]

§1. Horizontal Mergers

381. Horizontal mergers, i.e., mergers between actual or potential competitors, are a primary focus of merger control. The assessment of horizontal mergers is detailed in the European Commission's horizontal merger guidelines,[484] which are also considered an important resource under Austrian merger control.[485]

382. In a horizontal merger, the Cartel Court will consider concentrations involving both actual and potential competitors. In the *Lyocell* case, for instance, the Supreme Cartel Court blocked a merger because the acquirer, Lenzing, was intending to purchase a competitor that was, at the time of the proposed merger, not yet

479. KG 9.2.2016, 27 Kt 2, 3/16 – *UNIQA/Privatklinik Goldenes Kreuz*; confirmed in KOG 7.7.2016, 16 Ok 5/16w – *UNIQA/Privatklinik Goldenes Kreuz*.
480. KG 6.10.2015, 29 Kt 44, 45/15 – *Europapier/PaperNet I*.
481. European Commission, Case M.8677 *Siemens/Alstom* [2019] OJ C300/14.
482. On 4.2.2020, France, Germany, Italy and Poland addressed a letter to Executive Vice-President Margrethe Vestager asking for more lenient EU merger rules in order to allow for the creation of so-called European champions, as reported by Michael Acton, '"European champions" policy likely to focus on more competition, not less' *MLex* (17.2.2020).
483. Bundeswettbewerbsbehörde, 'Position Paper on National and European Champions in Merger Control' (November 2019).
484. European Commission, Guidelines on the assessment of horizontal mergers under the Council Regulation on the control of concentrations between undertakings [2004] OJ C31/5.
485. Franz Urlesberger, '§ 12 KartG' para. 27, in: Alexander Petsche, Franz Urlesberger & Claudine Vartian (eds), *Kartellgesetz 2005* (2d ed., Manz 2016).

(or barely) active on the Austrian lyocell market.[486] Based on the restrictive granting of patents for the production of lyocell, this excluded virtually any potential competition in the foreseeable future.

383. In *Meta/Giphy*, the Federal Competition Authority was concerned that potential competition in advertising might be stifled when Facebook's mother company Meta, which held strong market positions in social media as well as in display advertising, acquired Giphy, the world's leading provider of free GIFs. Prior to the acquisition, Giphy had started a promising advertising service that would allow it to monetise its services, thereby representing possible competition for Meta. The transaction fulfilled Austria's transaction value threshold but was not notified. Due to this, Meta was ordered to pay a fine of EUR 9.6 million for gun jumping.[487] When it came to assessing the acquisition in substance, the Cartel Court conditionally cleared Meta's acquisition of Giphy subject to access commitments.[488] The conditional clearance was confirmed by the Supreme Cartel Court. [489] The UK's Competition and Markets Authority and, on appeal, the Competition Appeal Tribunal reached a different conclusion on the same transaction, finding that the acquisition was anti-competitive and Meta had to sell Giphy.[490]

§2. Vertical Mergers

384. Vertical mergers, i.e., mergers between companies that are active at different levels of the economy, are also considered under Austrian merger control. The European Commission has published guidance on non-horizontal mergers,[491] i.e., vertical and conglomerate mergers, which also constitutes an important practical resource under Austrian merger control.

385. In *Mediaprint*, the Cartel Court held that the extension of the merged entity into the downstream market of press wholesale distribution was susceptible to increase the entity's market power vis-à-vis its competitors.[492] In addition, the proposed concentration raised serious concerns related to media pluralism. The concentration was approved subject to conditions and restrictions.

486. KOG 14.2.2005, 16 Ok 1/05 – *Lyocell.*
487. KG 22.7.2021, 28 Kt 6/21y – *Meta/Giphy (gun jumping).* On this aspect of the case, *see also* Thomas Aldor, 'Die aktuelle Bedeutung des europäischen sowie des österreichischen Vollzugsverbots am Beispiel der Fusionsvorhaben von Illumina/GRAIL und Facebook/GIPHY – unter Berücksichtigung der neuen Transaktionsschwelle' (2022) *Österreichische Zeitschrift für Kartellrecht* 68.
488. KG 7.2.2022, 28 Kt 8/21t & 28 Kt 9/21i – *Meta/Giphy.*
489. KOG 23.6.2022, 16 Ok 4/22g – *Meta/Giphy.*
490. Competition & Markets Authority, *Meta/Giphy* (ME/6891/20-II, 6.12.2021); Competition Appeal Tribunal, *Meta/Giphy* [2022] CAT 26, 14.6.2022.
491. European Commission, Guidelines on the assessment of non-horizontal mergers under the Council Regulation on the control of concentrations between undertakings [2008] OJ C265/6.
492. KG 5.8.2004, 26 Kt 132/04 – *Morawa/Mediaprint.*

§3. Market/Product Extension Mergers

386. The European Commission's guidance on non-horizontal mergers is relevant for mergers in which markets or products are expanded.[493]

387. The Supreme Cartel Court has stated that the Cartel Court should take into account conglomerate effects that can occur when a company's product offerings are expanded or complemented. By way of an example, it referred to portfolio effects that arise when related product markets are combined into one market, and the product extension enables the purchaser to exclude competitors from this market. The Court also referred to spill-over effects that arise when, as a result of a merger, the purchaser obtains access to resources that further strengthen its position on its home market.[494] In *Lyocell*, possible post-merger portfolio effects were discussed as a restriction of potential competition, as the sale of lyocell could be tied to the sale of viscose.[495] In *Wrigley*, the Cartel Court emphasised the two-sided nature of portfolio effects: while portfolio effects could lead to cost advantages and efficiency gains by allowing for economies of scope, they could also have exclusionary effects on competitors if applied in a predatory manner.[496]

§4. Pure Conglomerate Mergers

388. The European Commission's guidance on non-horizontal mergers is relevant for pure conglomerate mergers.[497]

§5. Joint Ventures

389. A joint venture that fulfils all the functions of an independent economic entity on a lasting basis is considered to constitute a merger (§ 7(2) KartG). Therefore, agreements that lead to the creation of a fully functional (concentrative) joint venture do not first need to be assessed under § 1 KartG.[498] A merely cooperative joint venture, however, will be assessed under § 1 KartG (on aspects of this assessment, *see* already §§ 133 ff. above).

---

493. European Commission, Guidelines on the assessment of non-horizontal mergers under the Council Regulation on the control of concentrations between undertakings [2008] OJ C265/6.
494. KOG 17.12.2008, 16 Ok 15/08 – *Gratiswochenzeitung*.
495. KOG 14.2.2005, 16 Ok 1/05 – *Lyocell* (recounting the Cartel Court's competition concerns).
496. KG 17.6.2004, 29 Kt 90, 150/04 – *Wrigley*.
497. European Commission, Guidelines on the assessment of non-horizontal mergers under the Council Regulation on the control of concentrations between undertakings [2008] OJ C265/6.
498. Franz Urlesberger, '§ 12 KartG' para. 42, in: Alexander Petsche, Franz Urlesberger & Claudine Vartian (eds), *Kartellgesetz 2005* (2d ed., Manz 2016).

390. In contrast to EU merger control,[499] Austrian merger control only assesses the likelihood of coordination among the founders of a joint venture under § 12 KartG rather than under §§ 1 ff. KartG.[500] This means that these competitive effects must be considered when applying the SIEC test. At a later stage, these effects on competition may come within §§ 1 ff. KartG, unless they constitute an ancillary restraint to a joint venture that was previously considered compatible with competition law.[501]

391. In an early case on the joint production of asphalt mixture (1998), the Supreme Cartel Court held that in order to take into account coordination effects such as those described in the previous paragraph, at least two founders of the joint venture need to be active on the market served by the joint venture, or an adjacent market.[502]

392. In another case on the joint production of asphalt mixture, *Austria Asphalt* (2017), the Supreme Cartel Court had to rule on the question of whether the corporate changes in a production joint venture came under the EUMR.[503] As a preliminary step, it clarified with the CJEU under what circumstances a change in control in a joint venture needs to be assessed as a merger under the EUMR. In the case at hand, a production joint venture previously exclusively controlled by a defendant changed to joint control. The CJEU stated that the change in control of an existing joint venture only gives rise to a concentration within the meaning of Article 3 EUMR where the joint venture created through such a transaction is a fully functional one.[504] Subsequently, the Supreme Cartel Court quashed the Cartel Court's decision and remanded the case to that court.[505]

---

499. Under EU merger control, the European Commission appraises the likelihood of coordination among the founders of a joint venture through an ex ante appraisal and along the lines of Art. 101 TFEU; *see* Art. 2(4) EUMR.
500. KOG 27.1.2014, 16 Ok 11/13 – *Morawa/Pressegroßvertrieb*; KOG 16.12.2002, 16 Ok 9/02 – *O-GmbH & Co KG.*
501. For a critical appraisal, *see* Franz Urlesberger, in: Alexander Petsche, Franz Urlesberger & Claudine Vartian (eds), *Kartellgesetz 2005* § 12 KartG, para. 46 (2d ed., Manz 2016).
502. KOG 15.12.1998, 16 Ok 15/98 – *Asphaltmischanlage I.*
503. KOG 31.3.2016, 16 Ok 1/16g – *Austria Asphalt I.*
504. CJEU Case C-248/16 *Austria Asphalt v. Bundeskartellanwalt*, ECLI:EU:C:2017:643, para. 35. On that case, *see* Johannes P. Gruber, 'Gemeinschaftsunternehmen' (2018) *Österreichische Zeitschrift für Kartellrecht* 14.
505. KOG 19.10.2017, 16 Ok 3/17b – *Austria Asphalt II.*

Part III. Antitrust Procedure

Chapter 1. Administrative Investigations Before the Competition Authority

393. The rules on the administrative proceedings before Austria's principal competition authority, the Federal Competition Authority (Bundeswettbewerbsbehörde or BWB), are contained in the Competition Act (Wettbewerbsgesetz or WettbG).

394. The Federal Competition Authority has, among others, the power to act as an official party in proceedings before the Cartel Court and the Supreme Cartel Court, apply the EU and national competition law rules, conduct sector inquiries, and carry out a competition monitoring (§ 2(1) WettbG).

395. As the Supreme Cartel Court has found, there are two different types of duties that the Federal Competition Authority must fulfil: duties that are to be fulfilled ahead of judicial competition law proceedings or outside of such proceedings, and duties that the Federal Competition Authority fulfils within the context of judicial competition law proceedings.[506]

396. The Federal Competition Authority carries out its duties ex officio (§ 2(3) WettbG).

§1. Initiative

I. General Sector Inquiries

397. The Federal Competition Authority has the power to launch sector inquiries ('Branchenuntersuchungen') if it believes that competition may be restricted or distorted in a certain sector of the economy (§ 2(1) no 3 WettbG). This provision is modelled on Article 17 of Regulation 1/2003, which foresees a similar power for the European Commission.[507] While Article 17 of Regulation 1/2003 also extends to investigations into particular types of agreements, this is not provided for under § 2(1) no 3 WettbG. However, Article 17 of Regulation 1/2003 foresees specific

506. KOG 11.10.2004, 16 Ok 15/04 – *Presse-Großvertrieb.*
507. Peter Thyri, *Kartellrechtsvollzug in Österreich* para. 92 (Manz 2007).

powers that the Commission enjoys when carrying out a sector inquiry, while the Federal Competition Authority can make use of its general powers for the purposes of a sector inquiry.[508]

398. In its sector inquiry into the food retail trade, the Federal Competition Authority requested information from a company that produced sweets but was not active in the food retail trade. The Supreme Cartel Court found that the Federal Competition Authority had successfully demonstrated that it was investigating, with the help of its sector inquiry, substantiated allegations that had been brought to its attention. The information to be provided by the sweets-producing company could be of relevance in that endeavour.[509] However, the Supreme Cartel Court also emphasised that the Federal Competition Authority's powers only extended as far as was necessary to carry out its duties.

399. In recent times, the Federal Competition Authority carried out sector inquiries into ATM fees, cement and concrete, electricity, electric vehicle charging, fuels, the food industry, the food retail trade, gas, health, taxis, and mobile telephony. These can be accessed online.[510] The sector inquiries regularly lead to investigations into specific suspected competition law infringements, as is evidenced by cases in the food retail trade.[511]

400. The Federal Competition Authority may also cooperate with the European Commission in cases in which the Commission carries out sector inquiries under Article 17 of Regulation 1/2003. This cooperation is foreseen in Article 17(2) in combination with Articles 20(5) and 22 of Regulation 1/2003.

II. Ex Officio Investigations

401. The Federal Competition Authority can start investigations concerning infringements of the KartG or of EU competition law of its own volition. The Federal Competition Authority may conduct all investigations necessary to perform its duties under the WettbG (§ 11(1) WettbG). The Federal Competition Authority exercises its powers ex officio, and this also applies to the investigation of specific competition law infringements (§ 2(3) WettbG). The Federal Competition Authority may decide to investigate when a possible infringement is brought to its attention through complaints (on these, *see* below), leniency applications (on these *see* §§ 452 ff. of this monograph) or the media. In addition, sector inquiries (*see* the previous section) may provide the Federal Competition Authority with important insights into possible competition law infringements that it may wish to pursue.

---

508. Reaching the same conclusion, *see* Peter Thyri, *Kartellrechtsvollzug in Österreich* para. 95 (Manz 2007).
509. KOG 11.10.2006, 16 Ok 7, 8/06 – *Lebensmitteleinzelhandel I.*
510. On these, *see* Bundeswettbewerbsbehörde, 'Sector Inquiries' https://www.bwb.gv.at/en/sector_inquiries last accessed 8.8.2024. Note that a larger number of sector inquiries can be accessed through the German version of the website.
511. For example, *see* KOG 8.10.2015, 16 Ok 2/15b & 16 Ok 8/15k – *Spar.*

402. The Federal Competition Authority may only use the knowledge obtained during an investigation for the purpose pursued in that same investigation (§ 11(1) WettbG). At the same time, the Supreme Cartel Court has acknowledged that – in line with the jurisprudence of the CJEU – the competition authorities are not forced to pretend to have 'acute amnesia'; instead, they can use random finds in order to embark on new investigations.[512] While § 11(1) WettbG restricts the use of evidence for the purpose pursued in the investigation, its intention is not to protect competition law infringements.[513] The Supreme Cartel Court uses the following striking example: if a search warrant is granted for the investigation of theft and the inspectors stumble upon a corpse in the process, then this random discovery should lead to a murder investigation. The same, in the eyes of the court, applies in competition law cases.[514]

403. In the course of Austrian competition law proceedings, the Federal Competition Authority's competence ends with an application to the Cartel Court, e.g., asking the latter to terminate an infringement, make a finding of an infringement or review a merger. For this reason, the Federal Competition Authority's powers to investigate equally end with the initiation of proceedings before the Cartel Court. At the same time, however, the Federal Competition Authority continues to have a role in the proceedings before the Cartel Court as one of the two official parties (§ 40 KartG).[515]

404. Where the Federal Competition Authority initiates investigations based on Articles 101 or 102 TFEU, it must inform the European Commission thereof (Article 11(3) of Regulation 1/2003). Likewise, the Commission is committed to informing European national competition authorities when it initiates proceedings. This occurs through a database of the European Competition Network ('ECN-Interactive').[516]

405. The Federal Cartel Prosecutor, as the second official party in Austrian competition law enforcement, cannot carry out any investigations by itself but needs to ask the Federal Competition Authority to carry out investigations (§ 81(3) no 1 KartG).

406. Where the Federal Competition Authority acts on behalf of the European Commission, either in antitrust proceedings (Article 22(2) of Regulation 1/2003) or in merger proceedings (Article 12(1) EUMR), it needs to exercise its investigative powers in line with the national provisions.

---

512. KOG 20.1.2016, 16 Ok 10/15d and others – *Mehlprodukte (Hausdurchsuchung)*; KOG 26.11.2013, 16 Ok 5/13 – *NÖM (Hausdurchsuchung)*.
513. KOG 20.1.2016, 16 Ok 10/15d and others – *Mehlprodukte (Hausdurchsuchung)*.
514. OGH 26.11.2013, 16 Ok 5/13 – *NÖM (Hausdurchsuchung)*.
515. OGH 11.10.2004, 16 Ok 15/04 – *Presse-Großvertrieb*.
516. Georg-Klaus de Bronett, *Europäisches Kartellverfahrensrecht: Kommentar zur VO 1/2003* Art. 11, para. 2 (2d ed., Carl Heymanns 2012).

III. Complaints

407. The Federal Competition Authority can receive informal complaints from the general public, competitors, customers, consumers or their respective interest groups. These complaints may lead to investigations, as detailed in the previous section.

408. In 2018, the Federal Competition Authority set up a whistleblower system which allows for the anonymous sending-in of complaints in relation to competition law.[517] This system is based on the empowering provision in § 11b(6) WettbG. To ensure confidentiality, the whistleblower system is based on secured anonymous mailboxes that guarantee that information sent through the system cannot be traced back, neither by the Federal Competition Authority nor by third parties. The system allows for the entering of free text as well as for the attachment of documents.[518] Documents' metadata is removed to safeguard the sender's anonymity.

409. Even before the implementation of the whistleblower system, the Federal Competition Authority regularly received anonymous complaints (e.g., phone calls and letters). In cases involving such anonymous complaints in the sawmill industry and in the polystyrene industry, the Supreme Cartel Court acknowledged that the Federal Competition Authority could rely on such anonymous complaints when applying for a search warrant with the Cartel Court, even if such anonymous complaints had to be carefully assessed as the basis for a search warrant.[519]

410. Complaints addressed to the Federal Competition Authority do not entail the complainant's right for the authority to further investigate the case brought to its attention.

§2. Powers

I. Requests for Information

411. The Federal Competition Authority is authorised to request information from undertakings, associations of undertakings and other natural or legal persons (§ 11a(1) no 1 WettbG). This information needs to be submitted within a reasonable period of time to be set in each individual case. While an on-site search serves the purpose of discovering perhaps unknown documents, the request for information under § 11a WettbG does not allow the Federal Competition Authority to look for new sources of information; it requires that the documents being requested are

---

517. Bundeswettbewerbsbehörde, 'Whistleblowing System of the Austrian Federal Competition Authority' https://www.bwb.gv.at/en/cartels_and_abuse_control/whistleblowing_system last accessed 8.8. 2024.
518. For the whistleblowing system, *see* https://report.whistleb.com/en/message/bwb last accessed 8.8. 2024.
519. KOG 7.11.2013, 16 Ok 7/13 – *Sägeindustrie (Hausdurchsuchung)*; KOG 20.12.2001, 16 Ok 7 to 13/11 – *Polystyrolkartell I.*

already known or have been volunteered.[520] The Federal Competition Authority is under no special duty to instruct under § 11a WettbG.[521]

412. The Federal Competition Authority can issue simple requests in order to obtain information and business documents. § 11a(2) WettbG provides that owners of undertakings and the undertakings' representatives are under an obligation to submit business documents that the Federal Competition Authority requests under § 11a(1) no 2 WettbG, to provide electronic access to documents or, when requested, to provide them in a standard file format on a data carrier and to grant permission to analyse business documents and make copies and extracts thereof, unless they are at risk of criminal prosecution when doing so. Companies must ensure that their representatives comply with this obligation.

413. While this is not explicitly stated in the law, questions that aim at a confession do not need to be answered.[522] Purely factual questions, however, must be answered. Business secrets do not constitute a valid reason to refuse to answer a request for information.[523] Whoever provides wrong or misleading information to the Federal Competition Authority in contravention of § 11a(2) WettbG is liable to pay an administrative fine of up to 0.5% of their total turnover in the preceding business year (§ 11a(5) WettbG). The threat of a fine is, in the eyes of the Supreme Cartel Court, a clear indication that the legislator takes requests for information – and companies' compliance with these requests – very seriously.[524]

414. The Federal Competition Authority has the power to order the provision of information or the submission of documents by an administrative decision ('Bescheid', § 11a(3) WettbG). The Federal Competition Authority itself is responsible for enforcing its administrative decisions unless its decision is on an administrative penalty (§ 11a(4) WettbG). The General Administrative Procedure Act applies to such administrative decisions and their appeal.[525] The Federal Competition Authority's administrative decision can be appealed to the Federal Administrative Court (§ 11a(6) WettbG), but the appeal does not have a suspensory effect unless the Court grants such an effect within two weeks from the filing of the appeal.

415. Where the Federal Competition Authority has ordered the provision of information or the submission of documents by administrative decision, it can fine

520. KOG 9.11.2011, 16 Ok 5/11 – *Brauereikartell*.
521. KOG 20.12.2001, 16 Ok 7 to 13/11 – *Polystyrolkartell I*.
522. This is in line with EU case law; *see* KOG 11.10.2006, 16 Ok 7, 8/06 – *Lebensmitteleinzelhandel I*.
523. KOG 11.10.2006, 16 Ok 7, 8/06 – *Lebensmitteleinzelhandel I*.
524. KOG 21.1.2008, 16 Ok 8/07 – *Josef Manner*. However, before the 2012 competition law amendment, former § 35(1)I KartG foresaw additional periodic penalty payments to enforce requests for information; this was changed by the Kartell- und Wettbewerbsrechts-Änderungsgesetz 2012 (KaWeRÄG 2012), BGBl I 2013/13.
525. § 11a(3) WettbG; Allgemeines Verwaltungsverfahrensgesetz (AVG; General Administrative Procedure), BGBl 1991/51 as amended.

anybody who provides wrong, misleading or incomplete information, or who provides no information, up to 1% of their total turnover in the preceding business year (§ 11a(5) WettbG). The Administrative Penal Act[526] applies to this administrative offence.

416. Where the Federal Competition Authority requests information or documents for the purposes of a sector inquiry (§ 2(a) no 3 WettbG), an administrative decision (§ 11a(3) WettbG) must always be preceded by a simple request under § 11a(2) WettbG (§ 11a(8) WettbG). The Supreme Cartel Court has highlighted that companies' swift reply to requests for information that the Federal Competition Authority sends out in the course of sector inquiries is crucial in order for this instrument to be effective.[527]

417. The Federal Competition Authority must respect the principle of proportionality when considering whether the information requested is proportional to the duties it is charged with carrying out.[528]

418. While Austrian law does not explicitly contain a professional legal privilege as is established under EU competition law,[529] it is now widely held that such a privilege must also exist where Austrian competition law provisions are applied.[530]

419. During on-site inspections, the Federal Competition Authority has the power to request any information it needs in order to carry out its investigation (§ 11a(1) no 3 WettbG). This includes the Federal Competition Authority's power to ask representatives or employees of the undertaking under investigation for explanations on circumstances or documents which are related to the subject and purpose of the investigation.

420. For the purpose of competition monitoring, which is one of the Federal Competition Authority's duties according to § 2(1) no 5 WettbG, the Federal Competition Authority may only rely on publicly available data and not on the extensive investigative powers bestowed on it by the WettbG (§ 11a(9) WettbG).[531]

526. Verwaltungsstrafgesetz 1991, BGBl 1991/52 as amended.
527. KOG 21.1.2008, 16 Ok 8/07 – *Josef Manner*.
528. The Supreme Cartel Court assumes that the principle of proportionality found in the Telecommunications Act must be read into the WettbG; KOG 30.5.2005, 16 Ok 10/05 – *Lebensmittelhandel*. *See* § 90(1) Telecommunications Act.
529. *See* CJEU Case 155/79 *AM&S v. Commission*, ECLI:EU:C:1982:157; GC Joined Cases T-125 & T-253/03 *Akzo Nobel v. Commission*, ECLI:EU:T:2003:287; GC Case T-30/89 *Hilti v. Commission*, ECLI:EU:T:1991:70.
530. Axel Reidlinger & Isabella Hartung, *Das österreichische Kartellrecht: Ein Handbuch für Praktiker* 359 f. (5th ed., Linde 2024) (containing many further references); Judith Feldner & Dieter Thalhammer, *Die Hausdurchsuchung im Kartellrecht* para. 154 (Manz 2016).
531. The provision still wrongly refers to § 2(1) no 8 WettbG, which was transferred to no 5 by the 2021 amendment.

II. Investigating and Search Powers

421. The Federal Competition Authority is authorised to carry out all investigations necessary in order to perform its duties of enforcing competition law (§ 11 WettbG).[532] In particular, it may consult experts and call witnesses and other parties concerned. The Federal Competition Authority's powers in relation to requests for information were already detailed in the section above. The Supreme Cartel Court has emphasised that there is no hierarchy among the investigation powers that are afforded to the Federal Competition Authority. The authority can therefore choose which instrument it wants to rely upon at what point in time of the investigation.[533] In particular, it cannot be expected that the Federal Competition Authority will issue a request for information before asking the Cartel Court to grant a search warrant, as this would easily undermine the effectiveness of surprise on-site inspections ('dawn raids').[534]

422. The Federal Competition Authority can either ask a company subject to investigations to submit to a voluntary inspection, or it can search the premises based on a search warrant it has obtained from the Cartel Court. While submitting to a voluntary inspection will be seen favourably by the Authority as it indicates cooperation on the company's side (§ 30(3) no 3 KartG), it also means that the company will not be able to rely on its rights of defence in the same way as it could when confronted with a search warrant, as the latter limits the search to the subject matter that the Authority has indicated to the Cartel Court.[535]

423. § 12 WettbG sets out how the Federal Competition Authority may search premises. This provision is modelled upon Article 20 of Regulation 1/2003.[536] The Federal Competition Authority may obtain a search warrant from the Cartel Court where:

a. it reasonably suspects an infringement of §§ 1, 5 or 17 KartG or Articles 101 or 102 TFEU;
b. there are grounds for suspecting said infringement; and
c. a search of the premises is necessary and proportional to obtaining information from business documents (§ 12(1) WettbG).[537]

---

532. On this aspect of Austrian competition law, *see* Anna Wolf-Posch, Bernhard Kofler-Senoner & Michael Mayer, 'Austria', in: Nathalie Jalabert-Doury (ed.), *Competition Inspections in 25 Jurisdictions: A Practitioner's Guide* (2d ed., Concurrences 2024), 1.
533. This is established case law; *see* RIS-Justiz RS0127267.
534. KOG 7.11.2013, 16 Ok 7/13 – *Sägeindustrie (Hausdurchsuchung).*
535. Bundeswettbewerbsbehörde, 'Leitfaden zu Hausdurchsuchungen' para. 15 (2022); Judith Feldner & Dieter Thalhammer, *Die Hausdurchsuchung im Kartellrecht* paras 135–136 (Manz 2016); Astrid Ablasser-Neuhuber, Florian Neumayr, Gerhard Fussenegger & Sebastian Reiter, 'Austria' § 2.05[5], in: Frank L. Fine (ed.), *European Competition Laws*, vol. 1 (loose-leaf, Matthew Bender Elite Products, release 21-11/2022).
536. KOG 11.10.2012, 16 Ok 5/12 *E-Mail-Verkehr (Hausdurchsuchung).*
537. KOG 20.12.2001, 16 Ok 7 to 13/11 – *Polystyrolkartell I*; KOG 5.3.2013, 16 Ok 1/13 – *unverbindlich empfohlene Verkaufspreise*.

On the proceedings before the Cartel Court, *see* §§ 468 ff. of this monograph.

424. The Federal Competition Authority has issued guidance on how it intends to conduct searches of premises, with the latest version dating from 2022.[538]

425. Once a decision granting a search warrant is issued by the Cartel Court, the Federal Competition Authority is tasked with carrying out the search. § 12(3) WettbG states that the Authority needs to serve the search warrant to the owner of the undertaking concerned and its legal representatives (on these persons, *see* § 11a(2) WettbG) immediately or within twenty-four hours at the latest. However, this time limit only starts to run once the Federal Competition Authority has started its on-site inspection.[539] For instance, in a case in which the Federal Competition Authority only initiated its on-site inspection two months and three weeks after the Cartel Court had granted the search warrant, this was regarded as permissible by the Supreme Cartel Court, given that the Federal Competition Authority was simultaneously granted search warrants for eight different locations and it was the general holiday period.[540]

426. On-site inspections are usually carried out at the same time as the search warrant is served, to preserve the surprise element.[541] The object and purpose of a search of premises are determined by the search warrant, and this also determines the extent to which seized documents can be relied upon in due course.[542] If a further suspicion of a competition law infringement arises while the Federal Competition Authority is carrying out its search, then it may request an expansion of the search warrant for further purposes.[543] Exceptionally, the principle of the right to be heard[544] is limited in the case of a search of the premises under § 12 WettbG, as this is required to ensure this instrument's effectiveness.[545]

427. The Federal Competition Authority may seal premises or take possession of documents during the search of the premises, as far as this is necessary to ensure a successful investigation (§ 12(4) WettbG). The party concerned has the right to be present during the search with a person of their confidence.

---

538. Bundeswettbewerbsbehörde, 'Leitfaden zu Hausdurchsuchungen' (2022).
539. Judith Feldner & Dieter Thalhammer, *Die Hausdurchsuchung im Kartellrecht* para. 130 (Manz 2016).
540. KOG 20.12.2011, 16 Ok 7 to 13/11 – *Polystyrolkartell I.*
541. KOG 26.11.2013, 16 Ok 5/13 – *NÖM (Hausdurchsuchung).*
542. KOG 6.6.2012, 16 Ok 2/12 – *Polystyrolkartell II (Hausdurchsuchung).*
543. KOG 26.11.2013, 16 Ok 5/13 – *NÖM (Hausdurchsuchung).* On a case in which multiple expansions were requested and granted, namely KOG 20.1.2016, 16 Ok 10/15d and others – *Mehlprodukte (Hausdurchsuchung), see* Philipp Maunz, Maximilian Diem & Anastasios Xeniadis, 'KOG zur mehrfachen Erweiterung eines Hausdurchsuchungsbefehls' (2017) *Österreichische Zeitschrift für Kartellrecht* 34.
544. On this principle ('rechtliches Gehör'), *see* § 15 AußStrG and Johann Höllwerth, § 15, in: Edwin Gitschthaler & Johann Höllwerth, *AußStrG* I^2 (1.6.2019, rdb.at).
545. OGH 20.1.2016, 16 Ok 10/15d and others – *Mehlprodukte (Hausdurchsuchung)*; KOG 14.2.2014, 16 Ok 8, 9/13 – *Brauereiwirtschaft (Hausdurchsuchung).*

428. Immediately before the search is carried out, the party concerned should be questioned on the prerequisites of the search, unless this may jeopardise the search's success (§ 12(5) WettbG).

429. The undertaking subjected to the search may object to the inspection or the taking possession of certain, individually identified documents (§ 12(5) WettbG). To do so, the undertaking must rely on a legally recognised obligation of secrecy or a right to refuse testimony, for instance, based on § 157(1) no 2 to 5 StPO. In that case, these documents are secured against unauthorised interference and brought before the Cartel Court. The Cartel Court then has the task of reviewing these individually identified documents. Upon inspection of said documents, the presiding judge at the Cartel Court decides whether and to what extent said document may be inspected, (fully or partially) copied or returned to the party concerned. The Cartel Court's decision can be appealed.

430. Where a person subjected to a search of the premises is not able to individually identify the documents that should not be inspected, they can request that certain categories of documents be secured from interference and separately kept at the Federal Competition Authority (§ 12(6) WettbG). The Federal Competition Authority then asks the person concerned to individually identify these documents within a time frame of at least two weeks. For this purpose, the person concerned may inspect the deposited documents. If they fail to do so, the documents become part of the authority's investigation file. If the party concerned individually specifies certain business documents, then the rules of § 12(5) WettbG apply.

431. In carrying out the search of premises, the Federal Competition Authority is supposed to cause as little sensation, nuisance or disturbance as possible, and to safeguard the property and personal rights of those being searched. The Federal Competition Authority needs to take minutes of the search and inform the Cartel Court thereof. The party concerned may be present during the search and can call a person of their confidence. The Federal Competition Authority may inspect business documents and request any information it needs to carry out its investigation, including interviewing the undertaking's staff. Where necessary, the Federal Competition Authority may seal premises and seize evidence (§ 12(4) WettbG). The Federal Competition Authority is under no special duty to instruct under § 12 WettbG.[546]

432. In order to clarify the Federal Competition Authority's search powers related to e-discovery in the course of a search, § 11a(1) no 2 WettbG specifies that the Federal Competition Authority's power to inspect documents extends to any business documents that can be accessed in or by the undertaking under investigation, irrespective of the format in which those documents are stored.[547] The Federal

546. KOG 20.12.2001, 16 Ok 7 to 13/11 – *Polystyrolkartell I.*

547. § 12(4) WettbG on the Federal Competition Authority's powers during a search of the premises explicitly refers to § 11a(1) nos 2 and 3 WettbG.

Competition Authority can rely on qualified experts – such as IT experts – to inspect and analyse such documents. The Federal Competition Authority can also make (digital) copies of these documents. This question had already been settled through case law dating from 2014 and 2015 regarding the Austrian food retailer Spar, in which both the Austrian Supreme Cartel Court and the Higher Administrative Court had held that the Federal Competition Authority's search powers extended to data that was accessible from the place which was detailed in the search warrant, even if the data was stored elsewhere (access approach), and that the Federal Competition Authority was entitled to use forensic software in its search.[548] Against the background of technological innovations, the Austrian legislator held that it would be useful to explicitly include a provision to this effect in the WettbG, while at the same time keeping the provision as technology-neutral as possible.[549]

433. Based on § 11a(1) no 3 WettbG, the Federal Competition Authority is authorised to request all the information it requires to carry out its investigations (§ 12(4) WettbG). In particular, it can ask any member of staff or representative of the undertaking under investigation for explanations on facts or documents relating to the subject matter and purpose of the Federal Competition Authority's investigation.

434. The search of the premises carried out by the Federal Competition Authority is an administrative police action by an administrative authority. Where a company subject to such a search believes that the Federal Competition Authority did not exercise its powers within the limits of the law, it can ask for a review before an administrative court.[550]

III. Cooperation with other State Institutions

435. § 10 WettbG deals with the Federal Competition Authority's cooperation with other authorities or state institutions. It provides that the Federal Competition Authority is authorised to cooperate with the Cartel Court, the Supreme Cartel Court, the Federal Cartel Prosecutor, sector-specific regulators, the Competition Commission, the European Commission and the national competition authorities of other EU Member States, if the cooperation is needed so that these other bodies can

548. Before the entering into force of that provision, *see* already KOG 14.2.2014, 16 Ok 8, 9/13 – *Brauereiwirtschaft (Hausdurchsuchung)*; VwGH 22.4.2015, Ra 2014/04/0046–0051 – *Spar*. On this, *see* Viktoria H.S.E. Robertson, 'The Spar Cases in Austria: Shaping the Legal Framework for Digital Evidence Gathering During Competition Dawn Raids' (2016) 7 *Journal of European Competition Law and Practice* 205.

549. Introduced by Kartell- und Wettbewerbsrechts-Änderungsgesetz 2017 (KaWeRÄG 2017), BGBl I 70ort he; for the legislative materials *see* 1522 der Beilagen XXV. GP (Erläuterungen zur Regierungsvorlage), p. 18.

550. RIS-Justiz RS0128003.

fulfil their duties (§ 10(1) WettbG). The cooperation may, for instance, consist in the provision of information or the transmission of documents.

436. When cooperating with the European Commission, the Federal Competition Authority may also apply for a search warrant with the Cartel Court. Such an application must include the original or a sworn copy of the Commission's investigation decision (§ 12b(2) WettbG). Based on previous case law from the CJEU (*see Roquettes Frères*,[551] subsequently taken up in Article 20(8) and 21(3) of Regulation 1/2003), the Cartel Court may only check the authenticity of the Commission's investigation decision and whether the intended search of the business or the private premises might be arbitrary or unreasonable.

437. While § 10(1) WettbG lists those bodies that the Federal Competition Authority is authorised to cooperate with, it also provides for a list of bodies whom the Federal Competition Authority can ask for information or statements: the Federal Cartel Prosecutor, sector-specific regulators, the Competition Commission, the European Commission and the national competition authorities of other EU Member States. Notably, the Federal Competition Authority cannot make such requests vis-à-vis the courts. § 10(2) WettbG, however, provides that the Cartel Court and the Supreme Cartel Court may request that the Federal Competition Authority provide them with information or submit well-founded statements.

438. In the application of Articles 101 and 102 TFEU, Article 12(1) of Regulation 1/2003 provides that the European Commission and the Member States' competition authorities can provide one another with and use in evidence any matter of fact or of law, including confidential information. In addition, under Article 22(1) of Regulation 1/2003, national competition authorities may carry out inspections or other evidence gathering under their national law on behalf and for the account of another Member State's competition authority. One such case involved the Federal Competition Authority carrying out a dawn raid on behalf and for the account of the German Federal Cartel Office.[552] Article 22(2) of Regulation 1/2003 provides that the European Commission may also request that a national competition authority carry out inspections that the Commission deems necessary.

439. The Criminal Police Department, the Public Prosecutor's Office and the courts are entitled to provide the Federal Competition Authority with personal data that they obtained under the Code of Criminal Procedure, and which the Federal Competition Authority needs in order to prosecute infringements of the KartG or of Articles 101 and 102 TFEU (§ 10(1a) WettbG).

440. Where the Federal Competition Authority's investigations concern the aviation sector, the Federal Minister of Transport can submit a statement to the Federal Competition Authority (§ 10(4) WettbG). Where the media sector is affected, such a right is afforded to the Austrian Communications Authority (KommAustria).

551. CJEU Case 26/74 *Société Roquette Frères v. Commission*, ECLI:EU:C:1976:69.
552. KOG 11.5.2017, 16 Ok 8/16m – *Amtshilfe (Hausdurchsuchung)*.

441. As already set out above, the Federal Cartel Prosecutor has no investigative powers. Instead, it can ask the Federal Competition Authority to carry out investigations (§ 81(3) no 1 KartG). In turn, and where this is necessary for the performance of its duties, the Federal Competition Authority can request information from the Federal Cartel Prosecutor and inspect its files (§ 10(3) WettbG).

442. When searching premises under § 12 WettbG, the Federal Competition Authority is regularly accompanied by the police. This possibility is foreseen in § 14(1) WettbG, and the same applies under Article 20(6) of Regulation 1/2003. The Federal Competition Authority may also rely on forensic IT experts from the Federal Criminal Police Office (§ 14(2) WettbG). The Federal Competition Authority signed a cooperation agreement with the Federal Criminal Police Office in 2009.[553]

443. The Federal Competition Authority closely cooperates with the European Commission and the other national competition authorities of the EU Member States, all of which are connected through the European Competition Network.[554]

§3. Right of Defence

444. The rights of defence during the administrative investigation are limited, as the Federal Competition Authority does not adopt any substantive administrative decisions on the infringement of competition law. Instead, it is an administrative authority charged with taking up cases and investigating them. It can then make applications to the Cartel Court, where the rights of defence are safeguarded based on the Non-contentious Proceedings Act.

445. Nevertheless, § 13(1) WettbG – as amended in 2021 – provides that the Federal Competition Authority needs to uphold the fundamental rights applicable in Austria, including the EU's Charter of Fundamental Rights[555] and the general principles of EU law. In particular, the law refers to the principles of proportionality and appropriateness, undertakings' rights of defence, and conducting investigations within an appropriate timeframe. The provision implements the ECN+ Directive and in large part is a verbatim copy of the latter's Article 3.[556]

553. Bundeswettbewerbsbehörde, 'Neue Wege zur Kartellbekämpfung – BWB verstärkt Ermittlungskapazitäten durch Kooperation mit dem Bundeskriminalamt' (20.6.2009) https://www.bwb.gv.at/news/news-2009/detail/neue-wege-zur-kartellbekaempfung-bwb-verstaerkt-ermittlungskapazitaeten-durch-kooperation-mit-dem-bun last accessed 8.8.2024.

554. *See* Joint Statement of the Council and the Commission on the Functioning of the Network of Competition Authorities (10.12.2002); European Commission, Commission Notice on co-operation within the Network of Competition Authorities [2004] OJ C101/43.

555. Charter of Fundamental Rights of the European Union [2016] OJ C202/389.

556. Matthias Ranftl & Natalie Harsdorf-Borsch, '§ 13 WettbG' para. 2, in: Alexander Egger & Natalie Harsdorf-Borsch (eds), *Kartellrecht – Kommentar* (Linde 2022).

I. Content and Notification of Opening Decisions

446. The Federal Competition Authority does not adopt any formal opening decisions of which the parties concerned would be notified. The Federal Competition Authority's proceedings are deemed to be initiated once it has taken its first official investigative measure against a company or an association of undertakings (§ 13a(1) WettbG).[557] Although this provision is contained in the realm of disclosure of evidence in proceedings for damages, it can be relied upon to mark the starting point of the Federal Competition Authority's investigations.

447. As set out above (§ 422 of this monograph), the right to be heard is limited in the proceedings leading to a search warrant, as this would jeopardise the effectiveness of this investigative tool. Where the Cartel Court issues a search warrant, the Federal Competition Authority needs to serve that decision to the undertaking concerned immediately or within twenty-four hours (§ 12(3) WettbG).

II. Administrative Proceedings: Hearings, Access to File, Briefs

448. Regular administrative proceedings that end with an administrative decision do not take place before the Federal Competition Authority nor before the Federal Cartel Prosecutor. Instead, the Federal Competition Authority as an administrative authority is charged with carrying out investigations that can result in an application to the Cartel Court (§ 36 KartG). The Federal Cartel Prosecutor, while not entitled to carry out its own investigations, can equally file applications addressed to the Cartel Court (§ 36 KartG). Even in cases in which it is neither the Federal Competition Authority nor the Federal Cartel Prosecutor that makes an application to the Cartel Court, the two official parties are always parties to proceedings before the Cartel Court and the Supreme Cartel Court (§ 40 KartG).

449. If the Federal Competition Authority intends to file an application with the Cartel Court requesting

- the termination of an infringement (§ 26 KartG);
- the declaration that commitments made by the undertaking concerned become binding (§ 27 KartG);
- the declaration that a prior infringement took place (§ 28 KartG);[558] or
- the declaration that a dominant position exists on a multisided digital market (§ 28a KartG);

557. While this provision is found within the realm of disclosure of evidence in damages proceedings, it can be of broader interest as the KartG and the WettbG do not otherwise state when administrative proceedings before the Federal Competition Authority are deemed to commence.

558. Under § 28 KartG, the Cartel Court may also declare whether or not a case comes under the KartG; *see* Johannes P. Gruber, 'Feststellungsentscheidungen (§ 28 KartG)' (2019) *Österreichische Zeitschrift für Kartellrecht* 122.

and if prior to this filing the Federal Competition Authority carried out investigations under

- § 11 WettbG (investigations);
- § 11a WettbG (requests for information and submission of documents); or
- § 12 WettbG (search of premises);

then it must afford the party concerned (i.e., the future respondent) the opportunity to take note of the results of the investigation and to make a statement related to them within a reasonable period of time (§ 13(1) WettbG). In practice, it is disputed whether the Federal Competition Authority always affords parties this right to be heard before making an application to the Cartel Court.[559]

450. Where the Federal Competition Authority has carried out investigations, but subsequently does not intend to file an application to the Cartel Court as set out above, it must inform the party concerned (i.e., the potential respondent) about this within a reasonable period of time (§ 13(2) WettbG).

451. Different circumstances can arise where access to the Federal Competition Authority's files may be of interest to a party. Where the issue of access to file arises in the realm of a claim for damages, provides that the Federal Competition Authority can disclose three types of evidence (§ 13a(1) WettbG):[560]

a. information that was prepared by a natural or legal person specifically for competition proceedings;
b. information that the Federal Competition Authority has drawn up and sent to the parties in the course of its proceedings; and
c. settlement submissions that have been withdrawn.

452. However, the Federal Competition Authority may only disclose such evidence upon order by a national court, and after proceedings on the corresponding infringement of competition law have come to an end – either by decision or in another way. § 13a(2) WettbG limits the disclosure of evidence by the Federal Competition Authority insofar as it is only supposed to disclose evidence if the latter cannot be obtained with reasonable effort from another party to the proceedings or, indeed, a third party. Leniency submissions and settlement submissions may not be disclosed by the Federal Competition Authority (§ 13a(3) WettbG). § 13a WettbG was amended to bring it in line with Article 6 of Directive 2014/104/EU.

453. On access to the file in cases involving damages claims for an infringement of competition law, *see* already §§ 237 ff. of this monograph (§ 13a WettbG and §§ 37j, 37k KartG).

559. Axel Reidlinger & Isabella Hartung, *Das österreichische Kartellrecht: Ein Handbuch für Praktiker* 299 (4th ed., Linde 2019; not contained in the 5th ed.).
560. This provision was introduced by BGBl I 2017/56.

454. In damages claims for competition law infringements that are brought before national courts, the national court can ask the Federal Competition Authority to submit a statement (§ 13b WettbG). The Federal Competition Authority is under no obligation to provide such a statement but can decide to do so when it sees fit.

III. Statement of Objections

455. Austrian competition law does not foresee a formal statement of objections as is known under EU law. This is also related to the fact that the Federal Competition Authority is not competent to adopt decisions, but can only apply to the Cartel Court to adopt a competition law-related decision ('Beschluss').

IV. Leniency Programme

456. While the Federal Competition Authority cannot itself adopt administrative fines for anti-competitive behaviour, it *can* decide to refrain from requesting the Cartel Court to impose a fine on an undertaking for engaging in an anti-competitive agreement (§ 1 KartG or Article 101(1) TFEU). This can be an impetus for cartelists to strike a deal with the Federal Competition Authority, thus providing the basis for the Austrian leniency programme.

457. The Austrian leniency framework (§ 11b KartG) closely follows the Leniency Model of the European Competition Network (ECN).[561] It was hoped that with the adoption of the ECN+ Directive,[562] the European leniency framework – comprised of the Member States' leniency frameworks and the European Commission's leniency framework – will become more harmonised and more interoperable. Based on the provisions as adopted in the ECN+ Directive, however, this wish may not materialise.

458. The Austrian leniency framework is detailed in § 11b WettbG and provides a possibility for an undertaking or association of undertakings ('applicant') to escape a fine. In order for the Federal Competition Authority to refrain from requesting that the Cartel Court impose a fine on the leniency applicant, the latter needs to fulfil the following cumulative conditions set out in § 11b(1) no 1 WettbG: the undertaking or association of undertakings:

1. have terminated their participation in the infringement unless exercising its reasonable judgment, the Federal Competition Authority is of the opinion that the continuation of the infringement is necessary in order to preserve the integrity of its investigation;

561. ECN Model Leniency Programme (November 2012).
562. Directive (EU) 2019/1 of the European Parliament and of the Council of 11 December 2018 to empower the competition authorities of the Member States to be more effective enforcers and to ensure the proper functioning of the internal market (ECN+ Directive) [2019] OJ L11/3.

2. subsequently cooperate with the Federal Competition Authority truthfully, promptly and without restrictions …,
3. (a) are the first to submit information and evidence to the Federal Competition Authority which enables it to immediately file a well-founded application pursuant to § 12(1) WettbG concerning a suspected infringement of § 1 Cartel Act or Article 101(1) TFEU, or
   b. are the first to submit any additional information and evidence to the Federal Competition Authority which, if it has already obtained sufficient information and evidence from other sources to apply for a warrant to search premises, enable it to immediately file a well-founded application pursuant to § 36(1a) Cartel Act with the Cartel Court; and
4. have not coerced any other undertakings or associations of undertakings to participate in the infringement.

459. Should the Federal Competition Authority request that the Cartel Court impose a fine on a company that is party to an anti-competitive agreement in which the leniency applicant also participated, then it files an application for a declaratory decision under § 28(1a) no 1 KartG against the leniency applicant that benefits from the leniency programme. § 28 KartG allows the Cartel Court to declare that an infringement took place, even if said infringement has already been brought to an end. This possibility explicitly covers cases in which no fine is requested because the infringer is a leniency applicant.[563]

460. Where an applicant does not meet the requirements in § 11b(1) no 3 a) or b) WettbG, but fulfils the requirements set out in § 11b(1) no 1, 2 and 4 WettbG, the Federal Competition Authority may request that the Cartel Court impose a reduced fine on the leniency applicant as per § 11b(2) WettbG. In order to qualify for the reduced fine, the applicant must submit information and evidence on the suspected infringement to the Federal Competition Authority that are of significant added value compared to the information and evidence already held by the Authority.

461. The WettbG's provisions on leniency are directed at the Federal Competition Authority, and the latter has some discretion in applying them. However, the Supreme Cartel Court has ruled that where the requirements set out in § 11b(1) WettbG are met, the courts are under an obligation to take this into account as a mitigating factor when deciding on the extent of the fine to impose (§ 30(3) no 3 KartG).[564]

563. Before the enactment of § 28(1a) KartG, this was disputed; *see* KOG 25.3.2009, 16 Ok 4/09 – *Industriechemikalien*. In the *Schenker* case before the CJEU, that Court clarified through a preliminary ruling that 'in the event that the existence of an infringement of Art. 101 TFEU is established, the national competition authorities [which, in Austria, includes the Cartel Court] may by way of exception confine themselves to finding that infringement without imposing a fine where the undertaking concerned has participated in a national leniency programme'; CJEU Case C-681/11 *Bundeswettbewerbsbehörde v. Schenker*, ECLI:EU:C:2013:404, para. 50. Following this ruling, *see* KOG 2.12.2013, 16 Ok 4/13 – *BWB/Schenker*. The possibility of a declaratory decision without the imposition of a fine is now explicitly provided for in § 28(1a) no 1 KartG.
564. KOG 4.10.2010, 16 Ok 5/10 – *Druckchemikalien*.

462. While the leniency provision used to foresee that the Federal Competition Authority should publish a leniency handbook on its website in which it sets out details on leniency applications and cooperation with the Authority,[565] it now foresees that the Federal Minister for Economic Affairs may adopt more detailed provisions in the form of a regulation (§ 11b(4) WettbG). Such a regulation was adopted in November 2021.[566] In addition, the Federal Competition Authority has continued to issue guidance on its leniency practice, last revised in 2022.[567]

463. Where an undertaking wishes to benefit from leniency, the Federal Competition Authority should issue a non-binding statement as to whether it intends to apply the leniency provisions (§ 11b(3) WettbG).

464. The Federal Competition Authority needs to inform the Federal Cartel Prosecutor when it intends to request a reduced fine or when it intends to refrain from requesting a fine altogether (§ 11b(3) WettbG). The Federal Cartel Prosecutor is no longer in a position to request the imposition of a fine after receiving the Federal Competition Authority's notice (§ 36(3) KartG). Should the Federal Cartel Prosecutor have already submitted such a request before receiving that information, then they must take it back.[568]

465. The Federal Competition Authority may not disclose leniency submissions at any time (§ 13a(3) WettbG).

466. Information that the Federal Competition Authority has obtained through the European Competition Network and that emanates from a leniency application may not be relied upon for the filing of an application requesting the imposition of a fine (§ 11b(5) WettbG). However, this does not preclude the Federal Competition Authority's ability to carry out investigations based on information obtained from outside the ECN, which in turn may lead to a request for the imposition of a fine.

467. While the intention of the leniency programme is to allow cartelists to share valuable information on cartels with the Federal Competition Authority and thereby receive immunity from fines, § 11b(6) WettbG contains a further mechanism through which the Federal Competition Authority can be informed of possible competition law infringements: an online whistleblower system. While the leniency programme only covers anti-competitive agreements, the whistleblower system covers anti-competitive agreements, abuses of a dominant position, retaliatory measures

565. *See* § 11b(3) WettbG before the 2021 amendment.
566. Verordnung der Bundesministerin für Digitalisierung und Wirtschaftsstandort über die Anwendung der Kronzeugenregelung des Wettbewerbsgesetzes, BGBl II 2021/487.
567. Bundeswettbewerbsbehörde, 'Leitfaden Kronzeugen' (2022).
568. Alfred Mair, '§ 36 KartG' para. 42, in: Alexander Petsche, Franz Urlesberger & Claudine Vartian (eds), *Kartellgesetz 2005* (2d ed., Manz 2016).

and the competition laws of other EU or EEA Member States.[569] This whistleblowing system is available at https://report.whistleb.com/en/bwb.

468. In the construction cartel case, the Federal Competition Authority had granted leniency status to the construction company STRABAG and therefore applied for a reduced fine before the Cartel Court, which the latter granted. In the course of further proceedings, however, the Federal Competition Authority became aware of the fact that the leniency applicant had not, as required by the law, fully cooperated with the authority. Against this background, it requested a review of the Cartel Court's fining decision. While the Cartel Court denied to review its already final decision,[570] on appeal the Supreme Cartel Court found that, given that the leniency requirements had not been met, the initial decision was again open to review.[571]

V. Settlement Procedure

469. Partially compensating for its lack of substantive decisional powers, the Federal Competition Authority has been relying on the settlement procedure in order to efficiently terminate competition law infringements in a binding manner. This procedure is gaining significant practical relevance.[572] To inform parties of the Federal Competition Authority's handling of settlements, it published a guidance paper to that effect that was last revised in 2023.[573]

470. In settlements agreed upon between the Federal Competition Authority and the undertaking(s) concerned, the Federal Competition Authority makes use of § 36(2) KartG. This provision states that the Cartel Court may not impose a fine on an undertaking that is higher than what the official party has requested. In practice, when entering into a settlement, the Federal Competition Authority and the undertaking concerned agree on the maximum fine that the Federal Competition Authority will request before the Cartel Court, and in return, the undertaking does not contest the allegations that the Federal Competition Authority makes in its application, declares that it does not wish to rely on an individual exemption and that it does not oppose the imposition of a fine. In such a case, the Cartel Court's hearing

569. On the distinction between different categories of informants, such as whistleblowers and leniency applicants, *see* Isabella Hartung & Sebastian Schwab, '"Whistleblower" versus Kronzeuge: Quo vadis, Informant?' (2019) *Österreichische Zeitschrift für Kartellrecht* 169.

570. KG 20.10.2022, 27 Kt 12/21y-65 – *STRABAG.*

571. KOG 25.5.2023, 16 Ok 8/22w – *STRABAG.*

572. *See* Hanno Wollmann & Franz Urlesberger, 'Im Fokus: Settlements mit der Bundeswettbewerbsbehörde' (2015) *ecolex* 47; Georg E. Kodek, 'Absprachen im Kartellverfahren' (2014) 67 *Österreichische Juristen-Zeitung* 443.

573. *See* Bundeswettbewerbsbehörde, 'Standpunkt zu Settlements' (2023) https://www.bwb.gv.at/fileadmin/user_upload/Standpunkt_zu_Settlements__2.Fassung__2023_.pdf last accessed 8.8.2024. On this standpoint, *see* Judith Feldner & Yvonne Handler, 'Settlements: Eine Analyse des aktualisierten Standpunkts der BWB' (2024) *Österreichische Zeitschrift für Kartellrecht* 8.

sometimes only lasts several minutes, and it can immediately announce its decision to impose a fine. Thereupon, the official parties and the undertaking concerned waive their right to an appeal.[574]

471. Settlements can relate to infringements of § 1 KartG or Article 101 TFEU, as well as to the abuse of a dominant position (§ 5 KartG or Article 102 TFEU) or non-compliance with the standstill obligation (§ 17 KartG) in mergers.[575] The settlement procedure can also be combined with the leniency procedure.[576]

---

574. Anastasios Xeniadis & Heinrich Kühnert, 'Einvernehmliche Verfahrensbeendigung in Kartellverfahren' (2012) *Österreichische Zeitschrift für Kartellrecht* 83, 92; Georg E. Kodek, 'Absprachen im Kartellverfahren' (2014) 67 *Österreichische Juristen-Zeitung* 443, 446.
575. Axel Reidlinger & Isabella Hartung, *Das österreichische Kartellrecht: Ein Handbuch für Praktiker* 357 (5th ed., Linde 2024).
576. Bundeswettbewerbsbehörde, 'Leniency handbook' 19 (2022).

Chapter 2. Proceedings at the Cartel Court

472. The Cartel Court is the decisional instance in competition law cases emanating from public enforcement as well as from private enforcement under the KartG. While the Federal Competition Authority as an administrative authority has broad investigative powers (on these *see* above, §§ 407 ff. of this monograph), it lacks decisional powers. It needs to apply to the Cartel Court for the imposition of an interlocutory injunction (§ 48 KartG), for the granting of a search warrant for on-site inspections (§ 12 WettbG), for the bringing to an end of anti-competitive agreements or unilateral conduct (§ 26 KartG), for the declaratory finding of an already terminated infringement (§ 28 KartG), for the declaratory finding of a dominant position on a multisided digital market (§ 28a KartG), for the imposition of penalty payments (§ 35 KartG) and fines (§ 29 KartG) for various types of competition law infringements, for the legal scrutiny of a merger (§ 12 KartG), and for the acceptance of binding commitments made by a party (§ 27 KartG).

473. The Cartel Court can also be called upon by private parties for the private enforcement of competition law, e.g., when the termination of an infringement or a declaratory decision on the previous existence of an infringement is at stake. However, private parties cannot request the imposition of a fine (§ 36(2) KartG). In addition, the Cartel Court is not competent to decide on damages claims for the infringement of competition law (on these, *see* §§ 209 ff. of this monograph) or on unfair competition law claims that are based on the infringement of competition law (on this, *see* § 96 of this monograph).

474. The Federal Cartel Prosecutor lacks investigatory powers but can apply to the Cartel Court in the same way as the Federal Competition Authority.

475. As per § 38 KartG, proceedings before the Cartel Court generally follow the Non-contentious Proceedings Act (Außerstreitgesetz).[577] The KartG, however, contains a number of special provisions on the specificities of proceedings before the Cartel Court (§§ 38 ff. KartG). In the following, some of the main rules applicable to the proceedings before the Cartel Court are set out.[578]

§1. Competent Court

476. The Higher Regional Court of Vienna (Oberlandesgericht Wien or OLG Wien) acts as the competent Cartel Court (Kartellgericht or KG) for Austria (§ 58(1) KartG).

577. Außerstreitgesetz (AußStrG), BGBl I 2003/111 as amended.

578. For a detailed monograph on competition law proceedings before the Cartel Court, *see* Sabine Völkl-Torggler, Iris Ingemarsson & Ludwig Majer, *Das Verfahren vor dem Kartellgericht* (3d ed., Verlag Österreich 2023).

477. The Cartel Court sits in panels of four judges, of which two are professional judges and two are expert lay judges (§ 59(1) no 1 KartG). A professional judge presides.

478. The expert lay judges are nominated by the Federal Minister of Justice in accordance with § 68 KartG. The Chamber of Commerce, the Chambers of Agriculture and the Chamber of Labour all get to nominate expert lay judges who are then appointed by the Minister of Justice. They must have studied law, business or economics in Austria and have long-standing professional experience in either law or business (§ 66 KartG).

479. The Cartel Court only decides upon application (§ 36(1) KartG). In its proceedings, it follows the rules of the Non-contentious Proceedings Act (§ 38 KartG).[579]

480. Decisions are taken by vote. In case of a tie, the vote of the presiding (professional) judge decides (§ 63 KartG).

481. The Cartel Court regularly requests the opinion of economic experts. In one instance, it requested the opinion of an economic expert who worked together with a research institute that had worked with one of the undertakings involved in the merger at issue on multiple occasions. It did not regard this as a reason to doubt the expert's impartiality; this was confirmed by the Supreme Cartel Court.[580] In order to ensure economic experts' impartiality, the Austrian legislator could consider implementing transparent rules on impartiality, as it appears that some guidance in this respect could improve the impartiality of competition law proceedings.

§2. Applications to the Cartel Court

482. As stated above, the Federal Competition Authority is an administrative authority that has broad investigative powers but lacks substantive decisional powers. This is in stark contrast to the powers of the European Commission, which has both investigative and decisional powers. The only decisional power the Federal Competition Authority has is to request the submission of documents by decision and to issue an administrative fine in case this decision is not complied with (on this, *see* § 191 of this monograph). Instead of directly deciding cases on which it has led investigations, the Federal Competition Authority is authorised to make an application to the Cartel Court (§ 36 KartG). This is also true for the Federal Cartel Prosecutor.

579. However, when imposing a fine the Cartel Court and Supreme Cartel Court may not rely on § 39(4) of the Non-Contentious Proceedings Act, which foresees that the reasons for the decision may be omitted when the decision is drawn up (§ 38 KartG).

580. KOG 23.6.2022, 16 Ok 3/22k – *BWB/Facebook*.

483. If the Federal Competition Authority wants to carry out on-site inspections, it needs to obtain a search warrant from the Cartel Court (§ 12 WettbG). On this, *see* §§ 490 ff. of this monograph.

484. If the Federal Competition Authority or the Federal Cartel Prosecutor believe that a company has committed an anti-competitive infringement, then they need to apply to the Cartel Court in order to bring that infringement to an end and/or to impose fines (§ 36 KartG).

485. Beyond the two official parties, sector-specific regulators, the Federal Chamber of Commerce, the Federal Chamber of Labour and the Standing Committee of Presidents of the Chambers of Agriculture as well as any undertaking or association of undertakings with a legal or economic interest in the decision also have standing to make an application to the Cartel Court (§ 36(4) KartG). However, only the Federal Competition Authority and the Federal Cartel Prosecutor are entitled to apply for the imposition of fines or to request the finding that a company has a dominant position on a multisided digital market. Similarly, only the two official parties may request a review of a merger (§ 36(2) KartG).

486. Where a private party has a legal or economic interest in the Cartel Court's decision ordering the termination of an infringement (§ 26 KartG) or finding that an infringement existed in the past (§ 28 KartG), it may itself bring a claim before the Cartel Court (§ 36(4) no 4 KartG). In practice, private parties more often address complaints to the Federal Competition Authority rather than bringing their own case before the Cartel Court, due to the authority's far-reaching investigative powers.

487. Where a party considers that the termination of a competition law infringement is a matter of urgency, it may apply for an interlocutory injunction with the Cartel Court (§ 48 KartG). On this, *see* §§ 496 ff. of this monograph.

488. The official parties are always parties to cases before the Cartel Court, even if the application was made by a private party (§ 40 KartG).

489. Once an application is made to the Cartel Court, hearings take place upon the request of a party (§ 47(1) KartG). While these are generally public hearings, parties can apply for an in-camera hearing if this is required to protect business or trade secrets.

§3. DECISIONS

490. The Cartel Court decides on applications by decision ('Beschluss'), in non-contentious proceedings (§ 38 KartG). Its decisions can be appealed to the Supreme Cartel Court (§ 49 KartG; *see* §§ 625 ff. of this monograph).

491. The Cartel Court can by decision:

- issue a search warrant (§ 12 WettbG);
- adopt an interlocutory injunction (§ 48 KartG);
- require the termination of an ongoing infringement (§ 26 KartG);
- render commitments made by undertakings binding (§ 27 KartG);
- find that an infringement that has already been brought to an end existed in the past (§ 28 KartG);
- find that an undertaking has a dominant position on a multisided digital market (§ 28a KartG);
- prohibit a merger or allow it to move ahead, also subject to conditions and restrictions (§ 12 KartG);
- dismiss an application, e.g., for lack of jurisdiction or lack of infringement; and
- impose fines or periodic penalty payments for an infringement of competition law or of certain provisions of the KartG (§§ 29, 35 KartG).

Since 2002, the Cartel Court has imposed fines exceeding EUR 408 million based on applications by the Federal Competition Authority.[581]

492. For antitrust proceedings, the KartG does not foresee any time limits and proceedings can last for a considerable amount of time. This is also due to the time necessary for expert opinions to be commissioned, received and taken into account.

493. Owing to the time-sensitive nature of merger control, there are time limits foreseen for the official parties' request for the examination of a merger (phase I, § 11 KartG: four or six weeks), for the Cartel Court's decision on a merger (phase II, § 14 KartG: five or six months), and for the Supreme Court's decision on an appeal to the Cartel Court's decision (§ 14 KartG: two months). On merger proceedings, *see* below §§ 577 ff. of this monograph.

I. Search Warrants

494. § 12 WettbG contains provisions on the search of premises to be carried out by the Federal Competition Authority. If it wants to search premises during its competition law investigations, the Federal Competition Authority must apply for a search warrant with the Cartel Court. It can do so where:

a. it reasonably suspects an infringement of §§ 1, 5 or 17 KartG or Articles 101 or 102 TFEU;
b. there are grounds for suspecting said infringement; and

581. Bundeswettbewerbsbehörde, 'Fines in Austria since 2002' (1.8.2024) https://www.bwb.gv.at/fileadmin/user_upload/Geldbussentabelle_gesamt__Stand_01.08_2024__CD_EN_final_.pdf last accessed 8.8.2024.

c. a search of the premises is necessary and proportional to obtaining information from business documents (§ 12(1) WettbG).[582]

495. On the reasonable suspicion ('begründeter Verdacht'), the Supreme Cartel Court has emphasised that this does not have to amount to a strong suspicion ('dringender Verdacht').[583] In the eyes of the Court, a suspicion is reasonable when it rationally allows for the conclusion that a competition law infringement was committed, based on the available facts.[584] The reasonable suspicion does not have to be directed at the person whose premises are being searched.[585] The initial suspicion may not be based on mere speculation or suspicions that are too vague or obviously unfounded.[586] As detailed above (§§ 403–406 of this monograph), anonymous complaints may, under certain circumstances, lead to a well-founded initial suspicion, as do leniency applications. Further instances that can lead to an initial suspicion and that have come before the Supreme Cartel Court include documents seized at a competitor's search,[587] email correspondence,[588] minutes of meetings,[589] website content,[590] witnesses[591] and observed payments.[592]

496. A search of the premises can also be carried out where the behaviour to be investigated lies in the past and has been concluded, as long as said behaviour is not time-barred from a competition law investigation.[593] The limitation period for the Federal Competition Authority is five years counting from the termination of a competition law infringement (§ 33(1) KartG).[594] The limitation period is interrupted as soon as the authority notifies at least one undertaking concerned with its investigation. After each interruption, the limitation period starts to run afresh. The absolute limitation period, however, is ten years counting from the termination of the infringement.[595]

497. On the necessity and proportionality of a search of the premises, the Supreme Cartel Court has held that the necessity is to be assessed based on the purpose that the search is set to fulfil, and that is made known to the addressee of the

582. KOG 20.12.2001, 16 Ok 7 to 13/11 – *Polystyrolkartell I*; KOG 5.3.2013, 16 Ok 1/13 – *unverbindlich empfohlene Verkaufspreise*.
583. KOG 11.10.2012, 16 Ok 5/12 – *E-Mail-Verkehr (Hausdurchsuchung)*.
584. This is established case law, *see* RIS-Justiz RS0125748.
585. RIS-Justiz RS0125748; KOG 7.7.2017, 16 Ok 1/17h – *Vergabeverfahren (Hausdurchsuchung)*.
586. KOG 19.4.2010, 16 Ok 2/10 – *Feuerwehrfahrzeuge II*.
587. KOG 7.7.2017, 16 Ok 1/17h – *Vergabeverfahren (Hausdurchsuchung)*.
588. KOG 5.3.2013, 16 Ok 1/13 – *unverbindlich empfohlene Verkaufspreise (Hausdurchsuchung)*; KOG 14.2.2014, 16 Ok 8, 9/13 – *Brauereiwirtschaft (Hausdurchsuchung)*.
589. KOG 20.1.2016, 16 Ok 10/15d and others – *Mehlprodukte (Hausdurchsuchung)*.
590. KOG 7.11.2013, 16 Ok 7/13 – *Sägeindustrie (Hausdurchsuchung)*; KOG 6.5.2014, 16 Ok 3/14 – *Online-Fahrradhandel (Hausdurchsuchung)*.
591. KOG 20.12.2001, 16 Ok 7 to 13/11 – *Polystyrolkartell I*.
592. KOG 19.4.2010, 16 Ok 2/10 – *Feuerwehrfahrzeuge II*.
593. RIS-Justiz RS0129421.
594. As per its wording, the provision applies to the imposition of a fine.
595. § 33(2) KartG foresees that the limitation period is suspended while another NCA within the ECN or the European Commission is investigating the infringement.

decision.[596] A search is regarded as necessary when it is needed in order to find sources of information on a suspected competition law infringement, or if the completeness of already obtained documents needs to be verified.[597] As a search of the premises has a more far-reaching impact on the addressees than a request for information, the requirement of proportionality ensures that the Cartel Court balances the search's impact on the individual sphere of the addressee and the authority's interest in clarifying facts through the search.[598]

498. The search warrant is issued by a decision of the presiding judge at the Cartel Court, in non-contentious proceedings. An appeal of that decision does not have a suspensory effect unless explicitly granted (§ 12(3) WettbG).

499. On the search of premises from the perspective of the Federal Competition Authority, *see* §§ 417 ff. of this monograph.

II. Interlocutory Injunctions

500. Any party can apply for interlocutory injunctions with the Cartel Court; § 48 KartG is not limited to applications by the official parties (i.e., the Federal Competition Authority and the Federal Cartel Prosecutor) but can also be relied upon by private parties bringing a claim before the Cartel Court. The Cartel Court may be asked to grant an interlocutory injunction before the initiation of the main proceedings, during these proceedings and up until the point in time when the execution for the issuing of preliminary injunctions has been initiated.[599] For the Cartel Court to have jurisdiction for the granting of an interlocutory injunction, corresponding main proceedings need to be pending before it.[600]

501. Where the KartG does not provide details for interlocutory injunctions, the Execution Act is applicable in a subsidiary manner (§ 378a EO).

502. In order to apply for an interlocutory injunction, the competition law infringement must be certified ('bescheinigt').[601] The applicant does not have to demonstrate the risk of a repeated offence, as this directly follows from the certified competition infringement.[602] Under Austrian law, this means that the applicant must

596. KOG 11.5.2017, 16 Ok 8/16m – *Amtshilfe (Hausdurchsuchung).*
597. KOG 16.6.2016, 16 Ok 6/16t – *Trockenbau I (Hausdurchsuchung).*
598. RIS-Justiz RS0127268; KOG 6.5.2014, 16 Ok 3/14 – *Online-Fahrradhandel (Hausdurchsuchung).*
599. Claudia Hainz-Sator, '§ 48 KartG' para. 7, in: Alexander Petsche, Franz Urlesberger & Claudine Vartian (eds), *Kartellgesetz 2005* (2d ed., Manz 2016).
600. KOG 16.7.2008, 16 Ok 3/08 – *Sägerundholz I. See also* § 387(3) Exekutionsordnung (EO; Execution Act), RGBl 1896/79 as amended.
601. KOG 11.10.2012, 16 Ok 1/12 – *ÖBB/Westbahn II*; KOG 16.7.2008, 16 Ok 6/08 – *Asterix bei den Olympischen Spielen.*
602. KOG 25.3.2009, 16 Ok 2, 3/09 – *Sägerundholz II.*

plausibly ('glaubhaft') show that the infringement occurred.[603] Only means of certification that are readily available may be relied upon.[604] Before issuing an interlocutory injunction, the Cartel Court must hear the defendant (§ 48(2) KartG). An appeal against an interlocutory injunction does not have a suspensory effect, although the opposing party can apply for such an effect when appealing the decision. When deciding upon the suspensory effect, the Cartel Court must take into account all interests concerned.

503. An interlocutory injunction based on § 48 KartG must contain the following elements:

- the object of protection, e.g., the disputed right (§ 381 no 2 EO);
- the means by which the right is secured (§ 382 EO);
- the period during which the injunction is applicable; and
- the period during which the injunction must be complied with.[605]

504. An interlocutory injunction issued by the Cartel Court constitutes an enforcement title (§ 34(1) KartG).

505. The Cartel Court's decision to issue an interlocutory injunction can be appealed within fourteen days (§ 49(2) KartG). As stated above, an appeal does not in itself have any suspensory effect.

506. If an interlocutory injunction is granted but later revoked on appeal, the party that was subject to the injunction cannot obtain damages from the other party. While such a rule exists under general Austrian enforcement rules,[606] the Supreme Cartel Court has ruled that this provision does not apply to competition law, as it would severely affect the public interest in antitrust enforcement.[607]

507. Where a competition law breach involves the FWBG, an interlocutory injunction can also be based on § 7(4) FWBG. That provision states that, in order to prevent imminent irreparable harm, the Cartel Court may be asked to issue an interlocutory injunction or a provisional order. It also contains the rule that the defendant must be heard before such an injunction is issued, and that an appeal does not have any suspensory effect unless such an effect is specifically granted.

603. On this *see also* § 274 ZPO (but note that this provision applies to civil proceedings, while competition law claims before the Cartel Court are led in non-contentious proceedings).
604. KOG 26.2.1996, 16 Ok 1/96 – *Power-Pack I*; KOG 1.7.2002, 16 Ok 5/02 – *Village Cinemas*; KOG 16.12.2002, 16 Ok 11/02 – *Red Bull*.
605. Sabine Völkl-Torggler, Iris Ingemarsson & Ludwig Majer, *Das Verfahren vor dem Kartellgericht* para. 381 (3d ed., Verlag Österreich 2023).
606. § 394 EO.
607. KOG 15.12.2003, 16 Ok 9/03 – *Power Pack IV*.

III. Decisions on the Termination and Finding of an Infringement

508. § 26 KartG concerns the termination of infringements. The Cartel Court needs to order the termination of an infringement related to the rules contained in §§ 1 to 25 KartG and Articles 101 and 102 TFEU and impose the necessary remedies in order to bring that infringement to an end. The remedies imposed may not be disproportionate in relation to the infringement. In particular, the provision foresees that structural remedies may only be imposed where no equally efficient but less intrusive remedy is at the Court's disposal.[608]

509. In order to make an application under § 26 KartG, that infringement must still be ongoing at the time at which the Court's decision is taken.[609] An application can neither be brought where an infringement has ceased[610] nor in order to prevent an infringement from occurring in the future.[611]

510. The Cartel Court can grant the party a deadline by which it must comply with the remedies imposed.[612]

511. In case an infringement of §§ 1 to 25 KartG or of Articles 101 and 102 TFEU has already been brought to an end, the Cartel Court may nevertheless issue a declaratory finding that such an infringement existed in the past where there is a legitimate interest in this decision (§ 28 KartG). Such an application can be combined with an application for the imposition of a fine by the official parties.[613]

512. A private party has a legitimate interest in making an application to the Cartel Court where the behaviour giving rise to the application has a direct legal effect on the legal position of the applicant or is directly capable of affecting the applicant's economic position.[614] It is not entirely clear how the legitimate interest under § 28 KartG relates to the legal or economic interest required for a private party's right to make an application under § 36(4) KartG.[615]

513. An official party has a legitimate interest pursuant to § 28(1) KartG where it may subsequently request the imposition of a fine under § 29 KartG.[616]

608. Emphasising structural remedies as an ultima ratio, *see also* KOG 4.4.2005, 16 Ok 20/04 – *Multiplex I.*
609. *See* KOG 6.9.2017, 16 Ok 10/16f – *BWB/Semperit*; KOG 16.9.2014, 16 Ok 13/13 – *Linz Strom.*
610. KOG 8.10.2008, 16 Ok 8/08 – *Aufzugs- und Fahrtreppenkartell II.*
611. KOG 19.1.2009, 16 Ok 13/08 – *Telekom 'KombiPaket'.*
612. KOG 12.7.2018, 16 Ok 1/18k – *Fachverband Reisebüros/Lufthansa.*
613. KOG 12.9.2007, 16 Ok 4/07 – *Bankomatvertrag III.*
614. KOG 27.2.2006, 16 Ok 1/06 – *OÖ Verkehrsverbund.*
615. KOG 8.10.2008, 16 Ok 8/08 – *Aufzugs- und Fahrtreppenkartell II.*
616. KOG 12.9.2007, 16 Ok 4/07 – *Bankomatvertrag III.*

514. A legitimate interest is also deemed to exist where such a finding should be made against a successful leniency applicant (§ 28(1a) no 1 KartG). Should the Federal Competition Authority request that the Cartel Court impose a fine on a company that is party to an anti-competitive agreement in which the leniency applicant also participated, then it files an application for a declaratory decision under § 28(1a) no 1 KartG against the leniency applicant that benefits from the leniency programme. This allows the Cartel Court to declare that an infringement took place, even if said infringement has already been brought to an end and will not be subject to a fine.

515. A legitimate interest by a private party is further deemed to exist where such a declaratory decision by the Cartel Court is requested in order to claim damages for an infringement (§ 28(1a) no 2 KartG). No such legitimate interest is deemed to exist where the Cartel Court has already adopted a decision to bring such an infringement to an end, has imposed a fine or has found such an infringement, or legal proceedings to these effects are pending in this respect.

516. The Cartel Court can be requested to decide whether the KartG applies to a specific case (§ 28(2) KartG), e.g., in the case of uncertainty regarding the notification requirements for a merger.

517. Non-appealable decisions by the Cartel Court or the Supreme Cartel Court, including settlements reached before these courts, represent enforcement titles (§ 34(1) KartG).

518. Where the Cartel Court or the Supreme Cartel Court has decided on the termination of an infringement pursuant to §§ 5, 6 KartG, this does not only permit the applicant to ask for the grant of the execution but also any company that is subject to the same abuse (§ 34(2) KartG).

IV. Commitment Decisions

519. The Cartel Court can render commitments made by undertakings binding rather than adopting a decision ordering the termination of an infringement under § 26 KartG (§ 27 KartG). It may only do so if it is likely that the commitments offered exclude future infringements, and after taking into consideration statements made by market participants ('market testing' of commitments).

520. The Supreme Cartel Court has accepted that it is a company's legitimate concern not to make any commitments that go further than the company's legal obligations do.[617]

617. KOG 8.10.2008, 16 Ok 9/08 – *Haftungsverbund IV*.

521. Commitments have, in the past, included the modalities of an exclusive distribution system,[618] specific modalities regarding the distribution of films to cinemas,[619] or restrictions of non-compete clauses.[620]

522. If commitments have been rendered binding, the proceedings may be reopened where there has been a material change in a significant fact on which the decision was based, where a company concerned does not comply with its commitments, or where the decision was based on incomplete, incorrect or misleading information provided by the companies concerned (§ 27(2) KartG).

523. In merger control, different types of commitments by the parties are possible: under § 17(2) KartG, the notifying parties can make a commitment towards the official parties to respect certain restrictions or obligations in return for the official parties to waive their right to apply for review to the Cartel Court or to withdraw such a request in case they have already made one. In such a case, the merger may only be implemented if the notifying parties adhere to the commitments they have made to the official parties. These commitments, however, are not declared binding by the Cartel Court in a separate decision. On these, *see* further §§ 605 ff. below.

V. Fines and Periodic Penalty Payments

524. Only the two official parties – the Federal Competition Authority and the Federal Cartel Prosecutor – may apply for the imposition of fines or periodic penalty payments with the Cartel Court (§ 36(2) KartG).

525. As the Cartel Court may not impose a fine on an undertaking that is higher than what the official party has requested (§ 36(2) KartG), the way is paved for settlements with the official parties (on this, *see* §§ 465 ff. above).

526. Based on § 29(1) no 1 KartG and following an application by one of the two official parties, the Cartel Court can impose a fine of up to 10% of the undertaking's worldwide turnover of the previous year in the case of:

- an anti-competitive agreement (§ 1 KartG or Article 101 TFEU);
- an abuse of a dominant position (§ 2 KartG or Article 102 TFEU);
- a retaliatory measure (§ 6 KartG);
- gun jumping (§ 17 KartG);
- failure to comply with an obligation pursuant to § 16 KartG; or
- failure to comply with binding commitments (§ 27 KartG).

618. KG 10.10.2018, 128 Kt 4/18k – *Medizinprodukte*.
619. KG 9.5.2011, 26 Kt 2/08 – *Constantin Filmverleih*.
620. KG 28.3.2008, 26 Kt 22, 134/07 – *Konkurrenzverbot*.

527. The turnover on which the fine is based needs to be calculated according to § 22 KartG. It includes the turnover of any parent companies of undertakings involved in the infringement.

528. According to the Supreme Cartel Court, the 'preceding business year' that § 29(1) no 1 KartG refers to for calculating the fine is the business year in which the last acts of infringement took place.[621]

529. In two recent cases, the Federal Competition Authority applied for a fine with the Cartel Court after private applicants had been successful in abuse of dominance cases ('follow-on fines'): In *Peugeot*, the authority applied for a fine against the carmaker for anti-competitive clauses in its car dealer agreements (on this case, *see* § 368 of this monograph).[622] And in *Info.Mail*, it applied for a fine against the Austrian Post for discriminatory clauses in agreements for bulk mail delivery.[623]

530. Based on § 29(1) no 2 KartG and following an application by one of the two official parties, the Cartel Court can impose a fine of up to 1% of the undertaking's worldwide turnover of the previous year where the undertaking:

- does not comply with decisions of the Cartel Court under § 19(3) KartG, a decision to terminate an infringement of Articles 101 or 102 TFEU pursuant to § 26 KartG or an interlocutory injunction under § 48 KartG; or
- provides wrong or misleading information in the notification of a merger (§ 9 KartG).

531. In *PaperNet*, for instance, a fine of EUR 750,000 was imposed because of wrong and misleading information provided in the merger notification.[624]

532. Fines are imposed on undertakings (§ 29(2) KartG) within the meaning of competition law. This includes the undertakings that operated the undertakings involved in the infringement at the time of the infringement, operate them subsequently as their legal successors or continue their economic activities. The fine can also be imposed on parent companies forming part of the same economic entity as an undertaking involved in the infringement (§ 29(3) KartG).

---

621. KOG 17.5.2024, 16 Ok 7/23z – *Karmasin*, § 2.2.1. On this question, *see* Thomas Aldor, 'Zum Begriff des "vorausgegangenen Geschäftsjahrs" gemäß § 29 Abs 1 KartG' (2024) *Österreichische Zeitschrift für Kartellrecht* 98.
622. Bundeswettbewerbsbehörde, 'Tätigkeitsbericht 2023' p. 53 (June 2024).
623. Bundeswettbewerbsbehörde, 'Marktmachtmissbrauch: BWB stellt Antrag auf Verhängung einer angemessenen Geldbuße gegen die Österreichische Post AG' (2.2.2024) https://www.bwb.gv.at/news/detail/marktmachtmissbrauch-bwb-stellt-antrag-auf-verhaengung-einer-angemessenen-geldbusse-gegen-die-oesterreichische-post-ag last accessed 8.8.2024.
624. KG 18.10.2016, 29 Kt 14/15 & 29 Kt 15/16 – *Europapier/PaperNet III*.

533. Fines can also be imposed on associations of undertakings. In that case, the fine is calculated based on the sum of the total turnover of each member of the association active on the market affected by the infringement (§ 31(1) KartG). Each member is liable for no more than 10% of the turnover it made in the preceding year.

534. When imposing a fine, the Cartel Court must take into account the gravity and duration of the infringement, the degree to which the infringer enriched itself through the infringement, the undertaking's culpability and its economic performance (§ 30(1) KartG).

535. § 30(2) KartG notes two aggravating factors, namely that: (i) the Cartel Court already imposed a fine on that undertaking because of the same or a similar infringement or has made a finding of such infringement; or that (ii) the undertaking participated as author or instigator in an infringement committed by several undertakings or has played a leading role in such an infringement.

536. In contrast, § 30(3) KartG contains four mitigating factors, namely that the undertaking: (i) only participated in an infringement committed by several undertakings to a limited extent; (ii) terminated the infringement on its own initiative; (iii) significantly contributed to the investigation of an infringement; or (iv) partially or fully repaired harm caused by the infringement.

537. In *Schenker*, the Supreme Cartel Court referred some questions on fines in competition law cases to the CJEU in Luxembourg. The CJEU confirmed that a national court could not take into account as a mitigating factor that the undertaking concerned erred about the unlawfulness of its behaviour based on wrong legal advice.[625] Following this preliminary ruling, the Supreme Cartel Court emphasised that the criteria for deciding on the amount of a fine under § 30 KartG were not a closed list. According to the Court, factors to take into account when deciding on the amount of the fine should also include the geographic scope of the infringement, the undertaking's market share, the nature of the infringement, and the undertaking's role in the infringement.[626] The decision on the amount of the fine is, according to the Supreme Cartel Court, one in which the court has some discretion as it must take into account all relevant circumstances, including the legal and economic context.[627] In its *Spar* case, the Supreme Cartel Court clarified that the amount of the fine must be such as to serve the goal of deterrence.[628]

538. The fine imposed by the Cartel Court cannot be higher than what was requested by the official party (§ 36(2) KartG). However, the official parties are not

625. CJEU Case C-681/11 *Bundeswettbewerbsbehörde v. Schenker*, ECLI:EU:C:2013:404.
626. KOG 2.12.2013, 16 Ok 4/13 – *BWB/Schenker*; *see also* KOG 4.10.2010, 16 Ok 5/10 – *Druckchemikalien*.
627. RIS-Justiz RS0122743.
628. RIS-Justiz RS0130389; e.g., in KOG 8.10.2015, 16 Ok 2/15b & 16 Ok 8/15k – *Spar*; KOG 31.3.2016, 16 Ok 7/15p – *BWB/Kühne + Nagel*.

obliged to propose the extent of the fine, but can instead request an adequate fine.[629] On the adequate level of a fine, the Supreme Cartel Court has emphasised that the fine should take into account an infringer's entire economic performance. Therefore, it should be calculated based on an undertaking's global turnover (§ 22 KartG), rather than being restricted to the turnover that was related to the infringement of competition law.[630] In the *Spar* case, the Federal Competition Authority requested an adequate fine, which the Cartel Court set at EUR 3 million. On appeal, the Supreme Cartel Court increased that fine by a factor of ten, ultimately imposing a fine of EUR 30 million.[631] In *Hygiene Austria*, the Cartel Court's initial fine of EUR 5,000 for gun jumping was increased by a factor of twenty, to EUR 100,000.[632] And in *REWE*, the Cartel Court's initial fine of EUR 1.5 million for gun jumping was increased by a factor of nearly fourty-seven, to EUR 70 million.[633]

539. Competition law fines paid go to the Federal Administration (§ 32 KartG). An amount of EUR 1.5 million, however, shall every year be used for the objectives pursued by the Federal Competition Authority and the Austrian Consumer Information Association ('Verein für Konsumenteninformation').

540. In a recent case involving a sugar cartel that had already been fined in Germany, the Supreme Cartel Court submitted a request for a preliminary ruling to the CJEU, asking how to apply the *ne bis in idem* rule in the parallel application of national and EU competition law by competition authorities from different Member States.[634] In its preliminary ruling, the CJEU answered that parallel proceedings in different Member States relating to the same set of facts but different geographic territories are possible, but require certain coordination among the authorities.[635] When applying the preliminary ruling to the sugar cartel, the Supreme Cartel Court decided that the *ne bis in idem* principle did not bar the finding of a cartel agreement in this case.[636] Subsequently, the Cartel Court decided on the fine for one of the cartelists.[637]

629. KOG 21.1.2008, 16 Ok 8/07 – *Josef Manner.*
630. KOG 25.3.2009, 16 Ok 4/09 – *Industriechemikalien.* This differs from the European Commission's practice of calculating the fine based on the infringer's sales to which the infringement directly or indirectly relates in the relevant geographic area within the EEA; *see* European Commission, Guidelines on the method of setting fines imposed pursuant to Article 23(2)(a) of Regulation No 1/2003 [2006] OJ C210/2, para. 13.
631. KOG 8.10.2015, 16 Ok 2/15b & 16 Ok 8/15k – *Spar*; *see* on this Maximilian Diem, Luca Schicho, Sebastian Schmid & Anastasios Xeniadis, 'Geldbuße verzehnfacht: KOG bestätigt Unzulässigkeit und Schädlichkeit vertikaler Preisabsprachen und signalisiert höhere Geldbußen' (2015) *Österreichische Zeitschrift für Kartellrecht* 220.
632. KOG 16.10.2024, 16 Ok 4/24k – *Palmers (Hygiene Austria).*
633. KOG 28.1.2025, 16 Ok 5/24g – *REWE.*
634. KOG 12.3.2020, 16 Ok 2/19h – *ne bis in idem*; CJEU Case C-151/20 *Bundeswettbewerbsbehörde v. Nordzucker*, ECLI:EU:C:2022:203.
635. *See also* CJEU Case C-117/20 *bpost v. Autorité belge de la concurrence*, ECLI:EU:C:2022:202.
636. KOG 21.10.2022, 16 Ok 2/22p – *BWB/Südzucker.*
637. KG 13.9.2023, 27 Kt 9/22h – *Südzucker.*

541. Where a company does not comply with certain obligations under the KartG, the Cartel Court can impose periodic penalty payments on the said company until it complies (§ 35 KartG). The following are reasons for imposing such periodic penalty payments:

- failure to comply with a decision to terminate an infringement made under § 26 KartG;
- failure to comply with subsequent measures in merger proceedings under § 16 KartG;
- failure to comply with an interlocutory injunction under § 48 KartG;
- failure to comply with binding commitments under § 27 KartG;[638]
- failure to grant access to evidence available electronically at the premises to be searched; or
- failure to submit to the authority's official acts during a dawn raid.

542. The periodic penalty payment may amount to 5% of the average daily aggregate turnover of the preceding business year and is calculated from the date set in the decision. Once a company complies, the Cartel Court will fix the definitive amount of the periodic penalty payment (§ 35(2) KartG). Again, only the two official parties may request that the Cartel Court impose such periodic penalty payments (§ 36(2) KartG).

543. Where the official parties request the imposition of a periodic penalty payment, the Cartel Court is obliged to do so if all the requirements for said penalty payment are fulfilled. It therefore has no discretion as to whether to impose such a payment or not.[639]

VI. Publication of Decisions

544. The Federal Competition Authority must publish the fact that it or the Federal Cartel Prosecutor filed an application with the Cartel Court under §§ 26, 27, 28, 28a or 29 KartG on its website (§ 10b(2) WettbG).

545. Once the Cartel Court or, in appeal proceedings, the Supreme Cartel Court has rendered its final decision on an infringement (§§ 26 to 29 KartG) based on an application by the Federal Competition Authority or the Federal Cartel Prosecutor, and that decision has become binding, the Federal Competition Authority must publish said decision's ruling and the case number on its website (§ 10b(3) WettbG).[640] The names of the affected undertaking(s) and the relevant sector of the economy can

638. On commitments, *see* Stefan Krenn, 'Verpflichtungszusagen in Kartellverfahren' (2012) 23 *ecolex* 795.

639. As the Supreme Cartel Court has noted, in that sense § 35 KartG differs from Art. 24 of Regulation 1/2003, upon which the Austrian provision is modelled; KOG 30.3.2007, 16 Ok 3/07 – *Lebensmitteleinzelhandel II*.

640. *See* Bundeswettbewerbsbehörde, 'Entscheidungen' https://www.bwb.gv.at/kartelle_marktmachtmissbrauch/entscheidungen/ last accessed 8.8.2024.

also be published. This ability to 'name and shame' is specific to competition law. The court's final decision must also be published where no fine was imposed because of a leniency application (§ 11b(1) no 1a WettbG); this will then indicate that the Federal Competition Authority definitely refrains from filing an application to impose a fine in that leniency case.

546. § 37 KartG contains a similar provision: the Cartel Court needs to publish its final decisions on the termination of an infringement (§ 26 KartG), a declaratory finding of an infringement (§ 28 KartG) or of a dominant position (§ 28a KartG), the imposition of a fine (§ 29 KartG), applications to issue interlocutory injunctions (§ 48 KartG) or merger applications and measures (§§ 11, 16 KartG). It must do so in the searchable Edicts Archive.[641] The publication shall include data on the parties concerned and the main content of the decision including the sanctions imposed. The Cartel Court's obligation to publish its decisions does not extend to commitment decisions.

547. Trade secrets and the companies' legitimate interests shall be taken into account when the Cartel Court publishes a decision. In particular, the Court shall give the parties concerned the opportunity to specify the parts of the decision they want to be excluded from publication. The presiding judge decides on the version of the decision to be published (§ 37(2) KartG).

548. In their appeal or their response to an appeal, parties may designate those passages of the Cartel Court's decision that they wish to see excluded from the text that is reproduced in the Supreme Cartel Court's decision (§ 49(2a) KartG).

§4. Access to File

549. Persons who are not a party to the proceedings will only be granted access to the file of the Cartel Court if all the parties concerned agree (§ 39(2) KartG). This, of course, poses a significant obstacle to the access to file by private claimants that are considering the launch of a damages action, as they would usually require the consent of their future respondent.

550. With regard to the application of Articles 101 and 102 TFEU, the rule contained in § 39(2) KartG may no longer be applied, as it would make claims for damages based on an infringement of EU competition law practically impossible: even before the Damages Directive was adopted in 2014, the Cartel Court had sent a preliminary reference to the CJEU in the case of *Donau Chemie*, asking whether that Austrian provision might be precluded by European law, especially in light of the earlier *Pfleiderer* judgment. In *Pfleiderer*, the CJEU had concluded that under EU law, a party may very well be granted access to leniency documents. However, the court deciding upon such access must be able to weigh the interests protected under

641. *See* Justiz – Ediktsdatei, 'Entscheidungen des Kartellgerichts' https://edikte.justiz.gv.at/edikte/ek/ekedi17.nsf/suche!OpenForm&subf=e last accessed 8.8.2024.

EU law, in particular, the interests of the information voluntarily provided by the leniency applicant and the aggrieved party's interest in obtaining damages.[642] In *Donau Chemie*, the CJEU found that the rule foreseen in § 39(2) KartG was contrary to EU law, particularly the principle of effectiveness, as it does not afford the court the possibility to weight the interests at hand.[643] It may no longer be applied where an infringement of EU competition law is concerned.

551. While this issue should have been resolved by a change in the law,[644] it is currently in the hands of the court to apply the law in line with the *Donau Chemie* preliminary ruling. In that respect, the Supreme Cartel Court has ruled that not only can § 39(2) KartG no longer be applied where it concerns an infringement of EU competition law but that this also applies where the infringement of national Austrian competition law is at issue.[645] Where a question of access to the court file arises, the court must now examine the issue for each individual document, rather than categorically refusing access.[646]

552. On access to leniency statements and settlement submissions, § 39(2) KartG foresees that, apart from the official parties, only the undertaking concerned as a party to the proceedings may access these – and only so as to exercise its right to a fair hearing. Apart from this, the party concerned may only use information that it obtained from leniency statements and settlement submissions through its access to the file in proceedings on the splitting of a fine jointly and severally imposed on parties to a cartel.

642. Case C-360/09 *Pfleiderer v. Bundeskartellamt*, ECLI:EU:C:2011:389, paras 30–32.
643. Case C-536/11 *Bundeswettbewerbsbehörde v. Donau Chemie*, ECLI:EU:C:2013:366, paras 39, 49.
644. Dieter Thalhammer & Stefan Wartinger, 'Die Möglichkeit zur Akteineinsicht in kartellgerichtliche Verfahrensakten im Spannungsverhältnis zwischen Public und Private Enforcement' (2013) *Österreichische Zeitschrift für Kartellrecht* 143, 146. On this case, *see also* Stephan Polster & Iris Hammerschmid, 'Aktenzugang im österreichischen Kartellverfahren nach der Entscheidung *Donau Chemie*' (2013) *Österreichische Zeitschrift für Kartellrecht* 140.
645. KOG 28.11.2014, 16 Ok 10/14b – *Domestic Interchange Fee.*
646. KOG 28.11.2014, 16 Ok 10/14b – *Domestic Interchange Fee.*

Chapter 3. Notifications and Clearance Decisions in Merger Control

553. Over the past years, the Federal Competition Authority has received an increasing number of merger notifications, rising from 281 in 2013 to 495 in 2019. In 2020, 425 mergers were notified to the Authority; a decline for which the COVID-19 pandemic may be accountable. Considering the Federal Competition Authority's limited number of case handlers and the fact that it is also expected to enforce §§ 1 and 5 KartG as well as Articles 101 and 102 TFEU, as well as reviewing merger notifications it receives from the European Commission, this is a considerable number of cases.[647]

554. In January 2022, a second national turnover threshold was introduced into Austrian merger control, now requiring at least two of the undertakings involved in a merger to reach a domestic turnover in Austria of over EUR 1 million (§ 9(1) no 2 KartG). This has subsequently led to the expected drop in merger notifications, to 340 in 2022 and 294 in 2023, respectively. Of the 294 merger notifications in 2023, 270 were concluded because the time period of four or – if extended – six weeks within which the official parties can ask the Cartel Court to review a merger expired (§ 11(1) and (2) KartG) and the merger was thus allowed to go ahead. In 13 cases, the official parties actively refrained from submitting the case to the Cartel Court (§ 11(4) KartG). Two mergers were allowed to go ahead based on commitments.[648]

§1. Preliminary Filing Obligations

555. Where a concentration is deemed to constitute a merger within the meaning of § 7(1) or (2) KartG and either surpasses the turnover thresholds foreseen in § 9(1) or the transaction value threshold of § 9(4) KartG, it must be notified to the Federal Competition Authority before being implemented – unless the exemption of § 9(2) KartG applies or the intended concentration would have no (potential) effect on the Austrian market (§ 24(2) KartG).

556. As already detailed above (§§ 153 ff. of this monograph), § 7(1) KartG establishes what constitutes a concentration for the purposes of Austrian merger control. This includes direct and indirect control that can be exercised over an undertaking, including asset and share deals, as well as control through a managerial takeover. A fully functional joint venture is also considered to constitute a merger (§ 7(2) KartG), and the interpretation of that provision generally follows the European practice.[649] Corporate restructuring within a group of companies does not constitute a merger (§ 7(4) KartG), as it is regarded as a single economic entity for

---

647. *See* Bundeswettbewerbsbehörde, 'Tätigkeitsbericht 2020' pp. 42–44 (June 2021) https://www.bwb.gv.at/fileadmin/user_upload/Downloads/taetigkeitsbereich/BWB_Taetigkeitsbericht_2020_barrierefrei.pdf last accessed 8.8.2024.
648. Bundeswettbewerbsbehörde, 'Tätigkeitsbericht 2023' p. 63 (June 2024).
649. KOG 27.1.2014, 16 Ok 11/13 – *Morawa/Pressegroßvertrieb*. But note that Austrian merger control only applies to the creation of a new joint venture; *see* on this § 384 in this monograph.

the purposes of competition law, meaning that structural changes within that company would not affect its market power.[650]

557. Austrian merger control knows several special provisions for media mergers. § 8(1) KartG defines what constitutes a media merger for the purposes of Austrian merger control (*see* §§ 89, 157, 374, 553, 559 of this monograph). § 9(3) KartG sets out specific turnover thresholds for media mergers, while § 10(1) no 2 KartG and § 13 KartG provide substantive rules on the competition law assessment of a media merger, which must take media pluralism into account. Although it has been suggested that this may not be compatible with the one-stop-shop principle under EU merger control,[651] a media merger that comes within the jurisdiction of the European Commission because it reaches the turnover thresholds of Article 1(2) or Article 1(3) EUMR must in parallel be notified to the Federal Competition Authority so that the latter can make an assessment as to the concentration's compatibility with media pluralism.[652] In such a case, the Federal Competition Authority's assessment is limited to the aspect of media pluralism.

558. Where merging parties do not comply with the standstill obligation (§ 17(1) KartG), the Federal Competition Authority can apply for considerable fines amounting up to 10% of the previous year's turnover to be imposed by the Cartel Court (§ 29(1) no 1a KartG), in addition to the sanction that any contracts violating the standstill obligation are null and void as per § 17(3) KartG. In 2021, technology company Meta had to pay a fine of EUR 9.6 million for acquiring GIF library Giphy without notifying the acquisition to the Federal Competition Authority.[653]

I. Criteria and Thresholds

559. The European Union's Merger Regulation contains a one-stop-shop rule according to which any concentrations that reach one of the two turnover thresholds of that Regulation have a Union dimension (Article 21 EUMR). The European Commission is exclusively competent to assess mergers with such a Union dimension. Mergers that do not have a Union dimension may be assessed under national merger regimes, such as the Austrian one. While both merger regimes are based on turnover as a starting point,[654] an additional starting point was recently added to Austrian merger control, namely that of the transaction's value.

650. KOG 10.3.2003, 16 Ok 20/02 – *Postbus*.
651. Josef Drexl, 'Competition Law in Media Markets and Its Contribution to Democracy: A Global Perspective' (2015) 38 *World Competition* 367, 381–382; Stefan Holzweber & Christine Dietz, 'Einführung' para. 34, in: Stefan Holzweber & Christine Dietz (eds), *Fusionskontolle in Österreich: Kommentar zu §§ 7 – 24 KartG* (LexisNexis 2024). *See*, however, Art. 21(4) EUMR; Heinrich Kühnert, '§ 7 KartG' para. 32, in: Alexander Egger & Natalie Harsdorf-Borsch (eds), *Kartellrecht – Kommentar* (Linde 2022).
652. Axel Reidlinger & Isabella Hartung, *Das österreichische Kartellrecht: Ein Handbuch für Praktiker* 192, 205 (5th ed., Linde 2024). The problematic nature of the Austrian view on a parallel notification requirement is also noted by these authors.
653. KG 22.7.2021, 28 Kt 6/21y – *Meta/Giphy (gun jumping)*.
654. KOG 27.6.2013, 16 Ok 2/13 – *Schenker/DB Mobility II*.

560. § 9 KartG contains the Austrian thresholds that are relevant for the notification of a merger. Under § 9(1) KartG, to trigger Austrian merger control the turnover of the undertakings concerned in the preceding business year must amount to:

(a) an aggregate worldwide turnover exceeding EUR 300 million;
(b) an aggregate Austrian turnover exceeding EUR 30 million, with at least two undertakings concerned each exceeding a turnover of EUR 1 million in Austria; and
(c) an individual worldwide turnover exceeding EUR 5 million for at least two of the merging undertakings.

561. § 9(2) KartG foresees an exemption from the notification requirement as foreseen in § 9(1) KartG for undertakings that, in the preceding business year, achieved the following turnovers:

1. only one of the undertakings concerned achieved, on the domestic market, a turnover exceeding EUR 5 million; and
2. the combined aggregate worldwide turnover of the other undertakings concerned does not exceed EUR 30 million.

562. The Federal Minister of Justice can issue a regulation stating that sales revenues achieved on a specific market have to be multiplied by a specific factor when applying the turnover threshold of § 9(1) KartG and the exemption foreseen in § 9(2) KartG (§ 18(1) KartG). This provision shall apply if mergers on specific markets are thought to adversely affect competition despite low turnovers. To date, no such regulation has been adopted.

563. As stated above (§ 553 of this monograph), the KartG contains special provisions on media mergers. The merger between the only two active press wholesalers in Austria, for instance, was held to constitute a media merger within the meaning of § 8(1) no 2 KartG.[655] § 9(3) KartG foresees that the turnover of media companies and media services needs to be multiplied by a factor of 200 when applying the turnover thresholds under § 9(1) nos 1 and 2 and § 9(2) no 2 KartG. This provision intends to allow for a closer scrutiny of concentrations that might have a negative impact on media pluralism.[656] For the worldwide turnover foreseen in § 9(1) no 3 KartG and the turnover exemption of EUR 5 million foreseen in § 9(2) no 1 KartG, the turnover is not multiplied. Where media support companies are concerned, their turnover must be multiplied by a factor of 20.

564. Introduced in 2017, § 9(4) KartG contains an additional transaction value threshold. Even if a merger does not reach the turnover-based thresholds foreseen in § 9(1) KartG, the merger must be notified if the following four conditions are met:

---

655. KOG 27.1.2014, 16 Ok 11/13 – *Morawa/Pressegroßvertrieb.*
656. KG 19.11.2013, 27 Kt 140/13 – *Agrofert/Ecopress.*

1. the undertakings concerned achieved an aggregate worldwide turnover of more than EUR 300 million in the last business year preceding the transaction;
2. the undertakings concerned achieved an aggregate domestic turnover of more than EUR 15 million in the last business year preceding the transaction;
3. the value of the transaction is more than EUR 200 million; and
4. the undertaking to be acquired is active to a large extent on the domestic market.

565. In order to provide companies with guidance on how to apply the new transaction value-based threshold in § 9(4) KartG, the Austrian Federal Competition Authority and the German Federal Cartel Office (Bundeskartellamt) jointly developed guidance on this question.[657] The reason for this joint effort lies in the fact that the Austrian and German legislators adopted similar provisions on a new transaction value threshold in 2017,[658] prompting the two competition authorities to cooperate in providing this guidance. The guidance contains explanations on how to assess the transaction value and what constitutes substantial domestic operations.

566. The turnover and transaction value thresholds in § 9(1) and § 9(4) KartG are meant to establish when Austria has jurisdiction over a merger, thereby implementing the effects doctrine (§ 24(2) KartG). The aim of the exemption provision in § 9(2) KartG, however, is to ensure that concentrations that do not have an appreciable effect on the Austrian market are not caught by merger control.[659] This is also the reason why § 9(4) no 4 KartG provides that the transaction value threshold only applies where the undertaking being acquired has significant economic activity on the Austrian market.

567. Further substantiating the effects doctrine of § 24(2) KartG as it applies to mergers, the Supreme Cartel Court has in individual cases assessed whether the concentration in question could have any effect on the Austrian market. In one case involving an Austrian bank's acquisition of a Czech and Slovak bank that had no turnover whatsoever in Austria, it found this not to be the case and therefore held that the concentration was not subject to Austrian merger control.[660] According to the Supreme Cartel Court, it was not the legislator's intention to subject Austrian companies' acquisitions on foreign markets to Austrian merger control where not even a potential effect on the Austrian market could be ascertained. § 9(2) KartG

657. Bundeswettbewerbsbehörde & Bundeskartellamt, 'Guidance on Transaction Value Thresholds for Mandatory Pre-merger Notification (Section 35 (1a) GWB and Section 9 (4) KartG)' (January 2022) https://www.bwb.gv.at/fileadmin/user_upload/Guidance_Transaction_Value_Thresholds_January_2022_final.pdf last accessed 8.8.2024. On the 2018 edition of that guidance, *see* Judith Feldner & Lukas Cavada, 'Der Leitfaden zur Transaktionswert-Schwelle' (2018) *Österreichische Zeitschrift für Kartellrecht* 174.
658. Kartell- und Wettbewerbsrechts-Änderungsgesetz 2017 (KaWeRÄG 2017), BGBl I 2017/56; Neuntes Gesetz zur Änderung des Gesetzes gegen Wettbewerbsbeschränkungen, dBGBl I 2017/1416.
659. KG 19.11.2013, 27 Kt 140/13 – *Agrofert/Ecopress.*
660. KOG 27.2.2006, 16 Ok 49/05 – *Erste Bank.*

had to be interpreted accordingly. This interpretation by the Supreme Cartel Court is also reinforced by the new transaction value threshold, which explicitly requires the target's significant activity on the Austrian market (§ 9(4) no 4 KartG; on this *see* immediately above), and by the second domestic turnover threshold (§ 9(1) no 2 KartG). The Federal Competition Authority has underlined that it would interpret any exceptions to the merger thresholds restrictively.[661]

568. Where the question of Austrian jurisdiction arises, and upon the application of a party, the Cartel Court can issue a declaratory decision on whether a concentration needs to be notified (§ 28(2) KartG). If this decision is in the affirmative, then the concentration needs to be notified to the Federal Competition Authority.

569. § 19(1) KartG contains three exemptions from the notification requirement. It provides that the Austrian merger control regime does not apply to the acquisition of shares in an undertaking:

1. if a credit institution acquires shares for the purpose of reselling them;
2. if a credit institution acquires the shares with a view to restructuring an undertaking in difficulty or securing claims against such undertaking;
3. if the shares are acquired exercising equity or capital financing business (§ 1(1) no 14 and 15 Banking Act)[662] or are otherwise acquired by an undertaking whose only purpose is to acquire shares in other undertakings as well as to manage such shares and resell them.

570. Where one of the exemptions under § 19(1) KartG applies, several restrictions must be observed; e.g., the acquirer may generally not exercise voting rights in respect of the shares in question and must usually dispose of the shares within one year of the acquisition.

II. Turnover Calculation

571. Because § 9 KartG relies on turnover as its main starting point, turnover calculation is of particular significance in order to establish jurisdiction for merger control. § 9(1) KartG speaks of the turnover of the 'undertakings concerned'. Depending on the structure of the concentration, this may be the entire turnover of the buyer and the target – e.g., in the case of an acquisition under § 7(1) no 1 and 2 KartG, or in the case of a share deal under § 7(1) no 3 KartG –[663] or it may only relate to the target's turnover in a certain branch of a company that is being

661. Bundeswettbewerbsbehörde, 'Inlandsauswirkungen von Zusammenschlüssen' https://www.bwb.gv.at/recht-publikationen/standpunkte/inlandsauswirkungen-von-zusammenschluessen last accessed 8.8.2024.
662. Bankwesengesetz (Banking Act), BGBl 1993/532 as amended.
663. KOG 30.5.2005, 16 Ok 16/04 – *Brau Union.*

acquired.[664] However, the turnover of the company that is about to sell a part of its business is not taken into consideration in its entirety.[665]

572. On the calculation of turnover involving minority shareholdings, the Cartel Court has held that the turnover of companies in which the undertakings concerned have a direct (yet minority) stake of at least 25% must be included in the turnover for the purposes of merger control, even if these minority stakes do not amount to control within the meaning of merger control. On any subsequent level, however, control is required in order to include the turnover.[666]

573. In its joint provisions, the KartG contains rules affecting turnover calculation when applying this Act (§ 22 KartG). This, of course, primarily affects merger control.

574. Based on § 22 no 1 KartG, undertakings that are affiliated with each other as set out in the definition of a merger (§ 7 KartG) are considered to constitute one single undertaking. This means that their internal sales are not added to the calculated turnover. However, this wide understanding of a company means that many company links will lead to the inclusion of a company's (entire) turnover in the calculation.[667]

575. § 22 no 2 KartG contains a specific provision on revenue items that are deemed substitutes for the turnover of credit institutions. § 22 no 3 KartG states that the revenue from premiums is relied upon in place of turnover for insurance undertakings.[668]

III. Market Share Calculation

576. § 21 KartG provides rules for the calculation of market shares. It states that market shares should be calculated for specific goods or services (§ 23 KartG), that undertakings affiliated with each other as set out in the definition of a merger (§ 7 KartG) are considered one single undertaking for the purpose of calculating market shares, and that foreign undertakings' market shares on the Austrian market are also taken into account.

577. While Austrian merger control previously relied on market share, this was changed to turnover in preparation for Austria's accession to the EU in 1995.[669] Nevertheless, the provision of § 21 KartG is relevant under merger control as the

664. Axel Reidlinger & Isabella Hartung, *Das österreichische Kartellrecht: Ein Handbuch für Praktiker* 195 (5th ed., Linde 2024).
665. KG 17.12.2004, 26 Kt 358/04 – *Gewista.*
666. KG 13.11.1996, 25 Kt 435/96 – *Berechnung der Umsatzerlöse, ecolex* 1997, 272.
667. KOG 9.12.1996, 16 Ok 6/96 – *Burgenland.*
668. *See also* Art. 5(3) EUMR on these sectors.
669. KOG 9.12.1996, 16 Ok 6/96 – *Burgenland*; Kartellgesetznovelle 1993, BGBl 1993/693.

notifying undertakings need to inform the Federal Competition Authority of the market shares they hold on the relevant markets (*see* § 10(1) no 1(b) KartG).

IV. Other Relevant Notions

578. Austria's system of merger control requires certain mergers to be notified to the Federal Competition Authority before being implemented. Parties to a merger are subject to a standstill obligation and may not implement their merger until the official parties have either refrained from submitting a request for examination to the Cartel Court or have not filed such a request within the set time limit (§ 17(1) KartG). While EU law foresees the possibility of the European Commission granting a derogation from the standstill obligation to merging parties under Article 7(3) EUMR, there is no possibility of obtaining such a derogation under the Austrian merger control regime.

579. If a merger is implemented before obtaining antitrust clearance, thereby contravening the standstill obligation, the merging parties risk a fine of up to 10% of the previous year's aggregate turnover under § 29(1) no 1:a KartG (*see* §§ 520 ff. of this monograph). According to the Supreme Cartel Court, a merger through which another undertaking is acquired is implemented within the meaning of § 17(1) KartG as soon as the buyer obtains the possibility of exercising control. It is not relevant at what point in time the buyer makes use of this possibility for the first time.[670]

580. In the case of *Castanea Rubra Assets* (2019), the Federal Competition Authority successfully asked the Cartel Court to impose a fine of EUR 100,000 on the undertaking for breaching the standstill obligation.[671] Further fines for breaching the standstill obligation were recently imposed on Hamburger (EUR 40,000)[672] – who was wrongly advised by lawyers that the concentration did not have to be notified in Austria – and KTM (EUR 60,000),[673] as well as on Meta (EUR 9.6 million)[674] and OneMed Holding (EUR 30,000).[675]

§2. Structure of Proceedings

581. Merger proceedings follow two phases: in Phase I, the Federal Competition Authority receives the notifying parties' merger notification and forwards it to the Federal Cartel Prosecutor. The official parties then have a four-week time frame

670. KOG 7.12.2017, 16 Ok 2/17f – *Anmeldepflicht.*
671. KG 13.2.2020, 25 Kt 2/19k – *Castanea Rubra Assets.*
672. KG 26.11.2015, 29 Kt 38/15 – *Hamburger/Peters.*
673. KG 1.10.2019, 26 Kt 5/19h – *BWB/KTM.*
674. KG 22.7.2021, 28 Kt 6/21y – *Meta/Giphy (gun jumping).*
675. KG 4.6.2021, 24 Kt 6/21v – *OneMed Holding/SMEDICO.*

within which they can apply for the Cartel Court to review the merger. Such a request triggers Phase II of the merger proceedings, which takes place before the Cartel Court.

I. Preliminary Assessment and Full Investigation

582. Before a merger is notified, the Federal Competition Authority encourages undertakings to enter into pre-notification talks in order to ensure that the merger proceedings can be carried out in a timely fashion. To this effect, it has issued guidance on pre-notification talks.[676]

583. Each company involved in a concentration may submit a merger notification (§ 10 KartG) to the Federal Competition Authority. This includes the target company,[677] but generally not the seller.[678] A merger notification initiates Phase I of the merger proceedings, taking place before the Federal Competition Authority.

584. The Supreme Cartel Court has held that merging parties may notify their (planned) concentration as soon as they seriously intend to implement it within a foreseeable period of time. In addition, they must have agreed – in principle – on how to structure the concentration and when to implement it.[679] In any case, a concentration must be notified before it is implemented (§ 17(1) KartG).

585. The notification requirements in § 10(1) KartG ensure that the Federal Competition Authority, to whom the notification is addressed, receives all relevant information in order to assess the merger from a competition law point of view. For this purpose, the notification must include:

1. exact and exhaustive information on circumstances which might create or strengthen a dominant position or might otherwise significantly impede effective competition, especially
   a) company structure, and in particular for each undertaking concerned information on
      – the ownership structure of the undertaking, including mergers as defined in § 7,
      – the turnover (quantities and revenues) achieved in the business year preceding the transaction, separately specifying certain goods and services as defined in § 23
   b) for each undertaking concerned information on the market shares it holds regarding the goods and services as specified in (a),
   c) the general market structure;

676. Bundeswettbewerbsbehörde, 'Guidance on pre-notification procedures in merger control' (February 2023) https://www.bwb.gv.at/fileadmin/user_upload/Leitfaden_Praenotifkationsverfahren_Barrierefrei_en.pdf last accessed 8.8.2024.
677. KOG 12.10.2016, 16 Ok 9/16h – *Novomatic/Casinos Austria I.*
678. KG 17.12.2004, 26 Kt 358/04 – *Gewista.*
679. KOG 23.6.1997, 16 Ok 4/97 – *Versicherungszusammenschluss.*

2. in case of a media merger, furthermore exact and exhaustive information on circumstances that might affect media pluralism.

586. The Federal Competition Authority immediately forwards merger notifications to the Federal Cartel Prosecutor (§ 10(6) WettbG; § 10(3) no 1 KartG). The Federal Competition Authority also publicly announces any merger notification, including the names of the merging parties, a brief description of the nature of the merger, which economic sector is affected and other relevant circumstances (§ 10(3) no 2 KartG). Within fourteen days of this publication, third undertakings whose legal or economic interests are affected by the merger may submit a written statement to the Federal Competition Authority and the Federal Cartel Prosecutor (§ 10(4) KartG).

587. At the time of notifying a merger, a lump sum fee of EUR 6,000 must be paid to the Federal Competition Authority (§ 10a(1) WettbG).

588. While the Federal Minister of Justice, in agreement with the Federal Minister for Economic Affairs, can issue regulations detailing the format and content of merger notifications (§ 10(2) KartG), no such regulation has been issued to date. However, the Federal Competition Authority has published a form for merger notifications that it urges notifying parties to use.[680]

589. Only the Federal Competition Authority or the Federal Cartel Prosecutor – as official parties – can ask the Cartel Court to review a notified merger ('Prüfungsantrag'; § 11 KartG). If such a request is made, then the Federal Competition Authority must publicly announce this without delay. Third parties cannot make such a request. The official parties' request triggers Phase II of the merger control procedure.

590. Should the merger notification not meet the requirements set out in § 10(1) and (2) KartG, it is for the Cartel Court – once it has been asked to review a merger – to order the notifying party to rectify the notification within an appropriate period of time (§ 43(1) KartG). Particularly where an incomplete merger notification nevertheless triggers the time limits for the Phase I investigation, the Federal Competition Authority may either directly request further information from the notifying parties or ask the Cartel Court to move to a Phase II investigation.[681]

591. In order to dissuade the two official parties from making a review request before the Cartel Court, the notifying parties can make a commitment towards them to respect certain restrictions or obligations in return for the official parties to waive their right to make a review request to the Cartel Court or to withdraw such a

680. Find this form at Bundeswettbewerbsbehörde, 'Formblatt für die Anmeldung von Zusammenschlüssen gemäß § 10 KartG' (2020) https://www.bwb.gv.at/fileadmin/user_upload/Formblatt_202010.docx last accessed 8.8.2024.

681. *See* Bundeswettbewerbsbehörde, 'Mangelhafte/unvollständige Anmeldung eines Zusammenschlusses – Vorgehen der Amtsparteien' (17.11.2011).

request in case they have already made one (§ 17(2) KartG). In such a case, the merger may only be implemented if the notifying parties adhere to the commitments they have made.

592. The Federal Competition Authority's investigation powers in merger proceedings are generally the same as under the antitrust provisions (§§ 11 ff. WettbG), including the power to request information and documents (§ 11a WettbG) or the possibility to request a search warrant with the Cartel Court to ascertain that the standstill obligation (§ 17 KartG) has not been breached (§ 12(1) KartG).

II. Time Framework

593. As stated above, a fee of EUR 6,000 needs to be paid to the Federal Competition Authority for each merger notification (§ 10a WettbG). The period of time within which the Federal Competition Authority or the Federal Cartel Prosecutor can file a request for review with the Cartel Act is only triggered once that lump sum has been paid; in any case, it does not start before the merger notification has been received.

594. The official parties must make their request for a review by the Cartel Court within four weeks from the receipt of the notification (or later if the notification fee has not been paid; § 11(1) KartG). This short time period of Phase I of the merger proceedings is justified by the notifying parties' need for clarity and legal certainty as concerns the implementation of their planned concentration.[682] As stated above, a request to the Cartel Court triggers Phase II of the merger proceedings.

595. The notifying party can request that the four-week period for Phase I of the investigation may be extended to six weeks (§ 11(1a) KartG). Once such a request for an extension is made, the Federal Competition Authority needs to transmit it to the Federal Cartel Prosecutor without delay.

596. The Competition Commission can make a well-founded written recommendation to the Federal Competition Authority on whether or not to file a request with the Cartel Court for the review of a notified merger (§ 17(1) WettbG). This recommendation must be received by the Federal Competition Authority at least one week before the deadline for filing such a request expires. Where the Federal Competition Authority does not file a review request despite the Competition Commission having issued a recommendation to that effect, the Federal Competition Authority must inform the Commission of its reasons for not filing said request. These reasons as well as the Commission's recommendation are published on the Federal Competition Authority's website while observing legal secrecy obligations (§ 17(4) WettbG).

682. KOG 10.3.2003, 16 Ok 2/03 – *Verbesserungsantrag.*

597. Even before the four- or six-week period of Phase I has lapsed, the official parties may waive their right to submit a request for a review by the Cartel Court (§ 11(4) KartG). If they have not waived that right but did not submit a request to the Cartel Court within the given time frame, they must inform the notifying party of this without delay.

598. If one of the official parties submits a review request to the Cartel Court, it thereby initiates Phase II of the merger proceedings. If the Cartel Court wants to prohibit the merger, it needs to do so within five months of receiving the request for review. If both official parties submit such a request, it is the first of the two that triggers the time limit. If the notifying party requests this, then the time frame can be extended to six months (§ 14(1) KartG). If this time limit has lapsed, or if the request for review is withdrawn, the Cartel Court needs to terminate its merger proceedings.

599. The Cartel Court's merger decision can be appealed before the Supreme Cartel Court. The Supreme Cartel Court needs to decide on the case within two months of receiving the court files (§ 14(2) KartG).

III. Right of Defence

600. As for antitrust proceedings, the rights of defence during the administrative merger investigation are limited, as the Federal Competition Authority does not adopt any substantive administrative decisions on the notified merger. Instead, it is an administrative authority charged with receiving merger notifications and reviewing those with a view to requesting a review by the Cartel Court. Before the Cartel Court, the rights of defence are safeguarded.

601. If the Federal Competition Authority intends to file an application with the Cartel Court requesting the termination of an infringement (§ 26 KartG) or the declaration that a prior infringement took place (§ 28 KartG), for instance, of the standstill obligation (§ 17 KartG), and if prior to this filing the Federal Competition Authority carried out investigations under § 11 WettbG (investigation), § 11a WettbG (request for information and submission of documents) or § 12 WettbG (search of premises), then it must afford the party concerned the opportunity to take note of the results of the investigation and to make a statement related to them within a reasonable period of time (§ 13(1) WettbG).

602. During Phase I, third parties whose legal or economic interests are affected by a notified merger can submit a written statement to the official parties within a timeframe of fourteen days counted from the publication of the merger notification (§ 10(4) KartG). No further third-party rights are associated with the submission of such a statement.

603. During Phase II, third parties whose legal or economic interests are affected by a merger that is being assessed by the Cartel Court can submit a written statement to the Cartel Court (§ 11(3) KartG). This does not give the intervener the status of a party to the merger proceedings. Through its intervention, the third party can therefore neither obtain the status of a party to the proceedings nor appeal the decision.[683] The Supreme Cartel Court applies this rule restrictively, as only parties whose legally protected position is directly influenced by a merger are admitted as parties to merger proceedings. This status does not apply to the seller of an undertaking.[684]

604. Where the Cartel Court has given conditional clearance to a merger, however, third parties may at a later stage bring a request before the Cartel Court asking it to enforce the clearance conditions (§ 36(4) in combination with § 16 no 2 KartG).

605. If a notifying party submits false or misleading information to the Federal Competition Authority in the merger notification, then a fine of up to 1% of the company's previous year's turnover may be imposed by the Cartel Court (§ 29(1) no 2:b KartG). If the standstill obligation (§ 17 KartG) is breached, then a fine of up to 10% of the company's previous year's turnover may be imposed by the Cartel Court (§ 29(1) no 1:a KartG). It is for the official parties to request the imposition of such a fine (§ 36(2) KartG). In recent years, considerable fines have been levied for gun jumping; most recently a fine of EUR 70 million on supermarket chain REWE.[685]

606. Where the Federal Competition Authority has carried out merger investigations but subsequently does not intend to file an application to the Cartel Court, it must inform the party concerned about this within a reasonable period of time (§ 13(2) WettbG).

§3. Clearance and Conditional Clearance

607. The Federal Competition Authority only has the power to ask the Cartel Court to review a merger; it does not adopt any substantive decision. §§ 12 and 13 KartG provide substantive guidance to the Cartel Court in its appraisal of a concentration.

608. By enabling the official parties to accept commitments in order to waive their right to request a review by the Cartel Court in Phase I, or in order to withdraw such a request in Phase II (§ 17(2) KartG), the KartG provides the official parties with some negotiating power for shaping notified concentrations that it regards as possibly anti-competitive.

683. *See* KOG 17.11.2003, 16 Ok 17/03 – *Tennisverband.*
684. KOG 29.5.2020, 16 Ok 2/20k – *Parteistellung Veräußerer.* On this, *see also* Anna Luger, Stefan Ruech & Anastasios Xeniadis, '(Kein) Veräußerer gesucht? – Zur Parteistellung des Veräußerers im Zusammenschlussverfahren' (2020) *Österreichische Zeitschrift für Kartellrecht* 179.
685. KOG 28.1.2025, 16 Ok 5/24g – *REWE.*

I. Conditions and Undertakings

A. Content

609. When requested to review a merger by the Federal Competition Authority or the Federal Cartel Prosecutor (Phase II), the Cartel Court can (§ 12(1) and (3) KartG):

- reject the request for a merger review because the merger is not subject to notification, either because it does not constitute a concentration within the meaning of the law (§ 7 KartG) or because it does not reach any of the applicable thresholds for notification (§ 9 KartG);
- prohibit the merger when it is likely that it will create or strengthen a dominant position within the meaning of § 4 KartG, or when it will otherwise significantly impede effective competition (SIEC);
- declare that the merger shall not be prohibited; or
- clear the merger subject to restrictions and conditions.

610. Where a merger is prohibited, the geographical reach of that prohibition has no limits. The Supreme Cartel Court does not regard this as an over-reach of the Austrian jurisdiction.[686]

611. § 12(2) KartG allows for some balancing in the substantive assessment of a merger: if the merger will improve competitive conditions that outweigh the disadvantages of market dominance, if the merger is necessary to maintain or improve the merging parties' international competitiveness and is economically justified, or if the merger's economic advantages significantly outweigh its disadvantages, then the Cartel Court may not prohibit a merger.

612. As mentioned above, undertakings whose legal or economic interests are affected by the notified merger can submit a written statement to the Cartel Court concerning the merger (§ 11(3) KartG).

613. In substantive terms, Austrian merger control now follows the European example and revolves around a significant impediment to effective competition (SIEC), with an emphasis on the creation or strengthening of a dominant position on a relevant market (§ 12(1) no 2 KartG). For the notion of a dominant position, the provision refers to § 4 KartG (on this notion, *see* above at §§ 121 ff. of this monograph). On the substantive assessment of a merger, *see* above at §§ 371 ff. of this monograph.

614. In the case of a media merger, the Cartel Court also needs to take into account whether the proposed merger is expected to be detrimental to media pluralism (§ 13 KartG). On media mergers, *see* §§ 89, 157, 374, 553, 559 and 553 of this monograph.

---

686. KOG 14.2.2005, 16 Ok 1/05 – *Lyocell*.

615. As set out above, the Cartel Court can, if it would otherwise prohibit a merger, attach restrictions or conditions to its clearance decision (§ 12(3) KartG). For instance, in a case involving press wholesalers, the Cartel Court required certain restrictions to be contained in the articles of association, as well as restrictions on access to data and terms and conditions.[687]

616. Regarding conditions, these can, for instance, relate to divestitures or behavioural commitments.[688] Such conditions have included the divestiture of parts of a business to third parties,[689] a non-discrimination commitment and an obligation to enter into a contract,[690] the commitment to continue operating a facility for a number of years,[691] or the commitment to ensure media pluralism through specified measures.[692] Where structural commitments are disproportionate, the Cartel Court will restrict itself to behavioural ones.[693]

617. It is the undertaking's responsibility to comply with the conditions imposed on it. Failure to do so – even if the responsibility of an individual employee – is imputed to the undertaking and might be relied upon by the official parties to apply for a fine for infringing the standstill obligation for conditional clearances (§ 17(2) KartG).[694]

618. Conditions and restrictions can also be agreed upon between the notifying parties and an official party, i.e., primarily the Federal Competition Authority (§ 17(2) KartG). Where such an agreement is reached, the official party that has previously applied for a merger review before the Cartel Court will usually withdraw its application (*see* § 36(5) KartG).

619. In order to counter possible competition concerns related to a notified merger, the merging parties can propose conditions or restrictions that the Cartel Court may then adopt under § 12(3) KartG. If competition concerns cannot be resolved, the notifying parties are free to abandon their merger plans and withdraw their notification at any stage.

620. § 12(3) KartG further gives the Cartel Court the possibility to change or lift restrictions and conditions imposed on merging parties, e.g., in the case that the circumstances significantly changed after such restrictions or conditions were imposed. Such a pronouncement by the Cartel Court requires a previous application

687. KG 5.8.2004, 26 Kt 132/04 – *Morawa/Mediaprint.*
688. Axel Reidlinger & Isabella Hartung, *Das österreichische Kartellrecht: Ein Handbuch für Praktiker* 219 (5th ed., Linde 2024); Franz Urlesberger, '§ 12 KartG' para. 91, in: Alexander Petsche, Franz Urlesberger & Claudine Vartian (eds), *Kartellgesetz 2005* (2d ed., Manz 2016).
689. KG 28.3.2018, 24 Kt 8/17g & 24 Kt 9/17d – *VTG Rail Assets/CIT Europe.*
690. KG 9.2.2016, 27 Kt 2, 3/16 – *UNIQA/Privatklinik Goldenes Kreuz.*
691. KG 24.2.2015, 26 Kt 73/14 – *Brau Union/Vereinigte Kärntner Brauereien.*
692. KG 16.4.2014, 27 Kt 164, 165/13 & 29 Kt 1, 2/14 – *Funke/News.*
693. KG 24.5.2004, 29 Kt 5/04 – *Agrana.*
694. For example, *see* KG 15.1.2015, 24 Kt 69/14 & 24 Kt 70/14 – *21 Centrale Partners/Ligier Group II.*

by the undertaking(s) concerned. For restrictions and conditions accepted by one of the official parties (§ 17(2) KartG), no such adaptation is foreseen in the law. However, it is generally assumed that the official parties may also waive certain restrictions or conditions.[695]

621. Even during Phase II of the merger proceedings, the Federal Competition Authority or the Federal Cartel Prosecutor may accept the parties' commitments to adhere to certain restrictions or obligations, and can then withdraw their review request before the Cartel Court (§ 14(1) KartG, § 17(2) KartG). This effectively ends any Phase II merger proceedings before the Cartel Court, as the latter can only decide based on an application (§ 36(1) KartG).

B. *Timing*

622. Once the official parties have requested a review of a merger by the Cartel Court, the Cartel Court must examine said merger within a time frame of five months, counted from the receipt of the request for examination (§ 14 KartG). Should both official parties make such a request, the time limit starts with the first such request. Within the five-month period, the notifying party may request that the time period be extended to six months.

623. In the case an appeal is lodged against the Cartel Court's merger decision, the Supreme Cartel Court must decide on the appeal within a short period of two months, counted from the receipt of the files (§ 14(2) KartG).

§4. Relations with Other Merger Control Authorities

I. Other Authorities Within the Local Jurisdiction

624. Should the Federal Competition Authority intend to declare that it will not file an application for the review of a merger with the Cartel Court or intend to withdraw such an application, it needs to grant the Federal Cartel Prosecutor the opportunity to give a statement (§ 10(5) WettbG). If the Competition Commission issued a recommendation in the merger proceedings concerned, the Competition Commission also needs to be afforded the opportunity to issue a statement.

625. In general, the European merger control regime and the EU Member States' national merger control regimes, both in procedural and substantive terms, are applied independently from one another.[696]

695. Franz Urlesberger, '§ 12 KartG' para. 79, in: Alexander Petsche, Franz Urlesberger & Claudine Vartian (eds), *Kartellgesetz 2005* (2d ed., Manz 2016); Raoul Hoffer & Johannes Barbist, *Das neue Kartellrecht* 65 (3d ed., LexisNexis 2017).

696. KOG 17.12.2001, 16 Ok 10/01 – *W-Beteiligungsgesellschaft II.*

626. The EU's Merger Regulation foresees a cooperation mechanism between national competition authorities and the European Commission. In particular, national competition authorities such as the Federal Competition Authority may, under Article 22 EUMR, refer concentrations to the European Commission where the concentration does not have a Union dimension but affects trade between Member States and threatens to significantly affect competition. In the following cases, Austria made or joined a referral under Article 22 EUMR: [697] *Adobe/Figma*,[698] *Facebook/Kustomer*,[699] *MasterCard/Nets*,[700] *Johnson & Johnson/Tachosil*,[701] *Knauf/Armstrong*,[702] *Apple/Shazam*,[703] and *Omya/Huber PCC*.[704] In all these cases, the jurisdictional criteria under Austrian merger control were fulfilled.[705]

627. Parties to a notified concentration that would not have a Union dimension under Article 1 EUMR, but that may be subject to merger control in at least three EU Member States, can request that their merger be reviewed by the European Commission (Article 4(5) EUMR). This provision is regularly relied upon, for instance, in cases in which a company wants to benefit from the European Commission's one-stop-shop principle, the European turnover thresholds are not reached but the national turnover or transaction value thresholds are. One such case was the *Facebook/WhatsApp* merger of 2014.[706] Unless one of the national competition authorities competent to assess such a concentration disagrees, the merger is referred to the European Commission and national merger control provisions may no longer be applied. However, the European Commission can also refer mergers that were notified to it to national competition authorities, where it regards the latter as in a better position to assess the notified concentration (Article 9 EUMR).

II. International Coordination

628. The national competition authorities of the twenty-seven EU Member States as well as the European Commission cooperate within the European Competition Network (ECN). Although the ECN was established as a forum to discuss antitrust enforcement, the authorities also cooperate on issues regarding mergers.

697. Stefan Holzweber, David Von der Thannen & Christine Dietz, '§ 9 KartG' para. 5, in: Stefan Holzweber & Christine Dietz (eds), *Fusionskontolle in Österreich: Kommentar zu §§ 7 – 24 KartG* (LexisNexis 2024).
698. European Commission, Case M.11033 *Adobe/Figma*, abandoned on 18 Dec. 2023.
699. European Commission, Case M.10262 *Facebook/Kustomer* [2022] OJ C417/8.
700. European Commission, Case M.9744 *MasterCard/Nets* [2020] OJ C118/50.
701. European Commission, Case M.9547 *Johnson & Johnson/Tachosil* [2020] OJ C124/1.
702. European Commission, Case M.8832 *Knauf/Armstrong* [2020] OJ C130/1.
703. European Commission, Case M.8788 *Apple/Shazam* [2018] OJ C417/4.
704. European Commission, Case M.3796 *Omya/Huber PCC* [2007] OJ L72/24.
705. Stefan Holzweber, David Von der Thannen & Christine Dietz, '§ 9 KartG' para. 5, in: Stefan Holzweber & Christine Dietz (eds), *Fusionskontolle in Österreich: Kommentar zu §§ 7 – 24 KartG* (LexisNexis 2024).
706. European Commission, Case M.7217 *Facebook/WhatsApp* [2014] OJ C417/4, para. 1.

For this purpose, an EU Merger Working Group was established in 2010,[707] which has adopted best practices on cooperation and carried out an inquiry into the public interest regimes in merger control across the EU.[708] The members of the ECN also cooperate with the national competition authorities of the European Economic Area (EEA) and the European Free Trade Association (EFTA).[709]

707. European Competition Network, 'Cooperation in Merger Control' https://competition-policy.ec.europa.eu/mergers/ecn-merger-working-group_en last accessed 8.8.2024.
708. EU Merger Working Group, 'Best Practices on Cooperation between EU National Competition Authorities in Merger Review' (8.11.2011) https://www.bundeskartellamt.de/SharedDocs/Publikation/EN/Others/BestPractices-EUmergerWorkingGroup.pdf?__blob=publicationFile&v=2 last accessed 8.8.2024; EU Merger Working Group, 'Public Interest Regimes in the European Union – Differences and Similarities in Approach' (10.3.2016) https://competition-policy.ec.europa.eu/document/download/88217c31-0ef0-4a08-82f4-7c1b3fe31c70_en?filename=merger-working-group_public_interest_regimes_en.pdf last accessed 8.8.2024.
709. European Competition Authorities, 'The Exchange of Information Between Members on Multi-jurisdictional Mergers – Procedures Guide' https://competition-policy.ec.europa.eu/document/download/9c7cec32-55f0-43aa-ab12-17c1fae234bc_en?filename=european-competition-authorities_information_exchange_procedures_en.pdf last accessed 8.8.2024.

Chapter 4. Challenging the Court's Decision

§1. Competent Courts

629. In both antitrust proceedings and merger proceedings, the Cartel Court is the competent court (on this, *see* above at §§ 468 ff. and 585 ff. of this monograph). The Cartel Court publishes any final decisions relating to the termination of an infringement, a finding of an infringement, applications to issue interlocutory injunctions or applications relating to mergers (§ 37 KartG). Should the Cartel Court's decision be modified by the Supreme Cartel Court, the decision of the latter shall equally be published.

630. An appeal ('Rekurs') against the Cartel Court's decision is heard by the Supreme Court (Oberster Gerichtshof or OGH), acting as the Supreme Cartel Court (Kartellobergericht or KOG).

631. As for the Cartel Court (*see* § 473 of this monograph), the panels of the Supreme Cartel Court must be composed of professional judges as well as expert lay judges. The Supreme Cartel Court sits in panels of five judges, of which three are professional judges and two are expert lay judges (§ 59(1) no 2 KartG). A professional judge presides. Should a reinforced senate be called upon to decide a case, the panel consists of seven professional judges and two expert lay judges (§ 59(1) no 3 KartG). On the nomination of expert lay judges, *see* already above at § 474 of this monograph.

632. Where a party wishes to challenge the Federal Competition Authority's administrative decision ('Bescheid') on a request for information, the General Administrative Procedure Act applies to the administrative decision and the appeal of that decision. Such decision can be challenged before the Federal Administrative Court (§ 11a(6) WettbG).

§2. Time Limits

633. Where a party wishes to appeal a final decision issued by the Cartel Court, the time limit is four weeks upon receipt of the Cartel Court's decision (§ 49(2) KartG).

634. In the case of interlocutory injunctions, the presiding judge's decision on which part of the decision to publish (§ 37(2) KartG) or interim decisions, the appeal must be brought within fourteen days.

635. In each case, the opposing party is granted the same time frame to respond to the appeal.

§3. Scope of Judicial Review

636. The Cartel Court issues a decision ('Beschluss'), and the appeal that can be lodged against such a decision before the Supreme Cartel Court is called a 'Rekurs'. The rules of the Non-contentious Proceedings Act apply to appeals of the Cartel Court's decisions.[710]

637. The appeal generally has a suspensory effect.[711] The Supreme Court only reviews questions of law and not questions of fact. As a rule, this also applies when it acts as the Supreme Cartel Court.[712] However, § 49(3) KartG as amended in 2017 states that an appeal may also be based on the fact that the files raise significant doubt as to the correctness of the relevant facts upon which the Cartel Court based its decision. However, this should be limited to exceptional cases.[713] This was recently emphasised by the Supreme Cartel Court.[714]

710. Sabine Völkl-Torggler, Iris Ingemarsson & Ludwig Majer, *Das Verfahren vor dem Kartellgericht* paras 309 ff. (3d ed., Verlag Österreich 2023).
711. Sabine Völkl-Torggler, Iris Ingemarsson & Ludwig Majer, *Das Verfahren vor dem Kartellgericht* para. 309 (3d ed., Verlag Österreich 2023).
712. Established case law; *see* RIS-Justiz RS0123662.
713. Sabine Völkl-Torggler, Iris Ingemarsson & Ludwig Majer, *Das Verfahren vor dem Kartellgericht* paras 336–341 (3d ed., Verlag Österreich 2023). This does not apply to the appeal of an interlocutory injunction; *see* § 48(2) KartG.
714. KOG 11.11.2021, 16 Ok 3/21h – *Post.*

Selected Bibliography

Literature on Austrian Competition Law in English

Ablasser-Neuhuber, Astrid, Florian Neumayr, Gerhard Fussenegger & Sebastian Reiter, 'Austria', in: Frank L. Fine (ed.), *European Competition Laws*, vol 1 (loose-leaf, Matthew Bender Elite Products, release 21-11/2022), § 2

Robertson, Viktoria H.S.E. (ed.), *Kodex Competition Law* (Collection of legal materials, 3d ed., LexisNexis 2024)

Tautscher, Katja, Martin Abram & Bernhard Wychera, 'Austria', in: Marjorie Holmes & Lesley Davey (eds), *A Practical Guide to National Competition Rules Across Europe* (Kluwer Law International 2007), 39–67

Vartian, Claudine, 'Austria', in: Ioannis Kokkoris (ed.), *Competition Cases from the European Union: The Ultimate Guide to Leading Cases from the EU, Member States and EFTA* (2d ed., Sweet & Maxwell 2010), § 3

Wolf-Posch, Anna, Bernhard Kofler-Senoner & Michael Mayer, 'Austria', in: Nathalie Jalabert-Doury (ed.), *Competition Inspections in 25 Jurisdictions: A Practitioner's Guide* (2d ed., Concurrences 2024), 1–17

Literature on Austrian Competition Law in German

Becka, Marcus (ed.), *Wettbewerbs- und Kartellrecht* (Collection of legal materials, 7th ed., Linde 2024)

Brand, Michael, *Schadenersatz im Kartellrecht: Praxishandbuch Private Enforcement* (Linde 2017)

Egger, Alexander, & Natalie Harsdorf-Borsch (eds), *Kartellrecht – Kommentar* (Linde 2022)

Feldner, Judith, & Dieter Thalhammer, *Die Hausdurchsuchung im Kartellrecht* (Manz 2016)

Gruber, Johannes P., *Österreichisches Kartellrecht* (3d ed., Manz 2020)

Gugerbauer, Norbert, *Kartellgesetz und Wettbewerbsgesetz* (3d ed., Verlag Österreich 2017)

Hoffer, Raoul, & Johannes Barbist, *Das neue Kartellrecht* (3d ed., LexisNexis 2017)

Holzweber, Stefan, & Christine Dietz (eds), *Fusionskontolle in Österreich: Kommentar zu §§ 7 – 24 KartG* (LexisNexis 2024)

Koppensteiner, Hans-Georg, *Österreichisches und europäisches Wettbewerbsrecht* (3d ed., Orac 1997)

Petsche, Alexander, Franz Urlesberger & Claudine Vartian (eds), *Kartellgesetz 2005* (2d ed., Manz 2016)

Selected Bibliography

Reidlinger, Axel, & Isabella Hartung, *Das österreichische Kartellrecht: Ein Handbuch für Praktiker* (5th ed., Linde 2024)

Thyri, Peter, *Kartellrechtsvollzug in Österreich* (Manz 2007)

Völkl-Torggler, Sabine, Iris Ingemarsson & Ludwig Majer, *Das Verfahren vor dem Kartellgericht* (3d ed., Verlag Österreich 2023)

Wijckmans, Frank, Filip Tuytschaever, Moritz Lorenz & Andreas Zellhofer, *Vertriebsverträge im Kartellrecht: Deutsche, österreichische und unionsweite Rechtspraxis vertikaler Vereinbarungen* (C.H. Beck 2019)

Winner, Martin, & Stefan Holzweber, *Kartellrecht Skriptum* (3d ed., LexisNexis 2024)

Österreichische Zeitschrift für Kartellrecht / Austrian Journal for Competition Law, ISSN 2218-6271 [mainly containing contributions in German, but occasionally also in English]

Table of Cases

Court of Justice of the European Union

CJEU Case 26/62 *van Gend en Loos*, ECLI:EU:C:1963:1
CJEU Case 6/64 *Flaminio Costa v. ENEL*, ECLI:EU:C:1964:66
CJEU Joined Cases 56 & 58/64 *Consten and Grundig v. Commission*, ECLI:EU:C:1966:41
CJEU Case 56/65 *Société Technique Minière v. Maschinenbau Ulm*, ECLI:EU:C:1966:38
CJEU Case 14/68 *Walt Wilhelm v. Bundeskartellamt*, ECLI:EU:C:1969:4
CJEU Case 26/74 *Société Roquette Frères v. Commission*, ECLI:EU:C:1976:69
CJEU Case 26/76 *Metro v. Commission*, ECLI:EU:C:1977:167
CJEU Case 27/76 *United Brands v. Commission*, ECLI:EU:C:1978:22
CJEU Case 85/76 *Hoffmann-La Roche v. Commission*, ECLI:EU:C:1979:36
CJEU Case 155/79 *AM&S v. Commission*, ECLI:EU:C:1982:157
CJEU Case 322/81 *Michelin v. Commission (Michelin I)*, ECLI:EU:C:1983:313
CJEU Case C-62/86 *AKZO Chemie v. Commission*, ECLI:EU:C:1991:286
CJEU Case C-41/90 *Höfner & Elser v. Macrotron*, ECLI:EU:C:1991:161
CJEU Case C-364/92 *SAT Fluggesellschaft mbH v. Eurocontrol*, ECLI:EU:C:1994:7
CJEU Case C-7/97 *Oscar Bronner v. Mediaprint*, ECLI:EU:C:1998:569
CJEU Case C-453/99 *Courage v. Bernard Crehan*, ECLI:EU:C:2001:465
CJEU Case C-105/04 P *Nederlanske Federatieve Vereeniging voor de Groothandel op Elektrotechnisch Gebied v. Commission*, ECLI:EU:C:2006:592
CJEU Joined Cases C-295 to C-298/04 *Vincenzo Manfredi v. Lloyd Adriatico Assicurazioni and others*, ECLI:EU:C:2006:461
CJEU Case C-273/06 *Petschenig v. Toyota Frey Austria*, ECLI:EU:C:2007:66
CJEU Joined Cases C-125, C-133, C-135 & C-137/07 P *Erste Group Bank & others v. Commission*, ECLI:EU:C:2009:576
CJEU Case C-280/08 P *Deutsche Telekom v. Commission*, ECLI:EU:C:2010:603
CJEU Case C-360/09 *Pfleiderer v. Bundeskartellamt*, ECLI:EU:C:2011:389
CJEU Case C-32/11 *Allianz Hungária*, ECLI:EU:C:2013:160
CJEU Case C-138/11 *Compass-Datenbank GmbH v. Republik Österreich*, ECLI:EU:C:2012:449
CJEU Case C-226/11 *Expedia*, ECLI:EU:C:2012:795
CJEU Case C-536/11 *Bundeswettbewerbsbehörde v. Donau Chemie*, ECLI:EU:C:2013:366

CJEU Case C-681/11 *Bundeswettbewerbsbehörde v. Schenker*, ECLI:EU:C:2013:404
CJEU Case C-295/12 P *Telefónica v. Commission*, ECLI:EU:C:2014:2062
CJEU Case C-557/12 *Kone and others v. ÖBB-Infrastruktur*, ECLI:EU:C:2014:1317
CJEU Case C-67/13 P *Groupement des Cartes Bancaires*, ECLI:EU:C:2014:2204
CJEU Case C-352/13 *CDC Hydrogen Peroxide v. Akzo Nobel*, ECLI:EU:C:2015:335
CJEU Case C-172/14 *ING Pensii*, ECLI:EU:C:2015:484
CJEU Case C-194/14 P *AC-Treuhand v. Commission*, ECLI:EU:C:2015:717
CJEU Case C-413/14 *Intel v. Commission*, ECLI:EU:C:2017:632
CJEU Case C-248/16 *Austria Asphalt v. Bundeskartellanwalt*, ECLI:EU:C:2017:643
CJEU Case C-595/17 *Apple Sales International*, ECLI:EU:C:2018:854
CJEU Case C-637/17 *Cogeco Communications v. Sport TV Portugal*, ECLI:EU:C:2019:263
CJEU Case C-724/17 *Skanska Industrial Solutions*, ECLI:EU:C:2019:204
CJEU Case C-435/18 *Otis v. Land Oberösterreich*, ECLI:EU:C:2019:1069
CJEU Case C-451/18 *Tibor-Trans*, ECLI:EU:C:2019:635
CJEU Case C-59/19 *Wikingerhof v. Booking.com*, ECLI:EU:C:2020:950
CJEU Case C-882/19 *Sumal v. Mercedes Benz Trucks España*, ECLI:EU:C:2021:800
CJEU Case C-117/20 *bpost v. Autorité belge de la concurrence*, ECLI:EU:C:2022:202
CJEU Case C-151/20 *Bundeswettbewerbsbehörde v. Nordzucker*, ECLI:EU:C:2022:203
CJEU Case C-333/21 *European Superleague Company*, ECLI:EU:C:2023:1011
CJEU Case C-611/22 P *Illumina Grail v. European Commission*, ECLI:EU:C:2024:677.
CJEU Case C-2/23 *FL und KM Baugesellschaft and S* (pending) [2023] OJ C127/17

General Court

GC Case T-30/89 *Hilti v. Commission*, ECLI:EU:T:1991:70
GC Case T-219/99 *British Airways v. Commission*, ECLI:EU:T:2003:343
GC Joined Cases T-125 & T-253/03 *Akzo Nobel v. Commission*, ECLI:EU:T:2003:287
GC Case T-99/04 *AC-Treuhand v. Commission*, ECLI:EU:T:2008:256
GC Case T-321/05 *Astra Zeneca v. Commission*, ECLI:EU:T:2010:266

***Oberster Gerichtshof* (Supreme Court)**

OGH 11.3.1965, 9 Os 85/64 – *Strumpfverkaufsautomaten*
OGH 29.3.1967, 9 Os 66/66 – *Haushaltsgeräte*
OGH 2.4.1985, 4 Ob 395/84 – *Baedeker's Reiseführer*
OGH 9.9.1997, 4 Ob 214/97t – *Filmverleihgeschäft I*
OGH 17.3.1998, 4 Ob 62/98s – *Servicegutscheine*
OGH 30.6.1998, 4 Ob 165/98p – *Reparatur von Leasingfahrzeugen*

OGH 22.6.1999, 4 Ob 90/99k – *Jahresbonus*
OGH 12.4.2000, 4 Ob 62/00x – *Fiat II (SAV)*
OGH 25.10.2000, 3 Ob 296/99x – *Discothèque*
OGH 22.2.2001, 6 Ob 322/00x – *Tankstellenbelieferungsübereinkommen*
OGH 15.10.2002, 4 Ob 187/02g – *Alfa Romeo*
OGH 29.4.2003, 4 Ob 79/03a – *Ö3 Millionengewinnspiel*
OGH 8.4.2004, 4 Ob 23/08y – *Tageszeitung Ö*
OGH 27.2.2007, 1 Ob 1/07i – *Kreditkarte*
OGH 28.1.2009, 9 Ob 66/07g – *Reisen*
OGH 14.7.2009, 4 Ob 60/09s – *Anwaltssoftware*
OGH 20.10.2009, 4 Ob 119/09t – *Suzuki*
OGH 16.11.2009, 9 ObA 59/09f – *Tankstellenpächter I*
OGH 13.7.2010, 4 Ob 191/09f – *Telefonverzeichnis*
OGH 23.3.2011, 4 Ob 34/11w – *Treuebonus*
OGH 13.3.2012, 10 Ob 10/12m – *Bierbezugsvertrag III*
OGH 2.8.2012, 4 Ob 46/12m – *Bankomatvertrag IV*
OGH 18.2.2015, 2 Ob 22/14w – *Mengenreduktionsklausel (Erdgas)*
OGH 30.8.2016, 4 Ob 120/16z – *Libormanipulation*
OGH 26.4.2017, 1 Ob 39/17t – *Eintrittskarten*
OGH 12.8.2020, 4 Ob 117/20i – *Verfahrensunterbrechung*
OGH 21.10.2020, 9 Ob 86/19s – *Otis*

Kartellobergericht (Supreme Cartel Court)

KOG 14.6.1993, Okt 3/93 – *Werbung mit Preisherabsetzungen II*
KOG 14.12.1993, Okt 6/93 – *Transportbeton*
KOG 26.2.1996, 16 Ok 13/95 – *Wettbewerbsverbote*
KOG 26.2.1996, 16 Ok 1/96 – *Power-Pack I*
KOG 9.12.1996, 16 Ok 3/96 – *Kiesabbau*
KOG 9.12.1996, 16 Ok 5/96 – *UFH-System II*
KOG 9.12.1996, 16 Ok 6/96 – *Burgenland*
KOG 9.12.1996, 16 Ok 11/96 – *UFS-Sammelsystem*
KOG 9.12.1996, 16 Ok 9/96 – *Hauszustellungssystem I*
KOG 23.6.1997, 16 Ok 4/97 – *Versicherungszusammenschluss*
KOG 23.6.1997, 16 Ok 14/97 – *Preisliste 2*
KOG 17.12.1997, 16 Ok 21/97 – *Preisliste 1*
KOG 18.6.1998, 16 Ok 5/98 – *Power-Pack III*
KOG 1.3.1999, 16 Ok 1/99 – *One*
KOG 15.5.2000, 16 Ok 10/99 – *Wiener Zeitung*
KOG 15.5.2000, 16 Ok 1/00 – *Mobilfunktelefone*
KOG 15.5.2000, 16 Ok 2/00 – *Flughafenfunktaxizentrale*
KOG 15.5.2000, 16 Ok 4/00 – *Hauszustellungssystem III*
KOG 9.10.2000, 16 Ok 6/00 – *Abonnementpreise*
KOG 9.10.2000, 16 Ok 7/00 – *Zonentarifsystem*
KOG 9.10.2000, 16 Ok 8/00 – *Regionalpartnerverträge*
KOG 5.9.2001, 16 Ok 3/01 – *Hausbrieffachanlagen*
KOG 5.9.2001, 16 Ok 4/01 – *Steinbruch*
KOG 5.9.2001, 16 Ok 5/01 – *E. L. Depotkosmetik*

KOG 17.12.2001, 16 Ok 9/01 – *W-Beteiligungsgesellschaft I*
KOG 20.12.2001, 16 Ok 7 to 13/11 – *Polystyrolkartell I*
KOG 1.7.2002, 16 Ok 5/02 – *Village Cinemas*
KOG 16.12.2002, 16 Ok 9/02 – *O-GmbH & Co KG*
KOG 16.12.2002, 16 Ok 11/02 – *Red Bull*
KOG 10.3.2003, 16 Ok 2/03 – *Verbesserungsantrag*
KOG 17.11.2003, 16 Ok 11/03 – *Schnurlostelefon*
KOG 17.11.2003, 16 Ok 14/03 – *Verschleißerprovision*
KOG 17.11.2003, 16 Ok 17/03 – *Tennisverband*
KOG 23.6.2003, 16 Ok 4/03 – *K-Hit-Radio*
KOG 10.3.2003, 16 Ok 20/02 – *Postbus*
KOG 10.3.2003, 16 Ok 1/03 – *Belieferung mit Regionaldaten*
KOG 17.11.2003, 16 Ok 11/03 – *Schnurlostelefon*
KOG 15.12.2003, 16 Ok 9/03 – *Power Pack IV*
KOG 15.12.2003, 16 Ok 12/03 – *Gebietskrankenkasse I*
KOG 14.6.2004, 16 Ok 5/04 – *Gebietskrankenkasse II*
KOG 11.10.2004, 16 Ok 9/04 – *Nicht adressierte Massensendungen*
KOG 11.10.2004, 16 Ok 11/04 – *TikTak Freiminuten*
KOG 11.10.2004, 16 Ok 15/04 – *Presse-Großvertrieb*
KOG 20.12.2004, 16 Ok 12/04 – *TikTak-Tarife*
KOG 20V.12.2004, 16 Ok 17/04 – *Wärmedämmverbundsysteme*
KOGV 14.2.2005, 16 Ok 1/05 – *Lyocell*
KOVG 4.4.2005, 16 Ok 20/04 – *Multiplex I*
KVOG 30.5.2005, 16 Ok 16/04 – *Brau Union*
VKOG 30.5.2005, 16 Ok 8/05 – *Flugscheinverkauf*
KOG 30.5.2005, 16 Ok 10/05 – *Lebensmittelhandel*
KOG 20.12.2005, 16 Ok 45/05 – *Honorarordnung der Baumeister*
KOG 27.2.2006, 16 Ok 49/05 – *Erste Bank*
KOG 27.2.2006, 16 Ok 1/06 – *OÖ Verkehrsverbund*
KOG 26.6.2006, 16 Ok 51/05 – *Asphaltmischanlage II*
KOG 11.10.2006, 16 Ok 7, 8/06 – *Lebensmitteleinzelhandel I*
KOG 21.3.2007, 16 Ok 12/06 – *Haftungsverbund II*
KOG 21.3.2007, 16 Ok 1/07 – *Haftungsverbund III*
KOG 30.3.2007, 16 Ok 3/07 – *Lebensmitteleinzelhandel II*
KOG 12.9.2007, 16 Ok 4/07 – *Bankomatvertrag III*
KOG 21.1.2008, 16 Ok 8/07 – *Josef Manner*
KOG 16.7.2008, 16 Ok 3/08 – *Sägerundholz I*
KOG 16.7.2008, 16 Ok 4/08 – *Radreisen*
KOG 16.7.2008, 16 Ok 6/08 – *Asterix bei den Olympischen Spielen*
KOG 8.10.2008, 16 Ok 5/08 – *Aufzugs- und Fahrtreppenkartell I*
KOG 8.10.2008, 16 Ok 8/08 – *Aufzugs- und Fahrtreppenkartell II*
KOG 8.10.2008, 16 Ok 9/08 – *Haftungsverbund IV*
KOG 17.12.2008, 16 Ok 12/08 – *Private Equity-Ausnahme*
KOG 17.12.2008, 16 Ok 15/08 – *Gratiswochenzeitung*
KOG 19.1.2009, 16 Ok 13/08 – *Telekom 'KombiPaket'*
KOG 25.3.2009, 16 Ok 14/08 – *Radiusklausel II*
KOG 25.3.2009, 16 Ok 1/09 – *Radiusklausel III*

KOG 25.3.2009, 16 Ok 2, 3/09 – *Sägerundholz II*
KOG 25.3.2009, 16 Ok 4/09 – *Industriechemikalien*
KOG 15.7.2009, 16 Ok 6/09 – *Pressegrosso I*
KOG 1.12.2009, 16 Ok 10/09 – *Pressegrosso II*
KOG 19.4.2010, 16 Ok 2/10 – *Feuerwehrfahrzeuge II*
KOG 9.6.2010, 16 Ok 1/10 – *Sägerundholz IV*
KOG 4.10.2010, 16 Ok 5/10 – *Druckchemikalien*
KOG 4.10.2010, 16 Ok 6/10 – *Holzhandel I*
KOG 9.11.2011, 16 Ok 5/11 – *Brauereikartell*
KOG 12.12.2011, 16 Ok 8/10 – *Radiusklausel IV*
KOG 6.6.2012, 16 Ok 2/12 – *Polystyrolkartell II (Hausdurchsuchung)*
KOG 11.10.2012, 16 Ok 1/12 – *ÖBB/Westbahn II*
KOG 11.10.2012, 16 Ok 4/12 – *Firmenbuch II*
KOG 11.10.2012, 16 Ok 5/12 – *E-Mail-Verkehr (Hausdurchsuchung).*
KOG 5.3.2013, 16 Ok 1/13 – *unverbindlich empfohlene Verkaufspreise*
KOG 27.6.2013, 16 Ok 7/12 – *Taxi-App*
KOG 27.6.2013, 16 Ok 2/13 – *Schenker/DB Mobility II*
KOG 7.11.2013, 16 Ok 7/13 – *Sägeindustrie (Hausdurchsuchung)*
KOG 26.11.2013, 16 Ok 5/13 – *NÖM (Hausdurchsuchung)*
KOG 2.12.2013, 16 Ok 4/13 – *BWB/Schenker*
KOG 2.12.2013, 16 Ok 6/12 – *BWB/Wiener Wohnen*
KOG 27.1.2014, 16 Ok 11/13 – *Morawa/Pressegroßvertrieb*
KOG 14.2.2014, 16 Ok 8, 9/13 – *Brauereiwirtschaft (Hausdurchsuchung)*
KOG 6.5.2014, 16 Ok 3/14 – *Online-Fahrradhandel (Hausdurchsuchung)*
KOG 26.6.2014, 16 Ok 12/13 – *Sports Direct/Asics*
KOG 16.9.2014, 16 Ok 13/13 – *Linz Strom*
KOG 28.11.2014, 16 Ok 10/14b – *Domestic Interchange Fee*
KOG 8.10.2015, 16 Ok 3/15z – *VAMED/NRZ Rosenhügel*
KOG 8.10.2015, 16 Ok 6/15s – *Radiusklausel V*
KOG 11.6.2015, 16 Ok 8/14h – *Verteilerboxen in U-Bahn-Stationen II*
KOG 8.10.2015, 16 Ok 9/15g – *Verpackungen II*
KOG 8.10.2015, 16 Ok 2/15b & 16 Ok 8/15k – *Spar*
KOG 8.10.2015, 16 Ok 3/15z – *VAMED/NRZ Rosenhügel*
KOG 8.10.2015, 16 Ok 6/15s – *Radiusklausel V*
KOG 1.12.2015, 16 Ok 4/15x – *Flüssiggas II*
KOG 20.1.2016, 16 Ok 10/15d and others – *Mehlprodukte (Hausdurchsuchung)*
KOG 31.3.2016, 16 Ok 7/15p – *BWB/Kühne + Nagel*
KOG 31.3.2016, 16 Ok 1/16g – *Austria Asphalt I*
KOG 16.6.2016, 16 Ok 6/16t – *Trockenbau I (Hausdurchsuchung)*
KOG 7.7.2016, 16 Ok 5/16w – *UNIQA/Privatklinik Goldenes Kreuz*
KOG 12.10.2016, 16 Ok 9/16h – *Novomatic/Casinos Austria I*
KOG 7.12.2017, 16 Ok 2/17f – *Anmeldepflicht*
KOG 21.12.2016, 16 Ok 11/16b – *Novomatic/Casinos Austria II*
KOG 11.5.2017, 16 Ok 8/16m – *Amtshilfe (Hausdurchsuchung)*
KOG 7.7.2017, 16 Ok 1/17h – *Vergabeverfahren (Hausdurchsuchung)*
KOG 6.9.2017, 16 Ok 10/16f – *BWB/Semperit*
KOG 19.10.2017, 16 Ok 3/17b – *Austria Asphalt II*

KOG 12.7.2018, 16 Ok 1/18k – *Fachverband Reisebüros/Lufthansa*
KOG 12.3.2020, 16 Ok 1/20p – *Simulcrypt-Vereinbarung*
KOG 12.3.2020, 16 Ok 2/19h – *ne bis in idem*
KOG 29.5.2020, 16 Ok 2/20k – *Parteistellung Veräußerer*
KOG 17.2.2021, 16 Ok 4/20d – *Peugeot*
KOG 12.10.2021, 16 Ok 1/21i – *ASFINAG*
KOG 11.11.2021, 16 Ok 3/21h – *Post*
KOG 23.6.2022, 16 Ok 3/22k – *BWB/Facebook*
KOG 23.6.2022, 16 Ok 4/22g – *Meta/Giphy*
KOG 21.10.2022, 16 Ok 2/22p – *BWB/Südzucker*
KOG 30.11.2023, 16 Ok 4/23h – *Rewe*
KOG 25.5.2023, 16 Ok 6/22a – *AMATIC*
KOG 25.5.2023, 16 Ok 8/22w – *STRABAG*
KOG 17.5.2024, 16 Ok 7/23z – *Karmasin*
KOG 17.5.2024, 16 Ok 5/23f – *Meinungsforschungskartell*
KOG 16.10.2024, 16 Ok 4/24k – *Palmers (Hygiene Austria)*
KOG 28.1.2025, 16 Ok 5/24g – *REWE*

Kartellgericht (Cartel Court)

KG 1.7.1996, 26b Kt 630/95 – *Hauszustellungssystem II*
KG 13.11.1996, 25 Kt 435/96 – *Berechnung der Umsatzerlöse*
KG 14.5.2002, 29 Kt 554, 555/00 – *Telekom Austria Wintertarif*
KG 19.12.2002, 26 Kt 369, 370/96-74 – *Benetton*
KG 11.7.2003, 27 Kt 456, 498, 499/02 – *Abwicklung des Zahlungsverkehrs*
KG 1.10.2003, 29 Kt 206/03 – *Kühlgeräteaufbereitungsanlage*
KG 24.5.2004, 29 Kt 5/04 – *Agrana*
KG 17.6.2004, 29 Kt 90, 150/04 – *Wrigley*
KG 5.8.2004, 26 Kt 132/04 – *Morawa/Mediaprint*
KG 17.12.2004, 26 Kt 358/04 – *Gewista*
KG 28.10.2005, 25 Kt 34, 253, 36, 42, 249, 250, 30, 32, 29, 35, 251, 252/05 – *Grazer Fahrschulen*
KG 3.3.2008, 29 Kt 129/07 – *Intersnack/Kelly*
KG 28.3.2008, 26 Kt 22, 134/07 – *Konkurrenzverbot*
KG 9.5.2011, 26 Kt 2/08 – *Constantin Filmverleih*
KG 20.3.2013, 26 Kt 17, 18, 27, 28/07 – *Preisbindung*
KG 26.3.2013, 29 Kt 26/13-6 – *Philips Austria*
KG 13.5.2013, 25 Kt 29/13 – *BWB/REWE*
KG 19.9.2013, 25 Kt 33, 34/13 – *Morawa/Pressegroßvertrieb*
KG 19.11.2013, 27 Kt 140/13 – *Agrofert/Ecopress*
KG 16.4.2014, 27 Kt 164, 165/13 & 29 Kt 1, 2/14 – *Funke/News*
KG 15.1.2015, 24 Kt 69/14 & 24 Kt 70/14 – *21 Centrale Partners/Ligier Group II*
KG 23.1.2015, 25 Kt 7/09 – *Radiusklausel*
KG 24.2.2015, 26 Kt 73/14 – *Brau Union/Vereinigte Kärntner Brauereien*
KG 6.10.2015, 29 Kt 44, 45/15 – *Europapier/PaperNet I*
KG 26.11.2015, 29 Kt 38/15 – *Hamburger/Peters*
KG 9.2.2016, 27 Kt 2, 3/16 – *UNIQA/Privatklinik Goldenes Kreuz*
KG 3.3.2016, 26 Kt 2/16 – *BWB/Rauch Fruchtsäft*

KG 30.6.2016, 29 Kt 10/16m – *BWB/Spar (Brauereiprodukte)e*
KG 18.10.2016, 29 Kt 14/15 & 29 Kt 15/16 – *Europapier/PaperNet III*
KG 26.1.2017, 27 Kt 12/16 – *BWB/Wagner & Jüptner (Trockenbau)*
KG 19.4.2017, 26 Kt 13, 14/16 – *Gewista/Ankünder*
KG 27.6.2017, 128 Kt 1/17t – *BWB/Tüchler (Trockenbau)*
KG 29.6.2017, 26 Kt 10/16i – *Akustik-Blasch*
KG 22.9.2017, 128 Kt 3/17m – *BWB/E+H Trockenbau*
KG 9.11.2017, 24 Kt 7/16h – *BWB/3P Trockenbau.*
KG 6.12.2017, 27 Kt 13/16p – *Fachverband Reisebüros/Lufthansa*
KG 19.12.2017, 25 Kt 2/17g & 25 Kt 3/17d – *Insight Health/IQVIA*
KG 28.3.2018, 24 Kt 8/17g & 24 Kt 9/17d – *VTG Rail Assets/CIT Europe*
KG 29.8.2018, 26 Kt 2/18s – *BWB/Devolo Austria*
KG 12.9.2018, 25 Kt 6/18x – *BWB/TCH*
KG 10.10.2018, 128 Kt 4/18k – *Medizinprodukte*
KG 11.4.2019, 25 Kt 1/19p – *Anker*
KG 14.6.2019, 24 Kt 7/19p – *Bose*
KG 1.10.2019, 26 Kt 5/19h – *BWB/KTM*
KG 8.4.2020, 128 Kt 2/19t – *Specialized Europe*
KG 13.2.2020, 25 Kt 2/19k – *Castanea Rubra Assets*
KG 12.5.2020, 27 Kt 5/18i – *Peugeot*
KG 4.6.2021, 24 Kt 6/21v – *OneMed Holding/SMEDICO*
KG 26.6.2020, 25 Kt 3/20h – *Zodiac Pool Cleaning Europe*
KG 15.7.2021, 24 Kt 5/21d – *Fond of*
KG 22.7.2021, 28 Kt 6/21y – *Meta/Giphy (gun jumping)*
KG 21.10.2021, 27 Kt 12/21y – *STRABAG*
KG 7.2.2022, 28 Kt 8/21t & 28 Kt 9/21i – *Meta/Giphy*
KG 17.2.2022, 26 Kt 5/21m – *PORR*
KG 12.5.2022, 24 Kt 1/22k – *Kastner & Öhler*
KG 21.6.2022, 27 Kt 14/21t – *AMATIC/Österreichische Lotterien.*
KG 1.7.2022, 25 Kt 4/22h – *Thalia*
KG 20.10.2022, 27 Kt 12/21y-65 – *STRABAG*
KG 5.12.2022, 25 Kt 8/22x – *Georg Hausmann KG*
KG 27.3.2023, 25 Kt 10/22s – *Swietelsky*
KG 20.6.2023,127 Kt 3/23p – *Kostmann*
KG 13.9.2023, 27 Kt 9/22h – *Südzucker*

Other Authorities and Courts

Competition & Markets Authority, *Meta/Giphy* (ME/6891/20-II, 6.12.2021)
VwGH 22.4.2015, Ra 2014/04/0046–0051 – *Spar*
LG Graz, 17 R 91/07p
BG Graz-Ost, 4 C 463/06h
Competition Appeal Tribunal, *Meta/Giphy* [2022] CAT 26, 14.6.2022

European Commission

European Commission, Cases COMP/34.657 *Sammelrevers* & COMP/35.245–35.251 *Einzelreverse* [2000] OJ C162/25

Table of Cases

European Commission, Case COMP/37.906 *Internetbuchhandel* Commission Decision of 22 March 2002
European Commission, Case M.3796 *Omya/Huber PCC* [2007] OJ L72/24
European Commission, Case M.7217 *Facebook/WhatsApp* [2014] OJ C417/4
European Commission, Case M.8788 *Apple/Shazam* [2018] OJ C417/4
European Commission, Case M.8677 *Siemens/Alstom* [2019] OJ C300/14
European Commission, Case M.9744 *MasterCard/Nets* [2020] OJ C118/50
European Commission, Case M.9547 *Johnson & Johnson/Tachosil* [2020] OJ C124/1
European Commission, Case M.8832 *Knauf/Armstrong* [2020] OJ C130/1
European Commission, Case M.10262 *Facebook/Kustomer* [2022] OJ C417/8
European Commission, Case M.11033 *Adobe/Figma*, abandoned on 18 December 2023

Table of Legislation

European Union

Primary Law

Treaty of Accession of Austria, Finland and Sweden [1994] OJ C241/1
Agreement on the European Economic Area [1994] OJ L1/3
Charter of Fundamental Rights of the European Union [2016] OJ C202/389
Treaty on European Union (TEU) [2016] OJ C202/13
Treaty on the Functioning of the European Union (TFEU) [2016] OJ C202/47

Regulations

Council Regulation 2821/71/EEC of the Council of 20 December 1971 on application of Article 85 (3) of the Treaty to categories of agreements, decisions and concerted practices [1971] OJ L285/46 as amended

Council Regulation (EC) No 1/2003 of 16 December 2002 on the implementation of the rules on competition laid down in Articles 81 and 82 of the Treaty [2003] OJ L1/1

Council Regulation (EC) No 139/2004 of 20 January 2004 on the control of concentrations between undertakings (EUMR) [2004] OJ L24/1

Regulation (EU) No 1215/2012 of the European Parliament and of the Council of 12 December 2012 on jurisdiction and the recognition and enforcement of judgments in civil and commercial matters [2012] OJ L351/1

Regulation (EU) 2018/302 of the European Parliament and of the Council of 28 February 2018 on addressing unjustified geo-blocking and other forms of discrimination based on customers' nationality, place of residence or place of establishment within the internal market (Geoblocking Regulation) [2018] OJ L60 I/1

Regulation (EU) 2019/1150 of the European Parliament and of the Council of 20 June 2019 on promoting fairness and transparency for business users of online intermediation services (P2B Regulation) [2019] OJ L186/57

Regulation (EU) 2022/1925 of the European Parliament and of the Council of 14 September 2022 on contestable and fair markets in the digital sector (Digital Markets Act) [2022] OJ L265/1

Commission Regulations

Commission Regulation (EC) No 2790/1999 of 22 December 1999 on the application of Article 81(3) of the Treaty to categories of vertical agreements and concerted practices [1999] OJ L336/21

Commission Regulation (EU) No 461/2010 of 27 May 2010 on the application of Article 101(3) of the Treaty on the Functioning of the European Union to categories of vertical agreements and concerted practices in the motor vehicle sector [2010] OJ L129/52
Commission Regulation (EU) No 316/2014 of 21 March 2014 on the application of Article 101(3) of the Treaty on the Functioning of the European Union to categories of technology transfer agreements (TTBER) [2014] OJ L93/17
Commission Regulation (EU) No 702/2014 of 25 June 2014 declaring certain categories of aid in the agricultural and forestry sectors and in rural areas compatible with the internal market in application of Articles 107 and 108 of the Treaty on the Functioning of the European Union [2014] OJ L193/1
Commission Regulation (EU) 2022/720 of 10 May 2022 on the application of Article 101(3) of the Treaty on the Functioning of the European Union to categories of vertical agreements and concerted practices (VABER) [2022] OJ L134/4
Commission Regulation (EU) 2023/1066 of 1 June 2023 on the application of Article 101(3) of the Treaty on the Functioning of the European Union to certain categories of research and development agreements [2023] OJ L143/9
Commission Regulation (EU) 2023/1067 of 1 June 2023 on the application of Article 101(3) of the Treaty on the Functioning of the European Union to certain categories of specialisation agreements [2023] OJ L143/20

Directives

Directive 2014/104/EU of the European Parliament and of the Council of 26 November 2014 on certain rules governing actions for damages under national law for infringements of the competition law provisions of the Member States and of the European Union [2014] OJ L349/1
Directive (EU) 2019/1 of the European Parliament and of the Council of 11 December 2018 to empower the competition authorities of the Member States to be more effective enforcers and to ensure the proper functioning of the internal market (ECN+ Directive) [2019] OJ L11/3
Directive (EU) 2019/633 of the European Parliament and of the Council of 17 April 2019 on unfair trading practices in business-to-business relationships in the agricultural and food supply chain [2019] OJ L111/59
Directive (EU) 2020/1828 of the European Parliament and of the Council of 25 November 2020 on representative actions for the protection of the collective interests of consumers [2020] OJ L409/1

Austria

Aktiengesetz (AktG; Stock Corporation Act), BGBl 1965/98 as amended
Allgemeines Bürgerliches Gesetzbuch (ABGB; General Civil Code), JGS 1811/946 as amended
Allgemeines Verwaltungsverfahrensgesetz (AVG; General Administrative Procedure Act), BGBl 1991/51 as amended
Audiovisuelle Mediendienste-Gesetz (Audiovisual Media Services Act), BGBl I 2001/84 as amended
Außerstreitgesetz (AußStrG; Non-contentious Proceedings Act), BGBl I 2003/111 as amended

Bankwesengesetz (Banking Act), BGBl 1993/532 as amended
Bundes-Verfassungsgesetz (B-VG; Federal Constitutional Act), BGBl 1930/1 as amended
Bundesgesetz gegen den unlauteren Wettbewerb (UWG; Unfair Competition Act), BGBl 1923/531 as amended
Bundesgesetz gegen den unlauteren Wettbewerb (UWG; Unfair Competition Act), BGBl 1984/448 (recast) as amended
Eisenbahngesetz (Railway Act), BGBl 1957/60 as amended
Elektrizitätswirtschafts- und -organisationsgesetz 2010 (ElWOG; Electricity Industry and Organisation Act), BGBl I 2013/6 as amended
Energie-Control-Gesetz (Energy Control Act), BGBl I 2010/110 as amended
Exekutionsordnung (EO; Execution Act), RGBl 1896/79 as amended
Faire-Wettbewerbsbedingungen-Gesetz (FWBG; Fair Conditions of Competition Act), BGBl 1977/392 as amended
Flughafen-Bodenabfertigungsgesetz (Ground-Handling Services Act), BGBl I 1998/97 as amended
Gaswirtschaftsgesetz 2011 (GWG; Gas Industry Act), BGBl I 2011/107 as amended
Gesetz über die Einrichtung einer Bundeswettbewerbsbehörde (Wettbewerbsgesetz or WettbG; Competition Act), BGBl I 2002/62 as amended
Gesetz über Erwerbs- und Wirtschaftsgenossenschaften (Act Concerning Commercial and Industrial Cooperatives), RGBl 1873/70 as amended
GmbH-Gesetz (GmbHG; Limited Liability Company Act), RGBl 1906/58 as amended
Hofkanzleidekret vom 6. Juni 1838 über die Ungültigkeit von Verabredungen bei öffentlichen Versteigerungen (Court Chancellery Decree on the invalidity of agreements at public auctions), JGS 1838/277
Jurisdiktionsnorm (JN; Jurisdictional Norm), RGBl 1895/111 as amended
Kartellgesetz 1951 (Cartel Act 1951), BGBl 1951/173 as amended
Kartellgesetz 1972 (Cartel Act 1972), BGBl 1972/460 as amended
Kartellgesetz 1988 (Cartel Act 1988), BGBl 1988/600 as amended
Kartellgesetz 2005 (KartG; Cartel Act 2005), BGBl I 2005/61 as amended
Koalitionsgesetz (Coalition Act), RGBl 1870/3 as amended
KommAustria-Gesetz (Austrian Communications Authority Act), BGBl I 2001/32 as amended
Konvention zum Schutze der Menschenrechte und Grundfreiheiten (European Convention on Human Rights), BGBl 1958/210 as amended, and BGBl 1964/59 (constitutional rank)
Mediengesetz (Media Act), BGBl 1981/314 as amended
ORF-Gesetz, BGBl 1984/379 as amended
Postmarktgesetz (Post Market Act), BGBl I 2009/123 as amended
Privatradiogesetz (Private Radio Act), BGBl I 2001/20 as amended
Staatsgrundgesetz vom 21. December 1867 über die allgemeinen Rechte der Staatsbürger für die im Reichsrathe vertretenen Königreiche und Länder (Basic Constitutional Act), RGBl 1867/142 as amended
Strafgesetzbuch (StGB; Criminal Code), BGBl 1974/60 as amended
Strafgesetzbuch 1803 (Criminal Code), JGS 1803/626 as amended
Strafgesetzbuch 1852 (Criminal Code), RGBl 1852/122 as amended

Strafprozessordnung (StPO; Code of Criminal Procedure), BGBl 1975/631 as amended

Telekommunikationsgesetz 2003 (TKG; Telecommunications Act), BGBl I 2003/70 as amended

Unternehmensgesetzbuch (UGB; Commercial Law Act), dRGBl 1897/219 as amended

Verbandsklagen-Richtlinie-Umsetzungs-Novelle, BGBl I 2024/85

Verbandsverantwortlichkeitsgesetz (Law on the Responsibility of Associations), BGBl I 2005/151 as amended

Verbraucherbehörden-Kooperations-Gesetz (Law on Cooperation among Consumer Protection Authorities), BGBl I 2006/148 as amended

Vereinsgesetz 2002 (Associations Act), BGBl I 2002/66 as amended

Verwaltungsstrafgesetz 1991 (Administrative Penal Act), BGBl 1991/52 as amended

Zivilprozessordnung (ZPO; Code of Civil Procedure), RGBl 1895/113 as amended

Verordnung der Bundesministerin für Digitalisierung und Wirtschaftsstandort über die Zustellung und Vollstreckung im Europäischen Wettbewerbsnetz, BGBl II 2021/486

Verordnung der Bundesministerin für Digitalisierung und Wirtschaftsstandort über die Anwendung der Kronzeugenregelung des Wettbewerbsgesetzes, BGBl II 2021/487

Germany

Gesetz gegen Wettbewerbsbeschränkungen (GWB; Act against Restrictions of Competition), dBGBl I 2013/1750 as amended

Table of Soft Law Instruments

European Commission

European Commission, Notice on the definition of relevant market for the purposes of Community competition law (Market Definition Notice 1997) [1997] OJ C372/5

European Commission, Guidelines on the assessment of horizontal mergers under the Council Regulation on the control of concentrations between undertakings [2004] OJ C31/5

European Commission, Notice on co-operation within the Network of Competition Authorities [2004] OJ C101/43

European Commission, Commission Notice on restrictions directly related and necessary to concentrations [2005] OJ C56/24European Commission, Guidelines on the method of setting fines imposed pursuant to Article 23(2)(a) of Regulation No 1/2003 [2006] OJ C210/2

European Commission, Consolidated Jurisdictional Notice under Council Regulation (EC) No 139/2004 on the control of concentrations between undertakings [2008] OJ C95/1

European Commission, Guidelines on the assessment of non-horizontal mergers under the Council Regulation on the control of concentrations between undertakings [2008] OJ C265/6

European Commission, Notice on agreements of minor importance which do not appreciably restrict competition under Article 101(1) of the Treaty on the Functioning of the European Union (*De Minimis* Notice) [2014] OJ C291/1

European Commission, Guidance on the application of the referral mechanism set out in Article 22 of the Merger Regulation to certain categories of cases [2021] OJ C113/1

European Commission, Guidelines on Vertical Restraints [2022] OJ C248/1

European Commission, Guidelines on the applicability of Article 101 of the Treaty on the Functioning of the European Union to horizontal co-operation agreements [2023] OJ C259/1

European Commission, Notice on the definition of relevant market for the purposes of Union competition law (Market Definition Notice 2024) [2024] OJ C1645

Table of Soft Law Instruments

Federal Competition Authority[715]

Bundeswettbewerbsbehörde, Federal Competition Authority treatment of anonymous submissions (Behandlung anonymer Eingaben durch die BWB)
Bundeswettbewerbsbehörde, Issuance of waivers of investigation (Abgabe von Prüfungsverzichten)
Bundeswettbewerbsbehörde, Notification requirement for concentrations – turnover calculation at the time of the acquisition (Anmeldebedürftigkeit von Zusammenschlüssen – Umsatzberechnung zum Zeitpunkt des Erwerbs)
Bundeswettbewerbsbehörde, Withdrawal of a request for investigation following the withdrawal of a notification (Zurückziehung eines Prüfungsantrages infolge der Zurückziehung einer Anmeldung)
Bundeswettbewerbsbehörde, Defective/incomplete merger notifications – actions by the official parties (Mangelhafte/unvollständige Anmeldung eines Zusammenschlusses – Vorgehen der Amtsparteien) (2011)
Bundeswettbewerbsbehörde, Position on vertical price-fixing (Standpunkt zu vertikalen Preisbindungen) (2014)
Bundeswettbewerbsbehörde, Position on media cooperation on the radio broadcasting market (Standpunkt zu Medienkooperationen im Hörfunkmarkt) (2015)
Bundeswettbewerbsbehörde, Working Paper Competition Monitoring (Arbeitspapier Wettbewerbsmonitoring) (2015)
Bundeswettbewerbsbehörde, Position on motor vehicle distribution (Standpunkt zum KFZ-Vertrieb) (2016)
Bundeswettbewerbsbehörde, Position on funeral services (Standpunkt zum Bestattungswesen) (2018)
Bundeswettbewerbsbehörde, Position Paper on National and European Champions in Merger Control (Positionspapier zu nationalen und europäischen Champions in der Fusionskontrolle) (2019)
Bundeswettbewerbsbehörde, Position on questions on the applicability of the group exemption under competition law (Standpunkt zu Fragen der Anwendbarkeit des kartellrechtlichen Konzernprivilegs) (2020)
Bundeswettbewerbsbehörde, Position paper – macroeconomic effects of mergers in the context of the COVID-19 crisis (Standpunkt – Gesamtwirtschaftliche Auswirkungen von Zusammenschlüssen im Kontext der COVID-19 Krise) (2020)
Bundeswettbewerbsbehörde, Proposition Paper Digitalisation and Competition Law (Thesenpapier Digitalisierung und Wettbewerbsrecht) (2020)
Bundeswettbewerbsbehörde, Guidelines – merger control and insolvency proceedings (Leitfaden – Zusammenschlusskontrolle und Insolvenzverfahren) (2021)

---

715. The Federal Competition Authority's up-to-date guidance can be accessed at Bundeswettbewerbsbehörde, 'Standpunkte der BWB' https://www.bwb.gv.at/recht-publikationen/standpunkte last accessed 8.8.2024. Many of the position papers are also available in English: Bundeswettbewerbsbehörde, 'Standpoints' https://www.bwb.gv.at/en/factual_information/standpoints last accessed 8.8.2024. To make sure you always access the most up-to-date version, please refer to the authority's German language website. Guidance without a date was ranked above the rest of the guidance.

Bundeswettbewerbsbehörde, Fairness catalogue for companies – position paper for good business conduct (Fairnesskatalog für Unternehmen – Standpunkt für unternehmerisches Wohlverhalten) (2022)
Bundeswettbewerbsbehörde, Guidance on transaction value thresholds for mandatory pre-merger notification in Austria and Germany (Leitfaden zur neuen Transaktionswert-Schwelle in der Zusammenschlusskontrolle in Österreich und Deutschland) (2022)
Bundeswettbewerbsbehörde, Guidelines on dawn raids (Leitfaden zu Hausdurchsuchungen) (2022)
Bundeswettbewerbsbehörde, Guidelines on the Application of Sec. 2 para. 1 Cartel Act to Sustainability Cooperations – Sustainability Guidelines (Leitlinien zur Anwendung von § 2 Abs 1 KartG auf Nachhaltigkeitskooperationen – Nachhaltigkeits-LL) (2022)
Bundeswettbewerbsbehörde, Leniency programme guidelines (Leitfaden zur Kronzeugenregelung) (2022)
Bundeswettbewerbsbehörde, Paper on fine reductions in the leniency programme (Papier "Geldbußenreduktionen im Kronzeugenprogramm") (2022)
Bundeswettbewerbsbehörde, Competition Law and Compliance (Kartellrecht und Compliance) (2023)
Bundeswettbewerbsbehörde, Focus paper on sector inquiry into food industry - Price comparison platforms (Fokuspapier Preisvergleichsplattformen) (2023)
Bundeswettbewerbsbehörde, Guidance on pre-notification procedures in merger control (Leitfaden Pränotifikationsverfahren in der Zusammenschlusskontrolle) (2023)
Bundeswettbewerbsbehörde, Position on settlements (Standpunkt zu Settlements) (2023)

Federal Ministry of Justice

Bundesministerium für Justiz, 'Handbuch zur Kronzeugenregelung: §§ 209a, 209b StPO in der Fassung des Strafprozessrechtsänderungsgesetzes II 2016' (1.1.2017)

Index

The numbers here refer to paragraph numbers.

www.ingramcontent.com/pod-product-compliance
Lightning Source LLC
Chambersburg PA
CBHW071446230926
51846CB00001B/355
9789403532394